all the lost girls

Deep South Books

all the

PATRICIA FOSTER

lost girls

confessions of a southern daughter

The University of Alabama Press

Tuscaloosa and London

Copyright © 2000
The University of Alabama Press
Tuscaloosa, Alabama 35487-0380
All rights reserved
Manufactured in the United States of America

1 2 3 4 5 6 7 8 9 • 08 07 06 05 04 03 02 01 00

Designer: Michele Myatt Quinn
Typeface: AGaramond
Printer and Binder: Thomson-Shore

∞

The paper on which this book is printed meets the minimum
requirements of American National Standard for Information
Science-Permanence of Paper for Printed Library Materials,
ANSI Z39.48-1984.

Library of Congress Cataloging-in-Publication Data

Foster, Patricia, 1948–
    All the lost girls: confessions of a southern daughter / Patricia
Foster.
        p. cm. — (Deep South Books)
    ISBN 0-8173-1047-9 (alk. paper)
    1. Foster, Patricia, 1948– 2. Mothers and daughters—Alabama—
Biography. 3. Alabama—Biography. I. Title. II. Series.
CT275.F6858 A3 2000
976.1'063'092—dc21   00-008355

British Library Cataloguing-in-Publication Data available

To my mother,
who gave me life and the breath of stories

". . . the past is never dead. It is not even past."

—William Faulkner, *Requiem For a Nun*

acknowledgments

I would like to express my gratitude to the PEN/Jerard Fund Award and the University of Iowa's Old Gold Award for financial support in writing this book. For their friendship and encouragement, I give profound thanks to Marilyn Abildskov, Julene Bair, Rick Campbell, Carol de St. Victor, Stan Gontarski, Meredith Horton, Jesse Lee Kercheval, Carl Klaus, Jay Lamar, Susan Lohafer, Patricia Stevens, Marly Swick, Sheila Taylor, Carol Tix, and Kris Vervaecke. To Nicole Mitchell, my editor, I extend thanks for her respect and insight into the heart of the book. To Barbara Golden, my aunt, I owe a debt in stories. And to my mother, that very private person who opened up her life to me, a gift of love.

I have used the given names of family members who agreed to be part of this book; names of others in the book have been changed to protect their privacy.

Excerpts from the book have been published in the following journals: *The Chattahoochee Review, Cream City Review, The Gettysburg Review, The Iowa Review, Puerto Del Sol, Southern Humanities Review,* and *The Tampa Review.*

preface

In southern Alabama, very early, when the sky is pewter gray, the world still wrapped in its night cocoon, a heavy mist rises above the grass and hovers in a low blanket of fog. Beyond the grass there are farms, fields where cattle huddle together, where soybean crops and potato crops are waiting to be harvested, and beyond that, down the dirt roads that run straight as your finger into county highways, the rivers and bays—Fish River, Magnolia River, Perdido Bay, Soldier Creek—meander southward through gladed swamps towards the Gulf of Mexico.

I can lie on my bed in Iowa City and smell the dirt, the thick grainy coating on legs and knees, the sweep of red dust as the wind swirls it along a country road, blowing against my face in fine powdery silt. Southern Alabama is the sweetness of honey-suckle, the treachery of poison ivy. It's the place of childhood memories, of getting splashed under the hose on a steamy after-noon, the mystery of lightning bugs whose bodies strobe inside a mason jar, the smell of okra and cornbread, of gumbo and shrimp cooking on the stove. I ask myself how a tiny patch of soil can hold such longing, and why the longing is so violent, like a terrible sore just beneath my skin.

To begin to answer that question I have to go back in time, to memories of childhood, particularly memories of my mother and me. I could begin almost anywhere—my mother's birth, my birth, my first day at school—but as I close my eyes, waiting to see the scrub pines and the kudzu crawling up ditches and circling trees, what emerges are the stories my mother told me about her own childhood in a little mining town called Praco.

prologue

1935. Praco, Alabama

It was early fall, the leaves fluttering down from the trees as I passed the elderberry tree, the halfway mark between home and Girl Scouts. I loved Girl Scouts more than anything, but because I was only twelve, I wasn't allowed to walk the five miles alone, and one of my older brothers sauntered up ahead, hands in his pockets, kicking at the leaves. He had this shock of black hair across his forehead, patched overalls like the other mining kids wore. He was smart but sullen, with dark outraged eyes that frightened me a little. At home I stayed out of his way, but here in the woods he had to protect me from snakes and dogs and the bogeymen hiding in the ditch.

Like always, we picked our way through cedar trees and pines and an old outhouse falling in on itself. Beyond the woods there was nothing but slag heap and dirt hills, little camp houses packed tight in the hollows. They were built on stilts, one side squatting low on the hillside, the other propped up on spindly legs. They were ugly, but I wasn't thinking about that. I was thinking about the tiny cocktail forks

Mrs. Elgin showed us in Etiquette class. Like doll forks. Shiny and smooth. You'll use them for parties when you grow up, she said, so I pretended I was picking up a cocktail fork, piercing a tiny shrimp, holding it up to the light. I'd never seen a shrimp before, not until Mrs. Elgin showed us a picture from a magazine. The shrimp looked like little pink commas curled around a splash of sauce. In the advertisement the woman's hands were smooth and soft like rubbed velvet, so different from Mama's. Hers were red-raw and wrinkled from washing dishes and clothes. I guess I was dawdling, catching glimpses of dead grass poking through the leaves, lifting that shrimp to my mouth, feeling the tiny prong of the fork on my bottom lip. I couldn't wait to grow up! I closed my eyes, already tasting the salty brine, about to swallow it whole when I stumbled over something. I didn't know what, only that I was thrown to the ground. And there was my brother.

I don't remember much more. I don't know if he grabbed my arms. I don't know if I resisted. I only remember the leaves matted on the ground, and sticky white discharge seeping into the earth. Then the sun fading at the top of the trees. My sock had been pushed into the heel of my shoe. And there was this awful silence, as if the hills had been lulled to sleep. I didn't hear anything. No mining trucks rumbling down the grade towards Birmingham. No miners on their porches getting ready for the night shift. No dogs yelping or barking at the trees. Then I was running, bursting through the woods, hurrying up the steps of the house, a leaf stuck to my thigh.

"Get on in here," Mama yelled at the sound of my feet. Mama was calling from the kitchen, her face wet with sweat as she stirred pots steaming with potatoes and turnip greens. She already seemed old. With bunions and varicose veins and a thudding heart. "Get the table set, get the kids ready, then pour the milk."

Though I knew better, I started towards her, needing to touch her, hoping she wouldn't be so mad. The day before she'd beat me with a

hickory stick; I don't remember what for, only that I almost cried. I'd
hated her for that! But now everything was different, if only she'd look
up and see.

"Mama?"

"Get in there and get busy. I've got supper to finish and clothes to
iron."

"Mama?"

"Now hurry!" She never turned around.

There was nothing to do but get out silverware, napkins, the hard,
mismatched plates. Each fork felt clumsy, stupid. Only the knives felt
good. Sleek and clean. I ran my finger down the edge, feeling the
rounded curve, then the little grated section. I wanted another kind
of knife, sharp, spear-shaped, pointed. I was too ashamed to think of
my brother, so I imagined moving towards Mama, quietly, on tiptoe,
thrusting the knife deep into those red-raw hands.

"I've never told anybody that," Mother says, her voice wobbly,
coming off sixty-two years of silence. It's 1997 and we're driving
past Piggly Wiggly, past the hospital, past Mr. Wally's Fruit stand.
The trees thin out, punctuated by fields and cattle grazing in pas-
tures of velvety green. The day is hot, thick with humidity, dense
with insects whirling in galaxies. The air-conditioner hums. We're
both astonished. It's as if we're all alone, orbiting the planet,
swirling in space. I stare at her as if struck dumb. What she's told
me changes everything I know about her, all the clever specula-
tions that have lived inside my head.

I watch the new stores come into view, K-Mart, Osco Drugs,
Videoland, then the shopping center off to the side of the road,
the buzz of motion as people wander in and out of the shops, dark
shadows frozen in the sun. The parking lot is dense with cars; heat
shimmers on the newly blackened pavement, making it look wet,
inviting. Silence fills the car.

"You never even told your mother?" I ask finally. My voice sounds weak and thin as if I can't catch my breath. I think of women today, how my students are taught to tell someone. Rape crisis numbers punctuate the inside of bathroom doors, and girls are encouraged to see counselors, to tell their stories, to punch pillows and scream, releasing their rage.

"No." She looks quickly at me, her lips pinched, all that's soft caught behind her eyes.

"But why not?"

She shakes her head. "It wouldn't have mattered. Nobody would have listened."

When I look out the window harsh sunlight pinches off the darkness. I nod, feeling the weight of those words in my mouth. *Wouldn't. Have. Mattered.* Even silence is better than irrelevancy. Better not to tell. Better to keep it to yourself. Hide it deep inside your flesh. *Better to leave, leave and BE somebody.* Leave and never come back.

I see her in bed that night as she turns away from her sisters. They are fitful, twisting and turning, trying to avoid sleep. "Be still," she says, her voice stiff and hollow. The three younger sisters turn to the left, snuggling deeper into the pillow. They snort and mumble in their sleep. But she lies awake, seeing patterns in the darkness, glints of light that lead out the window, down the graded road, past the Praco mines, past the blast furnaces and coke ovens of Birmingham. Out into the world. I imagine her running lightly through the patchy grass, down the steep winding road, then standing in the shadows, waiting until morning for the bus. She means to run away. To get free. But something holds her back, the imprint of a hand, hot and offensive, on her flesh. If she leaves she'll have to tell. Already she can imagine the woman at the YWCA standing before her, sad-faced, questioning, indignant, incredulous. Wait, a voice inside her says. Close your eyes. Pray to God. Wait.

And she waits and waits and waits.

For weeks I don't know what to do, where to put this information, for you see, it wasn't my mother I intended to write about. It was me. Me who wanted to leave and never come back. Me who wanted to BE somebody. Me who broke into pieces and had to put all the pieces back together again. Not my mother. She was my Jane Eyre, the one who triumphed and survived, the one who said the past was dead. "Dead, you understand. Who cares about the past?"

Then months later at my home in Iowa City, I wake to the sound of crying, shrieks like the cawing of birds trapped in the cellar, but when I get up to look out the window, there's only a branch beating against the side of the house. I sit in my living room shivering, pulling my legs tight beneath me, my arms wrapped loose around my chest. Outside, the ground is covered with snow, a white fleece blanket. The wind howls.

Earlier in the day my sister called from Alabama to say she was worried about Mother. "I think she's depressed," she said, and as always we tried to think of ways to console her. "Maybe a little trip," Jean said. "To New Orleans or Atlanta. Maybe if she can just get out of town and have some fun."

"No," I surprised myself by saying. "That won't do any good."

My sister was quiet on the other end of the line. "I know," she whispered, "but I just want to make her happy."

Now I get up and open the window, feeling the rush of cold air against my face. My body tightens and I draw my nightgown closer around me, tucking it between my legs. I think of how hopeful we used to be, small winds in the blackness of night, and then I breathe deeply, wondering if children ever recover from failing at what they most want to do. As I stand at the window I realize I've spent a good part of my life feeling that I've failed my mother and an equally insane part assuming she's failed me. But the truth is much more complicated.

A friend once told me that all the stories you *must* tell are love stories. I nodded, wanting it to be so. Tonight as I stand at the window, I decide that this is the story I can tell, the story of my mother and me, the story of invisible knives, of girls trapped in darkness. Though this story begins in the ugly depths of violation, it's not a book about sexual abuse, but a book about ambition, the story of two women who struggle to enter the world, determined to remake themselves, to leave behind the miserable past. For a long time I felt so attached to my family I couldn't see where they left off and where I began, as if there were hidden strings holding us together. And this is a story about that too. About the long, hard struggle for autonomy.

Outside the wind rages. I hear it rushing through bare branches, sprinting across plowed, empty streets. I imagine the fields damp beneath a sheet of ice, animals huddling close for warmth. Snow falls with a shudder from my roof, but as I watch the snow blow its white breath against the trees, I feel strangely hopeful, as if I'm beginning my real education, the only one that matters. Who am I? I've been asking all my life. And how did my ambition become so intertwined with my mother's?

Our story goes a long way back. It begins not with my mother, but with my grandmother, for she too was badly hurt. She too needed the feel of the knife. Maybe healing only comes from revealing the weapons, exposing the daggers buried deep inside the flesh. Or maybe it comes from recovering what disappeared so long ago in childhood, the life that's hidden, lost, unforgiven.

PART ONE

1951. Lineville, Alabama

I am three, lying in my mother's bed, the curtains floating and drifting, following the wind. Sunlight breaks through the windows, shattering the air, and I wonder how long I've been alone here, without my mother. If I turn my head, I can smell her skin on the pillow, see the shape of her body in the bed. But if I close my eyes, another woman comes to visit me, a woman who laughs and then takes out her teeth. Ha! she says. The other woman is old. I think she is my mother's mother, but I can't be sure.

"Where is your mother?" I ask later while Mother is dressing in the closet, the door open wide so I can see her slip the pale green dress over her thick, dark hair.

"Mama's at home in Praco."

I puzzle over this, not just the fact of Praco, but the idea that my mother has a mother she calls Mama.

"But why did you leave her?"

Mother is zipping up her green dress, stepping into high heel shoes. She's not looking at me, paying no attention, trying to get her feet wedged into those sleek, narrow boats. "You always have to leave your mother," she says casually. "You do that when you grow up."

I look back to the bed where I spent half the night, remembering how I had to creep into this room on tiptoe, avoiding my father—a light sleeper—creeping over to the side where my mother slept. I tapped her on the arm and she startled awake, then lifted the covers and let me in.

"I won't," I say. "I won't ever leave you."

"Sure you will," she says. "When. You. Grow. Up." She says it like a game.

But I don't intend to do such a thing. I intend to keep it a secret. I have all kinds of secrets. I never tell my mother that I dream of her mother, that she comes to me easily at night, her body shrouded in blankets, her hair a cap of snow. She seems pale, worried, the worry worked into the wrinkles of her face.

"Listen," the old woman always says. And then she garbles something I don't understand. The next morning, all I remember is that she was there. My mother's mother.

My mother had a mother. It surprises me still.

One night when it's storming, rain streaking the outside of the glass, beating its tense rhythm against the eaves of the house, I'm frightened and find my way into Mother's bed. I sleep cuddled next to her body, one finger curled around a lock of her hair. I listen to the rain. It murmurs and roars, seeping into the hollows of my dreams. Still, the old woman beckons. "Listen," she mutters without her teeth. "Be quiet and listen." No, I shake my head. No, I won't.

Then suddenly I'm older, much older, and once again I hear her voice wrapped in the darkness of dreams. "Listen," she repeats.

And this time I do.

rules of labor

My grandmother's story:

The mining slums of Mabren, Praco, Flat Creek, Bessie, thin red rivers of road traversing the hills, cutting through the dark mornings of hazy mist as the miners leave the boardinghouse, the smell of coffee in their nostrils, their hands clutching paper sacks and thermoses as they trek down the dirt roads to the mines. "Get movin'," one of the miners says, squinting in the pale, steamy half-light. By 6:00, there's a lull in the clatter, the rooms empty of the gruff noise of men. My great-grandmother Barbara stops in the dining room to catch her breath as the watery light seeps through the windows. The sky is lint gray, a faded blanket. She works as a cook in her sister Kate's boardinghouse in Pinckney City, Alabama, peeling potatoes, baking bread, stirring endless pots of stew. At night the stink of cabbage clings to her dark hair as she unpins her topknot, shaking loose her glory. But there's little time to think about such things. One shift has left, another is due within the hour, tired, hungry men, coal dust beneath their fingernails, clotted in the pores of their skin.

Barbara walks briskly from the dining hall into the kitchen where her three-year old daughter, Mary, my grandmother, sits in a corner, playing with a broom. Even Mary can be useful, can bring silverware from the tables, can pick up trash dropped on the floor. And she must be useful for they have nothing to give the world but their labor.

"Mary," Barbara calls. "Stop doing that. You go on and pick up the forks dropped around the tables."

The girl looks up from her play with the gratitude of a lover. She slaps her hands together for attention, but her mother, distracted, has already turned away.

Barbara stares at the pile of dishes, then briefly at her hands, rough and red, wrinkled from dishwashing, the knuckles thickening, nails clipped short, but there's no reason for vanity when you've come straight from a famine in Scotland, the hard knotting of the stomach, the dull ache of the brain. If she stares too long, she remembers the stench of steerage, that claustrophobic darkness. The smells waft over her: urine, shit, sweat, the stink of cramped bodies. She swallows quickly, stiffening, surprised when Mary brushes up against her, trying to nestle into her skirts. She swipes at her, an automatic defense. There's work to be done. "Go on now," she says brusquely, straightening, her fingers dipping into the greasy water.

As Mary slinks away, back to chores, to the shiny flash of a fork, that tiny place where her hand brushed her mother's body still tingles. She thinks of it greedily, a place she can lick, the smell of her mother embedded in the folds of her skin. But even these moments, too haphazard to be called attention, are numbered when Barbara meets Mr. Herron, a miner who likes the looks of the thin, pragmatic Barbara but has no use for a needy stepdaughter. "Mama," Mary whimpers, but it's no use. Once Barbara and Mr. Herron marry, Mary will no longer sleep beside her mother, but will be banished, like a character in Dickens, to a pallet behind the wood stove.

"It's time for you to get out and go to work," her stepfather says one night as he reaches for the steaming plate of potatoes she put before his plate. Mary, age eleven, nods, knowing there's no use to try to wheedle sympathy, to plead for mercy.

"Tomorrow," he barks and begins to eat.

It snows that night, a fine mist of white that covers the hills, the steep curve of the mountain now softened by drifts. Mary wakes at dawn, dresses and makes breakfast for the family, biscuits and eggs, thick coffee for her stepfather. She dresses as warmly as she can, woolen stockings, dress, sweater, coat handed down from her mother, working shoes that cover her ankles. Once the dishes are washed, the floor swept, she watches her mother bend over to feed the youngest boy, her nipples like darkened scars on a with-ered chest. Mary knows better than to try to kiss her mother, that tall, thin woman who never smiles. Instead, she says, "I'm leav-ing," and steps out into whiteness, gasps at the cold, and starts walking. It's so cold she can't stop, but walks quickly down the road the four miles from Pinckney City to Bessie, her hands beat-ing at her arms to keep them warm. She looks gratefully at the trees, snow nestled in the branches, the boughs thickened in their heavy white coats, then shivers, pulling her arms into her chest, cold seeping through her toes. She's still a child, her body quick and supple, a girl's body with the beginning indentation at the waist, her breasts flat, only the pucker of nipples. Her mind lifts only at the slice of blue sky she sees just over the hills. Perhaps by noon, a weak sun will shine, warming her shoulders, her knees.

But when the sun breaks through, it warms only the nape of

her neck, the tops of her shoulders. It never reaches the soft fold of her ears, the frozen tundra of her toes. She stops at the community store, relieved to be inside, near a fire and warmth. She huddles close to the fire, staring at the floor, then foolishly blurts, "I'm a good worker. Is anybody in these hills needing help?" She blushes, puts both hands inside her pockets. The manager, a soft-hearted man, takes pity on her, and sends her home to tend his sick wife and care for his children.

Bessie is a thriving community, serving the Bessie Mine, the Risco Mine, the Porter Mine, workers coming and going, moving into the shed-like houses, buying food and clothes at the Commissary, whites living up in the mountains, blacks down in the hollow, closer to the mines. The Ku Klux Klan is already entrenched, kicking out unmarried couples "living in sin," "doing their dirt," and guarding the separation between blacks and whites. There's only a remnant of a union and little regulation in the mines, but back-breaking labor is all most of the people know. For four years, Mary works for the family in Bessie, goes to church every Sunday, the only place besides the Commissary where people come together, the women in hand-sewn cotton dresses and flowered hats, the men in starched white shirts, grave-faced and solemn. Among them there's a young man, dark and intense, whose eyes shadow Mary's progress up the aisle. He's been raised by grandparents, reported to be petted, "spoiled rotten," though not spoiled enough to escape the mines. A hard worker, he's been doing a man's work since age thirteen. He's also a dark-haired flirt, a man who likes the ladies, who stares through Mary's clothes at church until she feels as though she's singing hymns dressed only in her bare skin.

One day he follows behind her, studying her as she walks down the aisle, the service over, women knotted together in bunches, the flowers on their hats faded, their bodies gone to fat, the men, often reed thin, tubercular, talking and smoking, furtively eyeing the pretty, young girls. She can feel him behind her, little jolts of electricity at her breasts, in her stomach, sudden nips of pleasure she can't explain.

"Can I walk you home?" he asks simply. His black hair is thick, brushed back from his face, the eyebrows dark and straight, the thick lashes meeting as he blinks. Only his smile curls in sexual expectation.

She turns away quickly. Lord, it's like a hungry animal breathing down her throat. "No," she says, trying not to stare into those hazel eyes, to get lost in that wicked thrill. It's the first time she's said no to an invitation, no to affection. Oh, to see his face buried in her neck, those hands reaching inside to undo the stiffening she's worked so hard to preserve! Imprinted on her brain is the day her stepfather drug her outside and made her lay her head on the chopping block, the wood cold with frost, her cheek going numb. At seven, she was so frightened, her body shook uncontrollably like a chicken's. Her stepfather's face was red, blotched with anger, the ax beside his feet, ready for use. "I'll learn you," he roared while her hands trembled as she held onto the wood, waiting, knowing the world only as a dark, devouring place and yet having no words for her fears. Of course, he didn't do it, didn't need to now that she understood she was at his mercy, bound to him even for permission to live.

The good-looking miner catches her answer like a player fielding a ball. He smiles, waits only a second, then says, "Hell, I didn't want to do it anyway," and strides ahead of her into the white heat of a summer afternoon.

But the good-looking miner is persistent, his appetite whetted. And eventually she submits—an old story—perhaps giving him first a shy smile, lifting dreamy eyes to stare at the gleaming whiteness of his neck. She isn't pretty as he is, isn't the "catch of the community," but merely a girl never loved, a girl starved, trained for endurance.

How they slip off together no one has ever told me. But in their early moments of desire, their unprotected passion, a child is conceived. Maybe what the good-looking miner gives her is warmth, the heat of bodies lying together on a soft bed of leaves. I want to imagine that she felt beautiful that night, that all the warmth her mother had withheld came flooding through her body, a puddle of delight tongued into the soft membrane of her ear, exploding inside her chest, and spreading to that gap between her legs. I want the sex to have been worth it, a hot needle of passion she'd hoped all of her life to have. Now she's had it and more.

After she discovers her pregnancy, her life turns a corner, for the only certainty now is that she'll be humiliated, gossiped about, dismissed, maybe even run out of town. I wonder if she thought about that first trek from Pinckney City to Bessie—the journey begun when she was eleven, a mere girl sent out, unconsoled and alone, to wrestle with the world. I imagine her sitting outside, staring at coal dust blowing its black breath into the air and wishing she'd walked further, to the next town or the next, no matter the hunger, the distance. Why hadn't her stepfather demanded this of her? Not four miles, but six, eight, ten. She feels the tingle in her neck, the ax ready to strike. But her torment is yoked to silence: an infant, a baby, when she's yet to wonder at the stars thick across a winter sky. She's only a child herself, groping and blind at the bottom of a pitcher until that one moment she was lifted up. Lifted up and held.

But inevitably, it happens. Mr. Holt sends her home. "It's best," he says. She doesn't plead or beg mercy. No carrying on, no fuss, just the trek back to Pickney City, one foot in front of another. "I'm going to have a baby." She stands before her mother, saying it quickly, unemotionally, looking at the hem of her dress. It's mid-morning, the men gone to work, to school, the clock on the stove ticking its infernal time. When she looks up, it's only to stare at the curtains at the window, dove white, so clean the threads seem illuminated, separate.

"Slut," her mother finally says, voice low, her face twisted with malice. "Whore." It's barely a whisper, but behind it the cold creeps through the bottom of her shoes, moving up her ankles, her legs into the hidden bones of her hips. Snow. Exile. The hard knot of resistance.

Barbara sits upright, a poker of stiffness. She will *not* have a bastard held up before the community. And the next day she marches off to the sheriff, makes him find the good-looking miner and bring him to justice. "There's a bairn coming, and a marriage has to be forced."

Now the outer darkness closes in: my grandfather agrees to marry Mary but he refuses to love her, and every year makes her pay for her sins. My aunts said he kept her "barefoot and pregnant" while he played "bull of the woods," having affairs with neighboring women which made her cry late into the night when her children were in bed, the covers pulled up to their chins. I close my eyes, sitting outside my Iowa house where the earth is damp and sweet-smelling and try to see my grandmother, wishing I could comfort her. She's a woman who knows so little of affection, who's never learned to give it willingly or receive it with joy. When I look at the cheap watercolor portrait painted after their wedding, my grandmother's hair is light auburn, swept upward in a Gibson Girl style that flatters her full face. And yet already the eyes betray an uncertainty, a pensiveness to her stare that hints at defeat. Beside her, my grandfather stares jauntily at me, sure of himself, his gaze direct, his hat pushed slightly back on his head to reveal a shock of thick black hair. Unlike my grandmother's eyes, his eyes are curious, piercing. He has work to do, a life to construct.

Of course I know my grandmother could have refused my grandfather, could have denied him her body, and yet from the women in my family it's agreed that she loved him, perhaps even adored him though there was little affection and much arguing between them. "She washed the house inside and out when he came home from Hot Springs, Arkansas, after treatment for arthritis," my mother once told me. And I can imagine Mary cleaning the floor, the rugs, turning the mattresses, washing the curtains, the linens, all for the homecoming of a man who gave her no softness, no visible love.

"When she died at fifty-seven," my aunt tells me, "Daddy was called from night duty at the mines. He worked the 11–7 shift as mine foreman." I imagine him at the beginning of his work, the damp, chemical smells filling his nostrils after the cool summer night air. He has walked to work as he has every night for thirty years. Now he's begun overseeing the shift, checking the last shift's production, flicking on the lamp atop his hat. When they call him home, he's surprised, then inexplicably frightened. He runs from the mines, scrambling up that graveled road, the pebbles skittering beneath his feet, his heart shuddering with fear. When he bursts through the door, he sees her corpse lying on the sofa, the doctor standing beside her. She is stone dead, turning blue. But he thrusts himself down beside her, throwing his tough arms over her body, his head resting on her belly. "Oh Mary," he blurts, his hands grabbing for her flesh, "I never loved anyone but you."

But, of course, she can't hear him, she, who never learned to turn her back, but waited patiently for him to hold her close in the curve of his arms. And this too is our legacy, this terror of emotion, of unburdening the heart.

Though my grandmother's death seems the proper end to the story, it's not the whole story. It says nothing about the sixteen children she bore, three of whom died at birth. It says nothing about how this family created dreams, how hopes were slyly sought and just as privately buried.

In the spring of 1919, a day when the trees are dressed with their new flesh of leaves, the sky clear blue, a great puff of cumulus clouds drifting towards the east, my grandparents cart their belongings to a new house, one with larger rooms, a back yard and a porch where my grandmother can brush her dog's white fluffy hair. With furniture stacked crudely inside the truck, with mattresses tied on top, the family begins their journey, down one set of hills into the valley and up another cluster of hills. It's only as they're driving into the new community that a wind springs up. The trees bend and whip, branches snapping. Dust drifts in thick, smoggy whorls. Screen doors bang against doorframes, clapping hard, wood against wood. As they cross Devon Bridge, my grandmother turns once, surprised to see the mattresses flap like wings and glide over the top of the truck. They rise for a moment before drifting slowly down to the river where they hit the creek with a thunderous splash. Maybe what she felt was a moment of lightness, an awe at the beauty of their flight, until she looked at the empty space now filled with a drenching rain. As she turns back to the road, rain slashes the red dirt; the hills begin to bleed.

They drive on. There's nothing else to do. The mattresses can't be retrieved. The night's comfort will be compromised but they have blankets, pillows, towels, clean sheets and food. The mattresses will never be mentioned. Like dreams, they're better left unnoticed, small hopes sinking deeper and deeper into thick, red mud.

It feels ridiculous to go to the graveyard and stand before my grandmother's grave. But still I do. It's just after Easter and someone has decorated the grave next to hers with giant, life-size Easter bunnies in lavender and pink. Their bunny ears bend stiffly in the wind. They hold bunches of browning lilies in their paws. Their whiskers are broom straws painted a snowy white. They're so absurd, I laugh.

"I hope Mary Baxter's getting a good chuckle over this one," I tell my aunt.

"She certainly better be," my aunt agrees, straightening the bunny's white satin tie. "There's not much else to do."

I stare at the grave, feeling nothing but this mild hilarity, and the sudden thought that I've never really known what my mother felt about her mother. Did she resent her? Was she ashamed of her? And was that all part of a complicated love? In a subtle way, I think Mother and I agreed not to talk much about Mary Baxter, this woman who was abandoned, who was both too hard and too vulnerable, who lived a life that couldn't be fixed. As I'm staring at the grave, the wind shifts, blowing wildly, and I see a flight of birds scatter noisily from a telephone wire. And suddenly I *do* feel something, an uneasiness as if I've brushed up against something hidden. I've always known my grandmother couldn't prepare my mother for the giant step of leaving the mines for life in the middle class. I see Mother earnestly trying to explain about vitamins and disease, the need for spinach and broccoli along with potatoes, her mother half-listening, too busy to give anyone her full attention. I see my mother sigh with exasperation, and then a restless anxiety grabs hold of my heart: neither could my mother prepare me for the life of an artist, that desperate fall into a more intimate place. We both left one world, the world of childhood familiarity, and could never really explain where we'd gone.

Three mothers. Three daughters. Can anyone prepare you for a life?

the merry thief

Always, my mother had dreams. Not dreams of becoming Miss America. Not dreams of passionate love. But dreams of independence, of escape from the heavy foot of her family. "Oh, she was the Golden One and we were the Slobs," my aunt confides to me late one night. "We all knew she'd get out. It was in everything she did, the way she went at her school work, even the housework, trying to make herself better, always better." My aunt sighs, closing her eyes. "God, it was a chore being next in line. Everything I did had to come up to her mark, and when I brought home a paper, Mama said, *Your sister would have gotten an A. What's wrong with you?* It made me so mad I'd run outside and build pine pole sleds with my buddies, sleds that sent us flying down the mountain, away from *her.*" The Golden One, the Princess, didn't even know her sister's anger because she was either feeding her mother's new baby or staring greedily at words on a page.

And that's the way I begin to see them: The Golden One vs. The Slobs.

It's 8:00 on Sunday morning when Mother pulls on a thin white slip, then her blue cotton dress, her best dress, the one she wears to church with the pearl buttons that look like eyes. She's just finished the buttons when she glances in the mirror and stares in horror at those "things" pushing through the bodice, peaking like shapely avocadoes. Until today she's bound them, wrapping them with a strip of old sheet, going round and round her chest, tightening, tightening, but they continue to grow, swelling like boils. What *are* these protuberances, these abnormalities that afflict her? How can she make them go away without confessing to her mother or calling a doctor? And won't they be mad at her, yelling, their voices crackling like ice in hot water? She leans closer to the mirror, afraid to touch them, to feel the gross swelling of flesh. On impulse, she opens the cabinet where her mother keeps medicines, takes out the bottle of Merthiolate, and precisely, starting at the nipple, paints each breast a hot glowing orange.

When they see her, the Slobs burst into laughter, clutching each other, thrilled at her misery. Though they don't quite understand what's wrong, they know it's secretive, funny, maybe even obscene. And when they overhear the explanation, they chant, "You're getting titties, you're getting titties," giggling at the bad word they've heard their brothers yell. They lie on the bed on their stomachs, laughing with delight while the Princess stands at the sink washing out her Sunday dress.

"Oh, honey, because we were girls, we were *nothing*," my aunt tells me, her voice weary, frazzled as if she's been shouting this sentence for years. "You weren't allowed to have an opinion. If you said anything, you got swatted. You learned to keep your skirt down and your trap shut." Nobody mentioned menstruation, pubic hair, breast development, or, god-forbid, sexuality, but how could you worry about such things when trouble splashed against your door, bills and illness and the inevitable babies; money was needed to fix the heater, the roof, to buy winter coats, to pay the damn doctor. Always in the background those blood-red hills, treeless, strip-mined, a father trudging home in a hard hat, the mother standing over a stove with flour in her hair.

Poor.

Even as FDR proclaims a third of the nation underprivileged in 1937, Mother at fourteen is lost in a fantasy world, dressed in a blue flared skirt and white cotton sweater, blue and white pom poms bouncing jauntily on her shoes. Beside her is Gayle Lattimer with her thick blonde curls, her doe-brown eyes, her joyous, squealing voice. Other girls twirl and jump. "Go, go, go," they scream, and when the crowd roars, they all jump high in the air, yelling the fight song, spurring their team to victory.

"Multiple fractions," Miss McAlilly snaps, her chalk scratching the board.

Mother sits up, startled, the daydream dropped from her mind. What was she thinking? The cheerleaders are all popular, pretty girls with straight white teeth and beautiful smiles. She ducks her head, stares at her book, embarrassed, ashamed, for she knows to stay in the background, quiet, observing. Now she puts her hand over her mouth, covering up her buck teeth, a shame she says "will haunt me forever."

"Go to the board," Miss McAlilly chides, and the next minute she's up from her seat working a math problem, her mind doing cartwheels, push-ups, everything forgotten but the pure beauty of math. To her surprise, she finishes before anyone else, and when she turns, Miss McAlilly beams at her, nodding.

"You're the best student in this class," Miss McAlilly tells her that afternoon, and she looks straight into Miss McAlilly's gray-blue eyes behind horn-rimmed glasses as if looking through a golden haze. No matter about her teeth. For the first time it occurs to her there are other ways to save yourself. She'll get an education! She won't be like the other women in Praco, old at forty, teeth gone, backs bent, hair gray and thin. She'll be an explorer, a scientist, a woman with outstretched wings.

"You must go to college," Miss McAlilly continues, holding her gaze while tucking a wayward hair back into her bun. "You must work hard and learn."

And that day on the bus in 1937 she forgets all about Gayle Lattimer and the blue flared skirt. She'll do what the other girls can't do. It seems so easy, for surely the mind is a sun that burns away fog. And of course, I want this to be an elaborate pantomime: Mother rising from the depths of poverty and shame into the lap of learning and culture, moving effortlessly from one social class to another, like tiptoeing into another room. It's the story we all yearn for, the one we crave, the story of transformation and recovery, everything that's messy nicely put to rest. But it doesn't happen that way. "The desire was there," Mother says, "but the navigation a black tunnel."

"I'll go to nursing school," she decides the next year, imagining herself in a starched white uniform, bending over a patient, expertly drawing blood. But to enroll you must be eighteen; Mother's just turned sixteen. "Goodness no, you must go to the university," Mrs. Elgin insists, but forget about that. Her father, a section foreman, makes more money than the average miner, but with all those children, there's nothing left for the luxury of college. She'll have to go to work, ironing for Mrs. O'Dell, taking care of Lally McGrundy's kids, scrimping and saving, caught in the underbelly of sacrifice, staying buck-toothed and patient and poor. At night she listens to the trucks screeching down the hills, brakes hard-pumped, the sound like a giant balloon being squeezed. Wind slaps against the side of the house, stealing through the cracks in the windows, twisting under the creaking door. "This can't be my life," she prays, while hiding in the background is that silenced twelve year old girl. "I've gotta leave. Leave and BE somebody."

And like a fairy godmother, Mrs. Elgin, produces the work scholarship.

A trip to Tuscaloosa. An interview. A chance.

"Don't be nervous now," Mrs. Elgin says, playing chords against her thigh while they wait in the front room of the Admissions' Office of the University of Alabama. "Just let me do the talking. I understand these things."

Mother nods, quiet, respectful. Even the air here has a sweetness that leaves her buoyant, almost gay. She's listening for Denny Chimes, memorizing the way the grass grows smoothly across the lawn of the quadrangle which she sees from this window. She says that word—"the Quad"—over and over in her mind. She can't wait to try it on her sisters back home. "Oh, I walked across the quad," she'll say nonchalantly, tossing her head, "past the library to the Admissions Office. Everybody noticed me." She blushes. Ridiculous! Even the dust here seems reverent. A tiny speck sits on the desk near a stack of papers, and she stares at it while Mrs. Elgin rattles off her accomplishments: valedictorian, all A's, Best Girl in the Community, Girl Scouts. Mother allows herself a slight smile, the brief hint of vanity—maybe she'll be a doctor or a lawyer—until she hears Mrs. Elgin say, "But she has no *talents*!"

And for a moment she can't breathe. There's no shame like the shame of knowing only the sink, the stove, the washboard, the floor.

But the admissions counselors don't even blink. "Well, that's fine, fine. She can work in the dining hall." And yet as they reach out to shake her hand, the desire for "talent" blooms like a deadly virus in her head. She's never really thought about talent before. It's like a foreign language, a secret closet, one buried in the folds of your brain. She looks at her fingers. Could they play patterns on the piano, flutter the keys of a flute? Could they draw a still life of toppled bowls and leftover fruit? Sketch a landscape, carve the solemn planes of a face? And what about her body? Could it move through air as if floating on a cloud . . . as if she could fly? But immediately she thinks of her twelve brothers and sisters, of the red road spiraling down the mountain, her mother in the kitchen with lard on her hands, and her mind breaks like a branch whipped in the wind. She steadies herself. Shoulders back. Head high. There are other ways to make your mark on the world.

A daughter never quite knows what a mother discovers, knows only what's emphasized, exalted in her own childhood, what's talked about in hushed voices in dressing rooms and hallways and late at night when sorrow comes unanchored from its moorings. I have only a hint at her terror—*never enough!* At my mother's center, it seems, is this inevitable conflict: the need to detach, to shed the body, the mind a small steel trap, clarifying and defining, assembling and modifying what she reads and hears, and yet behind that focus, there's a voluptuous need to dismantle it all, to explode into tenderness, into a delirium of helplessness, laughing and crying at that horrible past. Oh, to let yourself go, to crack open the awful secrets! But of course, she can't. It's as simple as that.

Instead she leaves for the university with two new dresses (one yellow, one pink), a pair of saddle oxfords, and four skirts Mrs. Elgin got from the Junior League. My "rich kid clothes," she tags them without irony, packing them carefully along with her shirts and underwear and nightgowns and socks. "Hand me downs," one sister snorts, zigzagging her fingers across the cloth. But Mother shakes her head, knowing it's much better to look like you belong in the world. And she's determined to belong.

It's in this other life that I see my mother studying in the library, working late into the night, her sleeves rolled up, her books spread out before her as she pushes through chemistry, biology, and anatomy, determined to be a scientist, to make A's. And she loves it. Every minute of it. "This isolated, inexperienced, underdeveloped, naive female had a lot of catching up to do so everything was exciting and worth my time," she writes me in 1998, then confesses she was the last one to bed at night because each evening there was a bull session where all the girls got together and gossiped about dating and clothes and campus politics, and of course, boys, boys, boys.

"Boys?" I ask. "*You* talked about boys?" Because as my mother she never once asked me about a single kiss. "Mother doesn't know *anything*," my sister and I used to whisper in the dark. "She just doesn't *know*." To us she'd arrived at adulthood intact, uncontaminated by the anguish and insistence of sexual desire.

It's true Mother had not one date in high school, didn't know what it meant to be liked, to be complimented or charmed, to have someone to talk to and laugh with, but that spring of her freshman year, her mother hired a young man to drive to the University and bring her home for the weekend. Tall, blonde, nice looking, he was a high school graduate working in the mines to save money for college. Though they'd never met—he'd grown up in another county—he spent the entire drive telling her how much he admired her for going to college, for overcoming the obstacles of poverty to get there, then quickly as she got out of the car, "And oh, yes," he said, "you've got good-looking legs."

"My little ego boost," Mother says. "He came up to see me when he could."

While in Europe the world is beginning to rupture—the Nazis entering Prague in 1939, Czechoslovakia collapsing, then in May, 1940, Holland and Belgium surrendering to the Nazis—on the

University campus in the Heart of Dixie, Mother doesn't worry about such things. It's not campus news, not about money or school. "I had no idea what was going on in the world," she says, "I had to worry about a job for the summer, work that might or might not come through. I was desperate. I'd do anything not to go back to Praco." And she's rescued by a hospital internship in Birmingham where she works for the head dietitian, a woman who takes such a liking to Mother, she introduces her fondly as, "my little baby," only her speech impediment makes baby into bebe, and that becomes her nickname—Bebe—the one the nurses and interns use when they sneak her into the labs and the nursery, introducing her to the infrastructure of the hospital, the Surgery Unit, the X-ray room, the Obstetrics Unit, the Orthopedic cast room until everything she's been studying begins to fall into place. *This is where she belongs,* this community of doctors and nurses and dietitians, all overworked and dedicated, with their in-jokes and parties, their late night coffee jams. If much of life is the anxious, ardent search for a spiritual home, a respite from boredom and anxiety, then Mother's just found her Eden.

And then wa-la! in her junior year Mother met Daddy, met him and married him in the space of a year. Actually my father stole my mother from another man, slipped into her mind like a merry thief and grabbed hold. I can imagine my father doing this, sneaking in, gay and scrappy, never taking no for an answer, keeping her laughing. Of course, Mother doesn't tell it this way at all when my sister and I beg her for the story of how they met. It's the middle of the afternoon in 1952 and Jean and I have been playing dress-up in fancy ruffled slips and long pearls all morning, but now it's too hot for being Audrey Hepburn and Kim Novak, for surviving a flood in the Amazon or rattlesnakes in Arizona, too hot to do anything but lie across Mother's bed in tennis shoes and shorts while she dresses in stockings and high heels to meet Bessie at her store. "Tell us again!" we plead, always longing for a repetition of how it all began: a job, a red-haired man, and then US. We know they met in college when mother was a junior and daddy in medical school, but we want the SECRETS, the sly details, the indelicate complications.

"Did you love daddy *right away?*" my sister asks, leaning up on her elbow, all the seriousness pushed forward in her face. When they kiss in front of us, they bunch their lips together like prunes. In the dark, my sister and I practice, kissing our pillows, or out in the back yard when we're Audrey Hepburn and Kim Novak, we kiss the oak tree, wrapping our arms around its trunk, scratching the inside of our knees. What we long for is the onslaught of emotion: did Daddy waltz you down the halls of the ward late at night when the patients were asleep, his arms around your thin waist, your hand at his neck? Did he stare at you so intently over each morning's scrambled eggs that you had to turn away in bewildered embarrassment? Did you laugh into your pillow at the little scrap of toast caught between his front teeth?

But Mother won't bend to our desires. "Well, I met your daddy and Joe Blair at the same time," she says matter-of-factly, telling us about that August afternoon of registration when she hurried across campus, dodging puddles, walking the half mile to the Men's Infirmary. It was raining, the sky opening up, pouring out its sins, when she appeared at the door, soaked, her jet black hair plastered to her head, rivulets of water streaming down her neck, her clothes damp, as she stepped inside. "The room was so white, white as a bone. White walls, white tables, white chairs, white cabinets," Mother laughs, "and two white men, first year medical students working as night nurses. A tall dark one who let me in and a red-headed man sitting at a table, looking up from his book, smiling at me as if he knew a secret." While they watched, Mother dried her hair with a towel, Joe, the handsome one, with the serious look of a med student, Daddy, wiry, his body pulsating with a kinetic energy.

"Joe was serious," Mother says. "Your daddy liked to joke." No matter that he was a short, curly-headed quirt from the backwaters of Pascagoula, he had this gift: he could make people laugh. But the jokes must not have intrigued her at first. "Let's see, I started dating Joe in October, going out to dances, to the Sweet Shop for cokes and sodas, sometimes to movies." She pauses, adjusting her slip. "But the three of us still went out together during the week, walking to the Post Office for mail, having lunch or big breakfasts of biscuits and eggs in the infirmary cafeteria." But at Christmas, Joe was called home to Mobile before the big Christmas dance, and it's here that Daddy elbows his way into Mother's life.

"What happened?" my sister asks. We're sitting up now, attentive, pulling on the bedspread's fringe. We know that this is a critical moment, a turning point, the beginning of our destiny.

"Well, when he asked me if I wanted to go to the dance"— Mother smiles—"I said 'sure.'" And then she turns away to powder her nose as if that's the end of the mystery, the story all wrapped up and put away.

"But weren't you in love with Joe? Hadn't you already *kissed* him?"

"Oh, no," Mother says. "I never thought going to the dance with your daddy would change my relationship with Joe." But maybe the jokes were beginning to take hold, maybe she needed to laugh after all those years in dreary old Praco. Like her, Daddy had scratched his way out of poverty which would mean a lot less explaining to do. There'd be no need to look back at those dank rooms, those lumpy beds, that mean-ass life, the faint brogue of Scotsmen swearing deep inside the mines. Together, they could turn to the future, carve out a middle class life of success and respect, money in the bank, the gas bill always paid. Throw away the chicken necks, the cornmeal, the turnip greens.

"But Joe was *furious*," Mother says, pride in her voice. She sits at her dressing table and presses her lips together, painting them a wild violet shade the color of wine. "But he forgave us," she says, blotting. "Because it was pretty clear we were a couple." What she doesn't say is that they were coasting wildly towards marriage, Daddy convincing Mother to give up her dietitian's internship at Peter Bent Brigham in Boston to elope with him. What she doesn't say is how little either reveals about the past. It's a closed door, a dead space, an empty cupboard full of heat and dust. Maybe, she thinks, my father's love is so great, the past can be erased, slipped silently like garbage into a deep, muddy hole.

And yet after they marry, Daddy does go home with Mother to that little mining town on the edge of nowhere with its bleeding red hills and its trucks roaring down the mountain. He meets her younger brothers and sisters—"this is Bobbie, Mary Jo, Eloise, Tiny, Sonny, Rosie, Bill"—who are introduced shyly and with great deference because he's a doctor and deserves their respect: he'll go to work every day in a coat and tie, park in a special spot, eat steak whenever he wants to and put his feet up on the couch with his shoes still on. "Hellooooo," they whisper and titter because he's short and grinning and staring at their sister.

That first afternoon, he descends with my grandfather into the mines (where no woman is allowed to go), then sits in the evening with the family at the large dining room table, the sisters still shy and awkward, the little girls poking each other beneath the table, staring at his nose and his eyes and the twist of red curls.

Who knows how my mother and father find time alone in that house full of children, or how my father persuades my mother to lift her dress, unhook her stockings and let him soap up her beautiful legs. "Be careful," she says, sitting on the closed seat of the toilet while my father bends towards her, a razor in his hand.

He holds my mother's leg out from the water, her calves shapely and muscled, pale as ivory, tapering to slender ankles, and glides the razor lightly over her skin. He grins, maybe even winks because he likes nothing better than to touch her and laugh, knowing he's the king here, knowing even as he shaves her legs his mother-in-law is in the kitchen making biscuits for *him*. "I want five boys and one girl," he whispers as he touches the razor just above her ankle bone. Her skin is clean and white and he imagines the little girl will have such skin. The boys will be tough and muscular, chock full of vitamins, one of them sure to be a football player, running the ball before cheering crowds. My mother laughs, pulling away. "Just *one* little girl," she says, while behind them there is the sudden noise of the household, kids in and out, screen doors banging, dogs barking, the clatter of pots and pans in the kitchen. But for the moment, they're alone, intimate, and my father leans towards my mother's knees, inhaling the dizzy lilac smell of her skin.

"Oh, they were so happy together," my Aunt Barbara says. "You should have seen them. I'd never known people could kiss so long. He was all over her and she loved it! That weekend they visited, they had to sleep on the fold-out couch in our living room. Of course we kids wanted to spy on them, so early the next morning we crept out to look at them, and wouldn't you know it, there they both were on the same side of the bed!"

Four years later, drafted and sent to the Phillipines and then to Korea, Daddy called Mother FLASH and DARLING and HONEYBUNNY in his letters, signing them ALL OF ME NOW AND FOREVER. From Korea, he writes: "*Our love will never be shamed or scarred on either end and for that I'm assured and made happy. Some day we will be close again and shut out the rest of the world and live for one another in our own little world."*

Their own little world. Maybe their life together was so good it was better than sliced bread, better than a goober found deep inside your pocket. Already they had education, professional expectations, two healthy children. And they wanted so much more! You could see it in their eyes: dining room tables set with roast beef and turkey, three-layer cakes and lemon meringue pies, a living room full of velvet drapes and upholstered chairs. A grand piano in one corner. A grandfather clock against the wall. Maybe for a little while my mother's life *was* golden. Maybe, just maybe, she'd found her prince. Or maybe there's always a dark side to happiness, and she was being lifted up in the late forties, full of girlish expectancy, for the backfire of the fifties. "Hush now, be good. Don't make trouble. Go back to the kitchen."

But we are still on the eve of the 50s, and first I need to be born.

rebellion

1948. FAIRHOPE, ALABAMA

Who would not want her birth to be miraculous, to coincide with the ides of fate? It's 1948, three years after the war, and yet the day before my birth, a Saturday in May, my sister's dumping sand on the living room chair, watching it spill in puddles to the floor. My brother's just learned the word quicksand and stands in the hall repeating it, *quicksand, quicksand,* struggling to get loose from its grip. The grass needs mowing and a breeze comes off the bay, fluttering the window shades in the upstairs room.

"But you must *hurry,*" Mother says over the phone to my father. He's just finished up his army duty in Augusta, Georgia, while she's been very pregnant and alone for three weeks in a white two-story house in Alabama.

"I'll be there tonight. Call my mother. Get her to take the children."

"No, Hally's taking them tonight. We'll use your mother after that." My mother is pale, tired. This has been her third pregnancy in four years, a pregnancy so fraught with nausea and bleeding that she's had a battery of metabolic tests which proved absolutely useless except that it revealed her blood type as A negative, something she hadn't known.

"Goodbye, love," my father says. "I'm leaving now." He'll begin practicing medicine on Monday morning, making $350 a month in this small coastal town, a tiny patch of beauty beneath the armpit of Mobile. It's here that pelicans swoop and dive on the piers, where the sun sets in a bruised halo over the bay. The days are warm and mild. It's a good place, I think, to be born. Fairhope. What more could a child want than the combination of these two words?

When the birth pains come at midnight, my father—who's arrived at 10:00—drives Mother to the clinic overlooking the bay, a small, private hospital with maternity beds, a delivery room and nursery, a doctor, a lab technician, and a small staff of nurses. It's in this clinic that my father will work alongside the doctor who will deliver me, an older man who will be his boss. As my mother's admitted to the clinic, I imagine her hopeful, anxious. She too wants a big family—boys rushing out to play baseball, girls with their tea sets, serving peanut butter sandwiches and tepid water, all of them sleeping at night like angels, their arms hanging limp over the sides of their beds. There will be brunettes, blondes and delicate redheads, their eyebrows a whisper of smoke. They will be doctors and lawyers and teachers. Maybe even a politician.

Once she's settled in her room, she looks quickly in the mirror, sees her dark hair falling in deep waves away from her face. Perhaps this next child will be a little boy with dark curls, hazel eyes, and lashes thick and velvety like her father's. Or perhaps some combination of her and my father, red hair but with hazel eyes and a pug nose, a boy who will run after Don, will help him build forts and fences, will sleep in the bottom bunk, too afraid to climb up to the top.

But she has little time to think, for I'm born at 5:30 the next morning, not the proposed boy at all, but a second daughter, so pale I'm almost no color at all. Fine blue veins spiral across my forehead, and bright orange spots begin to freckle my cheeks. I'm a silent, sleeping child, but as the day lengthens, Mother begins to worry; I seem so listless, so quiet, there's something odd in this absence of frustration. Why don't I cry when I'm hungry, when my diaper is changed? Where are those sly, subtle smiles, those gurgles of flirtation with the world? And what about the strange little freckles, orange spots sprinkling my cheeks like diluted Mercurochrome? She's read in medical journals about the Rh factor— the problem of blood type (my father is B positive)—how it can affect a child, resulting in brain damage and lethargy, and ultimately, death. She also knows that many doctors discount such a theory because it's an unproven hypothesis, still being researched. As she watches me sleep, she can't see me picking up my teacup or playing with my favorite dolls, but vanishing into the walls of the house, becoming ghostly, invisible, leaving only the faint rhythm of my breath.

"She doesn't cry," she says to the doctor when he arrives the next morning, "and that's not normal. There's something wrong." The doctor, grey-haired and gentle, a man well thought of in the community, leans over, examining me. He's so close Mother can see the part in his hair, can smell his aftershave, can hear the starchy crackle of his white coat. He feels my pulse, checks my lungs, studies my chart. "She's fine," he says confidently, straightening, his stethoscope gleaming in the light. "She's just pale, but she's eating well. Don't worry." Mother sighs, retreating into the world of hopeful endings, wondering if she might just be anxious, overzealous, *that kind of mother.* She's been well-trained to respect doctors. In every hospital where she's worked, the doctors are treated like gods, autocratic, omnipotent, their authority never questioned. At City Hospital in Mobile, the entire staff stood at attention when a doctor entered the room. If only she could talk now to my father, but he's kept busy, almost sleepless, with a round of new patients and checking on the kids at Hally's.

In the hushed early light of morning, Mother notices I'm ghostly white as if the blood flows weakly below the surface of my skin. Outside in the mimosa trees, the sharp cries of robins and bluejays make such a racket of noise they contrast sharply with my infinite stillness. Only occasionally do I whimper, as if too exhausted to protest. For the second time, Mother sees me leaving, a child who simply can't hold on, who turns her cheek to the wall and stops breathing. Is this madness, hallucination, some storm of depression, or is she seeing what no one else can see?

The next morning she's sitting up in bed, recovering well, the stitches healing, her bound breasts no longer leaking so much milk. "What about the Rh factor?" she asks bluntly when the doctor comes into her room. She doesn't give him a chance to interrupt. "Her father's B positive and I'm A negative. I know it's a new theory, but I think something's wrong with my baby. She's just too white. And she has those orange spots on her cheeks, described in journals I've read as one of the symptoms of this problem."

Again I see the doctor bend over my bed, his hands sifting through the delicate baby covers, pulling them away from my placid face. He's a kindly man, a man who wants to do good, a man my parents are bound to by employment. He's taken my father into practice when there are a glut of physicians returning from the army. And now he looks at Mother with something between egotism and sympathy, this woman so dark, so vibrant in her concern. "You just read too much, Mrs. Foster," he says in his soft-spoken, Southern voice. "There's nothing wrong with your baby." Then the nurse bustles in with water and fresh towels for her sponge bath. The doctor pats her hand.

An uneasy comfort settles around her. When finally she talks with my father, he says he doesn't know, he'll do some reading himself, but then he's called back to the emergency room. When he leaves, Mother goes quiet, her mouth prim, her breasts leaking. To divert her thoughts, she calls Hally to see about the other children. Of course, they're crying; they miss her. They want her to come home, want to know she's sleeping in the room down the hall, not in some faraway place they can't even recognize, doing something they don't understand. Today she sleeps in between feedings, falls into that trance of darkness where nothing is retrieved, a black hole, a hidden well. And yet something happens in the night, a change in the current of her thoughts as she watches the shadows of the trees brushing against a moonlit sky. It's as if she's waking up, seeing the world for the first time, knowing her impression of life is indispensible, and without it, I will die. She sees the frail structure of things, understands that knowledge is a tiny pinprick in the fabric of danger. And who is holding this structure up, defining its shape?

She dresses before the nurse comes into the room, putting on stockings, slip, skirt, white blouse over her bound breasts, willing to risk the doctor's censure, her husband's disapproval, their life together.

"Lord, what are you doing?" the nurse asks when she sees my mother stepping into her spectator high heels. "You can't be getting up yet. Things aren't ready, your stitches aren't set." The nurse is flustered, the tray rattling as she sets it down.

"I'm taking my baby to City Hospital in Mobile," Mother says, already turning away, clasping her belt.

Her announcement causes an uproar, an alarm clock shattering the clinic's peaceful sleep. The nurse rushes out to get the doctor. "Oh, Dr. Jenson, you better come quick," while Mother finishes dressing, putting tissue and lipstick in her purse. Almost immediately the doctor appears, trying to calm my mother—is she hysterical? does she need to be sedated?—agreeing to do a hemoglobin test, to satisfy this woman fully dressed and ready, all restraint thrown to the wind.

When the doctor discovers my hemoglobin is dangerously low (so low I'm expected to die), there is no joy in Mother's victory, only the powerful knowledge that something is definitely wrong. Now they must rush me in an ambulance to City Hospital, the shrill siren signifying trouble. I imagine my mother on that drive, young, frightened, her worst fears confirmed as she sits tensely in the ambulance with my father, thinking of the small delicate bootees, the tiny gowns, the white christening dress with its blue embroidered yoke.

After a series of tests are made at City Hospital, the specialist confirms my mother's diagnosis: I was an Rh factor baby, one whose own blood created antibodies to my mother's blood source. When the doctor explains what my mother already knows, she nods, understanding the danger, the threat inherent in the pregnancy itself. But what she couldn't have anticipated is the specialist's response.

"How could you have *allowed* this to continue, you, a mother, a scientist?" he asks. He's red-faced, vitriolic. He looks like he wants to slam a door. "A mother has *responsibilities,* Mrs. Foster. You must never forget that."

Stunned, Mother stares boldly at him but before she can speak, I'm whisked away to another part of the hospital where I'm bound like a mummy to a board, the transfusion needle inserted in a tiny vein in my forehead. The chance of my survival is slim. Transfusions to babies can be difficult for the very real possibility that the baby's blood will reject the red blood cells.

Only my father is allowed to watch. Mother is sent to the nurses' residence hall to await the results. As she walks towards the door, my life now in medical hands, the sister in charge of pediatrics places a firm hand on her arm. "Your baby's got grit," she says. "She held onto my finger as we took her in. Now you go into the chapel and if the transfusion goes well, I'll call the nurses' residence hall." Mother dutifully goes into the chapel, lit only by candles. The shadows deepen into velvet darkness, the light blooming in tiny pools. Mother prays that I will get well, that I will grow up to be strong and healthy, and that I will never know the terror of my birth.

As the night lengthens, she listens to the muffled sounds of the nurses moving down the residence hall, the soft scrape of doors closing, then the creak of cabinets opening, the night sounds of crickets buzzing in the trees. On the altar the candles flicker; the room grows small and close. Perhaps it's really years later that she hears the phone ringing, a sound no louder than the tinkling of bells. But it's here that she first listens to my voice: in that tiny chapel she imagines she hears me cry.

Three months later it's raining, waves of water flooding the yard. It's now that my father comes bounding into our house in Fairhope, his tie loosened, his body smelling like mildew and sweat. "Hellooooo," he calls out, rushing into the kitchen, shaking water from his hair. It's the energy of the move that's upon him. After worrying so much about finances, my parents have decided to return to northern Alabama where my father can enter a partnership, making the glorious sum of a thousand dollars a month. "There's even a house we might buy," he tells my mother, pulling her away from the sink and swinging her around. She's still light as a feather, like dancing a stick. "A brick house," he says, grinning, "with a big back yard." Neither of my parents has ever lived in a brick house, and more than anything else it signifies our mobility, our ability to embrace an American life.

And yet before we move I have to finish my transfusions. I've been kept alive with AB positive blood, but its AB negative that will do the trick, rendering the antibodies useless, as harmless as wet firecrackers. Now my parents wait anxiously for an unknown donor, for the man who will breeze through the hospital doors, carrying inside him a secret prize. "I hear you need some real rare blood," he'll say, already rolling up his sleeve. "Well, that's me. That's the kind I got."

And in another week, such a man will appear. In two months, I will be pronounced healthy and well, and in a flush of optimism, our family will move north, where for the first time we'll become "middle class."

the doctor's wife

Mother wakes me. "Get up, we're going." But I don't want to move, curled into the covers, peeking at the white lacy canopy of my bed. "Get up!" she rouses my sister. And then I remember! *Birmingham.* We're driving through downtown Birmingham where Vulcan, the Iron Man lives, then on to Praco, where Mother grew up. It will be Mother's first trip since she learned to drive, a feat accomplished only after birthing three children and settling down with my father in a place called Lineville, a town so rural you can say hello and goodbye in the same breath. "It's not even on the map," my brother complains, staring impatiently out the car window as the one stop light blinks red then green. I've never thought of this before. To me, Lineville's the biggest place in the world besides Anniston where my sister and I buy bright pink bathing suits, where we get our dolls re-wigged. There's Hudson's Drug Store where we slurp coke floats and eat banana splits, and the Methodist Church with its slender steeple across from the sprawling Baptist Church.

It's true, this is a hick town, a country town, held together by the Lineville Pants Factory, where women sit daily at Singer sewing machines sewing up a leg seam, a zipper, a waistband on thousands of pairs of pants. The women wear cotton print dresses and eat homemade pimento cheese on white bread for lunch, nibbling brownies as they file back to their tables. Because they sit in such confined positions, their necks bent like fragile stems, their eyes aimed straight down at their work, they get backaches and eye strain and sometimes they cry at the news of another pregnancy. And that's why we're here: they need a doctor, a jack-of-all-trades kind of general practitioner, like my daddy, who delivers babies, sets broken legs and arms, treats worms and pneumonia and drives up into the mountains to places with funny names like Shinbone and Cheaha.

But now that my mother can drive we can go *anywhere.* "Anywhere," she says proudly, having practiced at the cemetery, turning the steering wheel of the big black Lincoln to the left, then the right, concentrating on moving slowly around the circle, mashing down the Sweet William that Louise Hadley had so carefully planted for Arthur as she backed up—*so sorry! didn't mean to*—and then parallel parking by lining up with the markers of Dora Raeburn and Elwood McKinley.

"Get your hair brushed," she tells my sister. She knows that only she can brush my hair, me thrust between her soft knees, the brush held above me like a weapon. "Stay still," she says, brushing from the back forward, jerking gently through the knots, then trying to pat and smooth my thick curly hair. To tame it, she rolls my bangs over her fingers until, exasperated, she gives up, scrunching it close to my head. "That'll do." Across the room, my sister puts barrettes in her long wavy hair; my brother doesn't even bother to look at his. But Mother doesn't notice. She's rushing around, throwing things in suitcases, picking out high heels that will bend her ankles if she wears "those silly things" in Praco. She stops only to look out the window at our car, her eyebrows arched in that peculiar way as if "worry" has been stenciled on her brow.

I wonder now what she was thinking in that little protective silence as she gazes at the car, then beyond at Daddy's red brick office on the corner. Was she worrying about visiting her mother, who had suddenly gone limp, her stout hips and legs resistant to the weight of her body, her heart beginning its erratic whoosh inside her veins? Or did she worry instead about Jimmy Lingo, "Goose" Murphy, and Ray Boussarge, the rowdy crowd of men my father had discovered this past month as if he'd been blind to impulse for eight years and had suddenly gained sight? She can see that damn Coach Lingo on the sidelines of the football field, fidgety and heated, hustling his "boys," stirring them to heroic feats. What if he does that to her husband, riling him, arousing something angry, primitive, pulling him not forward but backwards into some boozy swamp?

If she thought about my father—and I'm almost sure she did— she must have remembered him coming in late last week, not from a house call as she'd expected but from Goose Murphy's poker game. *No, don't think about that,* she tells herself, don't think beyond this brick house with its four bedrooms and the pretty yard with its flower beds of iris and daisies, its sprawling oak trees; don't think back to Mama crying in the night, Daddy, such a dandy, coming in all liquored after a "date" with his lady friend down the road. Life, she knows, means holding tight to the reins, not looking off to the side, catching sight of shapes that turn too quickly into nightmares. *Young lady, you keep your eyes straight ahead and get busy!*

"Get in the car," she says while we drag out more and more toys to take. My sister and I need three dolls apiece, their suitcases jammed full of clothes and my brother wants to take his Lionel train.

"You can't take it *all*," Mother says. "Pick one car. You won't have the track to run it on." My brother screams, gets down on the floor and tries to bite the maid's ankles.

"Stop that!" Mother says and jerks him away; he's finally pacified by wearing his Roy Rogers jacket.

When we're finally ready, she calls one more time to see if my father's changed his mind, if he doesn't want to go with us. But of course, he can't. "Mrs. Simple's in labor," he says. "It could last all night." Patients stand around his office, hollow-eyed, coughing, crowding into that little space like people waiting for a lottery, anxious and stunned. When we moved here Daddy knew he'd have to work all hours, in some of the worst conditions, going out into damp, smelly shacks of the country people in rural Alabama where nightly he made house calls, driving out Wedowee Road into poverty and ignorance where people believed in turpentine cures and asafetida bags, where patients left their payment at the general store, believing a doctor wouldn't come if the $3 for a shot of "healing" wasn't left on the table. Sometimes he had to wade streams or climb steep hills, and when he came home he was tired and often irritable from exhaustion.

"You go on though," he says, "and have a good time."

Mother sits hunched over the wheel as we drive through Birmingham, making us all look for stop signs, for signals, for landmarks for the trip. "Remember that gas station," she says, "they had clean restrooms."

"Can we stop at Vulcan?" we beg, wanting to climb up into the fist of that huge steel arm.

"Not today. This is my first time through. Maybe on our way back."

The traffic surges like an animal and we move through slowly, then fly out onto the open highway, the windows rolled down, our hands waving in the stinging air. We tell each other stories until we hit the winding road to Praco, that rubbed red road that feels like a washboard. Here, we become silent. I lean into Mother's body, my hand on her thigh, listening for the trucks that come crashing down the mountains. There's something awful about the landscape, the hills strip-mined, nothing but stubble and brush with little houses perched in clusters as if protecting themselves from all this ugliness. It's hard for us to believe that Mother grew up here, Mother who wears high heels and jewelry, who won't even say 'damn.' We sit quietly as if an unknown enemy lurks nearby, a hidden power we can't describe. Only when we reach my grandmother's house does a sense of normalcy return: there are flowers in the yard, coffee cans full of daffodils and gladiolas growing in floating patches of grass. Dogs lounge on the wide porch, twitching their tails at some internal irritation. My grandmother, though dangerously fat for a woman with high blood pressure, sits beside her white Spitz, a bowl of ice cream in her lap.

"Mama, what?" my mother says as she climbs out of the car, her spike heels grinding tiny holes into the dirt.

"Chocolate," her mother says, not looking at the bowl, but at my mother with a leaden stare.

"But Mama—" I can hear the scratch of irritation in her voice.

"It's the last. Didn't save any, though I meant to. The children can get themselves some more down at the store."

"Well, you shouldn't. You know that—"

"Shouldn't isn't can't. Now let's get your stuff out of the car and get you settled."

On Sunday, we stand outside after lunch, saying goodbye, Mother's heels making her seem tall and stately beside the bulky peasant bodies of her parents. Parked in the red dirt driveway, our car looks expensive, foreign, and I feel smug with pride. *Our Car. Our Life.* As we drive away we seem separate, special, destined for luxury. Our mother has been named *Alabama's Most Gracious Lady* by the county newspaper, her picture so elegant and remote, you'd have thought she was brought up a socialite in Birmingham. Our father knows everyone in the county, patients and friends who bring us corn and cucumbers and watermelons, people who always wave when we drive by. Nothing threatens us; we're untouchable, safe, unlike our grandparents who have to worry about heating bills and flush toilets in a decrepit mining town.

As we wind our way through the small towns and communities outside of Birmingham, the landscape peppered with slag heaps, with sagging houses, we want only to get home to our brick house. I think of my dolls all squashed up in the car, hair mussed, dresses wrinkled, how I'll have to put Evelyn and Betsy to bed on the window seat with a linen napkin over their bodies. I'll sit beside them and watch the night creep over the back fence, spreading out like fog.

On the outskirts of Birmingham, Mother begins her nervous talk. "We'll have to stop for gas. When we stop, we'll get directions, just to be sure. We don't want to get lost." And she pushes back the jet-black hair that's fallen in her face. "It always looks different coming back, doesn't it? Any of you remember that Coca-Cola plant on the way in?" We stare mutely at it; I stick my thumb in my mouth. "Just think how glad your daddy'll be to see us!"

We troop into the filling station to go to the restroom, to line the toilet seat with paper, to buy cokes and peanuts and licorice candy, anything to tide us over until we get home. The day has turned sultry and hot, a thick moist heat that lies on the city like a blanket. In the distance, we can see Vulcan, the Iron Man, twenty feet high, that totem to Industry, that shiny steel myth. "Can we go there now?" I ask.

"I can climb up into the head," my brother says. "And I'm not gonna hold your hands."

"You have to," my sister says. "And the other hand has to be on the railing."

"Make me," he says, flattening out his lips like string.

"Stoppit!" Mother says. "We're not going anywhere. We've got to get through Birmingham, then get home to fix your daddy's supper."

Coming out of the filling station, we see that another car has pulled up next to ours. At first the sun's glare blinds us after the darkness of the filling station and makes everything white like the after-image of a flash, but as we walk towards the car, Mother stops so suddenly we bump against her thighs. There next to the car stands Coach Lingo, his feet planted slightly apart like parallel planks of wood, his face a mask of soundless hilarity. What he's laughing at is Daddy, trying to hide something—maybe a beer can inside his pocket—as he gets out of the car. Behind him lurks "Goose" Murphy in a Schlitz cap and Ray Boussarge needing a shave. Daddy looks like a teenager playing hooky, all cares thrown aside. Beyond him, the smoke from the steel mills leaks suddenly into the air, an exhaust of white steam polluting the sky.

Yet as my parents face each other, Daddy seems suddenly wary, defiant, his mouth set, chin out, a brash anger clouding his eyes. Mother gasps as if she's been slapped. And then something electric goes through her body. She straightens, looks coolly beyond him at Vulcan, and without speaking, walks to the driver's side of the car.

"Get in kids. We've got a long ways to go." Her pocket book hits the seat with a whack. "And take that thumb out of your mouth," she says to me as she puts the key in the ignition, her knuckles whitening where she grips the wheel. She stiffens in her seat, her eyes facing the highway, her brow so tight, it's like a china plate, hairline cracks ready to break.

No one says a word about my father. We all pretend he doesn't exist, that he is no one, unknown, some renegade man out for a lark. When we look back through the window, he's laughing at something the Coach has said, his head tilted back, his body loose, at ease in the moment.

"Poker," Mother mutters and stares straight ahead.

And yet nothing more happens. The next morning our lives continue as before—grits and eggs and orange juice for breakfast, hopscotch and kindergarten, the news at six—the model family, college educated parents, three kids, a brick house, all indications that we'll be riding into the sunset of success. If the doctor has pledged himself to the public, driving out into the county on dark nights of sleet and fog to see whether Mrs. Longstreet's kid Bobby has penumonia, the doctor's wife is meant to stay on the home front and pick up the pieces, put them back together so that everything looks just right.

And yet there's an image I can't get rid of.

I am three, dressed in underpants. My mother carries me on her hip as she answers the doorbell: we cling to one another as if each is an anchor for the other in a pitching sea. The heavy oak door swings back into the room and we stand, the two of us united before the dark night air. It's midnight and we've both been awakened from sleep. At first, we don't see anything, only the thick swell of mosquitoes and moths which cluster at the first hint of light. Then a hand swings into view followed by its body. A big black man, probably younger than my mother, stands on the steps, hat in hand, his eyes bloodshot, the smell of liquor on his breath. "Lookin' for Dr. Foster," he says in a slow, southern drawl, his eyes focused carefully at my mother's chin. I can feel my mother's body tighten as my legs swing free below her hips. The three of us stay in this tableau as if we're taking each other's measure. Finally, my mother says, "He's out on a house call. Would you like to go on over to the office and wait, or leave your name and telephone number and I'll have him call when he comes in?" There's a pause, my mother standing straighter, the strands of her hair curling around her neck. I put my head on her shoulder. "It may be awhile," she adds.

"No m'am," he says, still looking at her chin. "It ain't me. It's Retha gotta have a doctor."

I don't remember any more. I don't remember what happened to the man, to Retha, only that I'm carried by my mother, carried through the house like a baby to open the door at night. Perhaps I make her feel more secure, for in this small rural Alabama town our house is frequented at all hours of the night by men and women looking for a doctor. There are knife fights, women in labor, insulin reactions, migraine headaches, drunks and beat-up women who need care and attention. And though we open the door every night to strangers, we never add a protecting screen, but keep only the big, heavy oak door which separates us from the dark as if this is our challenge to the world: to meet it head on.

Much later in my life, my mother told me that she carried me until I was four, until people began asking if I could walk. It's why she carried me I'm curious about and why I let her. Surely I remember walking around the yard, playing at the beach, even running down the long slope of our back yard, then up the steep back stairs. I don't remember being carried except at night to the door. Yet my mother assures me she did carry me other places, and I've seen her since pick up grandchildren too old to be held and tote them like sacks while she stirs fried okra at the stove or washes the dirt from celery. In my mind, I became the replacement for my father, this man who was gone most of the night, whose life was interwoven with ours so erratically I often cried when I saw him, this intruder in the primary relationship between my mother and me. In my child's imagination, I was the owner of my mother's body, the one caressed, the one who had first place in her bed, mirroring her dreams, her anxieties, feeling the tension in her body as she opened the door at midnight.

Growing beside her, I'm like a root absorbing nutrients from her soil. I learn many things from her, perhaps the most important is that you can never say no, not to the community which hovers at your front door, not to your husband, overworked and demanding, nor to any of your children. No means you have an agenda, one beyond your service to others.

Even as a child I understood that women's lives in the 50's seemed fragile, unnaturally futile, while men took everything in stride. When frustration hit, Daddy could slam doors, kick chairs, then walk out into the night, going to Goose Murphy's house for a beer or riding alone on the idle back roads of Clay County where trees fluttered like huge dark fingers against the sides of the car. But for women there seemed only a void. They cried, curled up like animals, then went to each other to lick their wounds. It wasn't unusual for one of my aunts to come to live with us for a week or a month while a new life could be fitted around the ruins of the old one. It might be a divorce, a separation, or just a bad case of the jitters, the world closing in, a little windstorm of fear. One night Aunt Joanie plunked down her suitcase, her face puffy and red, devoid of sexual polish. In the kitchen she talked in a hushed voice to my mother and we were told to play in our rooms, to leave them alone. I didn't understand what had happened, hearing only faint references to husbands, money and inattention before their voices dropped to a whisper. They'd talk late into the night, and then sometimes the depression would lift and like a genie they'd spring free of their nagging doubts. The next morning they'd make fudge or chocolate chip cookies, resourceful busy-ness always the ultimate relief. The next year another aunt would come, suitcase in hand, her purse stuffed full of Kleenex and bills.

When Aunt Frankie, age seventeen, came to live with us for two years while her husband was stationed in Japan, she seemed the exception, rushing into our house with an old suitcase, a checked cloth coat, a teasing smile. Although already married, Aunt Frankie hadn't finished high school. She'd just "up and married," she said, tossing it off as if it were no more important than choosing your favorite flavor of ice cream. It was only through the finagling of my mother (who'd taken over that year for the science teacher) that she was allowed to enter eleventh grade two months late and make a push for her diploma. "A woman should have a chance at education," Mother always said. "Frankie too."

In bobby socks and circle skirts—poodle skirts the girls called them—Frankie acted like any other teenager, polishing her nails Desiree Blush, complaining about English and Econ. "I don't know why Mrs. Bryant has such a hissy about all those commas," she'd say, holding up an essay slashed with red marks. "I put one in every time I feel like it. Tom's never complained." Tom was her husband. At the time she didn't seem to have the divided loyalties of my other aunts; in fact, marriage appeared merely tacked on, an extra but irrelevant course she'd added to her schedule. Like the other local teenagers, she went to all the dances and football games at the school, caroused with the other fifty students in her class (by senior class this number would be whittled down to thirty-four), determined to be the class clown.

Putting on lipstick in front of the bathroom mirror the night of her senior prom, she let me stand in the doorway, watching her get ready. She dabbed my mother's White Shoulders behind each ear and into her cleavage. She turned every which way, assessing herself from different angles. Looking at her in her low-cut black prom dress, I forgot about her big nose, her wide forehead, thinking instead she was the most beautiful woman I'd ever seen. "Like a movie star," I said. I imagined myself in that dress, swaying sultrily with my Kim Novac hips. Then for a moment, Aunt Frankie leaned close to the mirror. "If only I weren't married," she whispered, more to herself than to me. "I could be—anything!"

"But you *are*," I said, remembering all the letters she'd written and received from Tom in Japan. I'd seen a picture of him on her bedside table where he smiled arrogantly at the camera as if he were looking right into your eyes. "You are," I repeated. At age five, there's nothing more definite than marriage.

"Well, just for a minute, let's pretend I'm not," she said, turning towards me, but still eyeing herself in the mirror. "How do I look?"

"Married," I screamed, drilling the word into her face. Then I fled down the stairs, out into the back yard, scared that Aunt Frankie was trying to pretend something you couldn't pretend.

Later that night a curious thing happened. Several months before Aunt Frankie had bought a canary at Hudson's Five and Dime, a small yellow bird, probably already sickly, nurtured indoors all its life. She named it Didi as if it were some rare, exotic species. "Didi loves me," she'd say. "Didi loves, loves, *loves* me." The bird rarely did more than hop from its swing to its feeder—it seemed perpetually frightened after my brother threw a firecracker near its cage—but to Aunt Frankie, Didi was a thing of wonder. She'd talk to it while she undressed, even explaining to it how a comma splice was "an unnatural act. It hurts Mrs. Bryant's ears," she told Didi. "She can actually *hear* it reverberating way down there, in her ear drums, Didi-bird. I want to make her have a big explosion on this next essay. What do you say, Didi? Aren't I awful?"

Though I don't know exactly what happened that night, this is what I imagined: sometime after midnight Aunt Frankie tiptoes into the room she shares with my ten year-old brother in her black cloud of a dress, her shoes in one hand so as not to wake him. The curls in her hair have sprung loose from all the dancing—she loves to jitterbug—and now hang limp around her neck, strands floating out in curious disarray. She's danced with every boy at school, flinging herself into the rhythm of the music as if metaphorically she can spin herself out of marriage. In fact, she's still swimming in the night's heartbeat. Dancing in a daring new dress, her thick, jet-black hair in a flood of waves and curls, she felt beautiful for the first time in her life, a beauty that's composed as much of the allure of freedom as the physical attractions of the dress and hair-do. For a silent moment, she stands beside the window. Outside the moon sheds a silvery light across the sloping lawn, silhouetting the big oak tree in the back yard; beyond are the woods, wildness. The sight draws her outward, onward. She sits for a moment on her bed, her dress unzipped but loosely caressing her body, its effect now of something lost, something to be remembered but no longer held. She tries to make herself sink back into reality. In two days she'll graduate from high school. In three months, her husband will come home from Japan. She hasn't seen him in two years. And even with a horde of letters, it's impossible to hear the secret sighs of his body, the things words can't express. In two years many things can change. A girl can grow into a woman. She can walk past the lawn into the woods. Aunt Frankie bows her head, breathing sadness, then lies back on her bed on top of the covers, the dress floating free of her breasts, rustling against the quilt on her bed. She doesn't notice that Didi is not in her cage, the door swung open as she sinks unwillingly into sleep.

Early the next morning my sister gets up to go to the bathroom and then the surprise occurs. In our room, she pulls my arm, waking me from a tight-knotted sleep. I jerk away, rolling over, but the pressure of her arm won't let me relax. "Come on," she insists, pinching. Reluctantly, I jump down from the bed, following her across the hall to my brother and Aunt Frankie's room. "What?" I whisper. I don't know what to look for. There's only the thick, heavy smell of sleep, the bluish light of early morning sneaking through the windows. My brother sleeps on his side, his mouth open, a ribbon of spittle connecting him to the pillow. I move past him to Aunt Frankie. And then my eyes register the shock: there on Aunt Frankie's smooth white breast lies Didi, frozen into the stiffness of death, her wings drawn close, her creepy little feet straight out, five inches from Aunt Frankie's chin.

My sister and I run back to our room, silent, shaken, jumping together into my sister's bed. I want desperately to giggle at this horror, but I know in my secret child's heart that Didi died in payment for Aunt Frankie's malicious wish. You cannot wish yourself out of marriage, cannot rebel against a southern lady's plight. You can only stay or leave. Very early in life I believe there's a price to pay for freedom: if you long for it, even musingly, something will be taken away. This, I think, is why so many women stay inside their houses, why Mother never rushes to climb the fence that separates the lawn from the woods. You have to choose one side or the other.

1998. FOLEY, ALABAMA

Tonight I'm standing at my old bedroom window, staring out at the black liquid sky when Mother comes in to tell me goodnight.

"Sleepy?" she asks and I shake my head. I've been thinking of Praco, of Mrs. Elgin and those four skirts laid out on the bed. Sometimes I don't know what to make of my mother's early life. I want to see it as something created, something contrived from another, more dangerous world. Earlier today while we were driving down the Greeno Road, past horse farms and the flat green fields of soybeans, Mother said how happy she'd been to get those four skirts for college, but when she saw the bulging suitcases of her granddaughter bound for Harvard, she wanted to laugh at how different things were today.

"Didn't you want to show them?" I ask now, turning from the window. "Didn't you want to throw all that misery right back in their faces?"

"Oh yes," Mother says quickly. She's sitting on the bed, working the catch on her robe, not looking at me. And then she smiles, a private, tight-lipped smile and glances pensively past me into the dark. "I used to love to go back to Praco in my new black Lincoln, with my nicely dressed children and my good clothes."

I nod. I can see us all in the Lincoln, driving up that graded hill to her mother's house, watching the land turn bleak and ugly, a single crow flying in a still white sky.

"You know the first time I came back with you kids, Mrs. Elgin insisted I stay with her—" Mother stops as if she's seeing herself climb out of the car in her new high heels, the sun setting in a stark summer sky "—because she had better facilities."

I'm shocked. "What do you mean?"

"You know, a bigger bathroom and nicer bedrooms."

"But what about your mother? Wasn't she embarrassed at that?"

"Oh no," Mother says, still fiddling with her robe, "Mrs. Elgin explained it to her, said it would just be so much easier. And Mama was grateful."

We're both quiet a moment. I turn back to the window, listening to the crickets making their racket of noise. I think of Mother parking her Lincoln in front of her parents' house, her mother fat and old in a flowered house dress coming out to greet us, the dogs yapping at her heels. For the first time I wonder if we made her sad. If we were just one more source of despair.

"And when your daddy came with us," Mother picks up the story, a smile puckering her lips as if she's seeing Daddy drive up that hill, then get out of the car with his little black bag, "I could introduce him as Dr. Foster, and all those people who'd made me feel ashamed . . . well, they had to be nice to me. Everybody respected a doctor."

Then suddenly I'm smiling too . . . because everything falls into place.

next door to the coloreds

Daddy stands in the darkened hall in his white doctor's coat, a syringe flashing silver in his hand. There are no windows in this hall, only squares of yellowish light from the examining rooms, and a dim overhead bulb which shines dully on his thinning red hair. I'm not sure it *is* a syringe, but I know that a shot—panties down, my face in my mother's lap—is the purpose of this visit. "Come on now, I haven't got all day," he says, the white doctor's coat moving stiffly towards us, shoes squeaking on the shiny polished floor. His voice thuds into my stomach like a bullet and I shy back into Mother's skirts, thumb jammed in my mouth. Sometimes he gives me shots in his bedroom, my bottom displayed like a target against the bumpy white bedspread; I'm pushed and pulled there like a prisoner, furious at this man who makes me cry.

"Okay, Pooch," he calls almost tenderly, moving closer, the stethoscope bouncing against his chest; his white coat crackles like hardened wax. For a moment, the hall brightens as the door behind us opens and a burst of sunlight plays on his face. Up close he looks less menacing, his mouth relaxing into a thin-lipped smile, tiny veins curling like commas across his nose.

As he fills the syringe, he holds the tip of his tongue between his lips. A nervous tic, Mother says, and I watch it, not the syringe, see the slick, bumpy surface of his tongue, mottled red like hamburger meat. But when he holds the boot of the syringe in his hand a roiling motion of seasickness starts in my stomach, taking over my body as I cling to Mother's knees. Hanging on for dear life, I feel the cold patch of alcohol and the searing sting of the needle before I go overboard, head first into the sea, every creature swimming from the depths to nibble on my nose, my ears, to twist through my hair. "Whaaaaa," I cry out, hands pushing and clawing at air. My anguish is unbearable; it flies out like so many pick-up sticks.

"There now, it's all over," Mother whispers, hands soothing my brow, fingers untwisting the curls. But I only squeal louder.

"Hush," he says, voice harsh. And I hide again in the skirt of Mother's dress, refusing to look at him until I'm safely outside the door, out of his reach.

"We're going to take Shirley to her father's," Mother announces as if nothing whatever has happened, a clean sheet dropped over the agony of the shot. She smiles at Nurse O'Brien, "Hello, Dorothy," and straightens Daddy's tie, patting it flat. "It'll probably take two hours, so expect supper to be late. Who knows what those roads will be like."

He nods, adjusts his stethoscope when Nurse O'Brien flicks a chart, summoning him down the hall to see Shorty Lipscomb, who has a fish hook embedded in his thigh.

And then, miraculously, we're outside the office, in the new black Lincoln, taking Shirley, Daddy's sister-in-law—who sits in front with Mother—to her father's house. Standing in the hump of the floor, I grab onto the seat behind Mother and stare at Shirley. Mother has already told us that Shirley is "country" and this so distinguishes her I forget about my father and spend most of the trip watching Shirley, waiting for whatever is "country" to come rushing out.

We're driving through land I've never seen. Past Barfield, a lonely two-lane road with fields on either side, occasionally a scarecrow, a run-down house, a barn, an old truck parked sideways in a ditch beside the fields. Near one house a hound dog chews on a piece of paper, then comes flying at our wheels, mouth foaming with fury, loud barks which break from its peeled-back mouth like high-pitched screams. Mother speeds up, rushing past broken-down fences, weedy yards, outhouses, barns, kudzu-filled ditches. When we turn off the main road onto a dirt-gravel road, I stare at Shirley. But Shirley looks self-absorbed, even stoical, and reaches inside her purse for another Pall Mall, the smoke floating out the window to merge with the dust.

We drive up hills, the road bumpier, narrower, the car bouncing us like horses in a trot. When we turn a corner, there's a chicken house and a gaping wire fence separating the raked dirt yard from the crumbly dirt road. A shack sits behind a scrawny tree. Chickens peck at the ground, nervous, bickering. A hawk flies nonchalantly over the roof. Mother stops the car, and Shirley looks peevishly at the house as if she wishes she hadn't seen it, then puts out her cigarette, stubbing it in the little silver ashtray where Mother keeps spare change.

This is it! The country!

As we open our doors, an old man, wearing a felt hat and overalls, walks towards us, his gait unbalanced, favoring one leg. His mouth looks as if it's been suctioned from the inside, and he chews on his toothless gums. I watch him with great interest, surprised and terrified that this is Shirley's father. "Howdy," he says to Mother, and then something to Shirley I don't understand. "Ain't you gettin out?" he leans in the window, staring at me, his face a wrinkled knot, the skin gray-colored as if he's been hiding under the house. I move closer to Mother, who laughs uneasily and pats my hand. "He's talking to you, honey. Can't you say hello?" But I hide in the dark fullness of Mother's hair and listen to the bubbles coming up inside my throat. If my father ever said *ain't*, we'd pack our clothes and leave him, getting in the car and driving all the way to Sylacauga.

But we *do* get out, the dust puffing in clouds when I jump from the back seat, my sandaled feet hidden from view. And once outside the car, in the open air, I surprise myself by splitting apart, becoming two people, something that happens quite frequently, though I never know what it means. One person is hugging Mother's leg, afraid to look at the old bag-of-bones father who might grab me and keep me prisoner in his chicken coop, putting a shotgun to Mother's back and making her drive all the way down the curving road without her daughter. If that happened I'd be left in the dark with chickens pecking at my hands and feet, feathers twirling around my head, my mind a bright constellation of fury. Then, without pause, the other me leaps ahead, bold and daring, watching keenly, freely curious about the motions of the old man's mouth. "You ain't seen nothing like this, has you?" he says, holding up a flour sack he's giving to Shirley, one with faded yellow flowers on the front and bloody smears on the back. He grins, exposing gray nubby gums. This other self wants to touch those gums, to walk around them with my fingers. I wish I could make him lie down in the middle of the dirt, then I'd sit on top of him and explore. I'd run my finger inside his mouth, pull out his tongue, look up his nose. I'd find out everything country about him. Teach him to say *isn't* instead of *ain't*. I'd be the teacher and he'd be the pupil, and I'd show him how to write P I G in the dirt with one finger. While exploring him from behind Mother's legs, I feel a moment of triumph that my father will never end up like this. Daddy gives me a dollar allowance so I can buy barrettes to keep inside my bureau drawer. He's clean and white. And despite my earlier indignation, he nudges a little bit forward like a hero pushing steadily across the page.

Still, I wish I could live alone with Mother in the bedroom with the twin canopy beds where the light splashes through the many-paned windows. There we wrap up in quilted blankets and tell stories, watching the squirrels leap from branch to branch, betting on which ones can jump the furthest.

Instead, we're all a family. "And we need each other," Mother says, cuddling me close as she puts me to bed. But I don't know how to tell her that my father expects a loyalty from me that I don't know how to give. I can see it in the way he looks quickly at me while he's sitting on the couch across from Goose Murphy, a beer in his hand. At first, he ignores me, takes a sip from his beer, the foam bubbling, the napkin stuck to the bottom of his glass, and he says something about Miss Hadley at the pants factory to Goose, a joke about her "weekend guests" which makes Goose laugh. I'm playing paperdolls on the floor and when I hear Goose laugh, I always smile, thinking that Goose is a funny name for this big man with a pointy head and fuzzy moustache. When my father gets up for a second beer, he suddenly notices me, though I've been here in the corner of the living room all along, making a nest with my doll's bed and my mother's straw hat turned over on its side. I keep the paperdoll clothes inside the hat, the dresses on one side, the sports clothes on the other, hats in the bottom. "Squeegy," he says with that note of propriety in his voice. I look up shyly, then boldly withhold myself. "Little Squeegy," he smiles a broader smile, an embracing smile, and I know instantly that my withholding is a sin because *when somebody is nice to you you're supposed to be nice back to them.* But somewhere deep inside, I believe he wants to take something from me, something that may be too fragile for me to give. And what's worse, the invitation might come in just this sneaky way, a smile and a kind word, and if I'm not careful, I'll forget to protect myself, and whatever is mine will quickly become his.

But what does my father feel? Does his heart beat rough inside his chest when he draws me near? I can't know, of course, and yet I need to know, need to imagine what rubs against the inner skin of his life.

A second beer in hand, he loosely holds his daughter, who's squirming against him like a nervous cat. He pats her tummy, and laughs at the story Goose is telling about Timmy Barker going out to his garage to sneak a beer. "Mary's a staunch Baptist, you know. Says she'll flat out divorce him if he drinks." Goose laughs. "And *she's* got the money."

He nods, noticing for the first time the paper doll his daughter holds in her hand, a glamourish Hollywood type, the feet ominously cut off at the ankle, one arm dismembered at the elbow. This absurd imperfection suddenly affects him, makes him want to hold on tighter, to protect his daughter from the inevitabilities of life, the very possibility of imperfectability. He wants nothing to happen to her, not even a scratch on the knee, a sprained ankle, a stubbed toe. And before he can stop himself, he remembers the premie, Mrs. Sebastian's first, incubated in diluted oxygen, the tiny fingers gripping air, mouth open in a silent howl. He can't forget that scream, wears it inside him like a blanket of pain. Blood he can stand. Guts, urine, razor cuts up the wazoo, skin sutured to skin, the ugly black thread crisscrossing the jaw. But save him from the premies.

"If that isn't hen-pecked," Goose goes on, "I don't know what is!" But the doctor isn't listening anymore, only nodding, still thinking about the way that tiny chest compresses and, like a burping frog, expands.

"A man's gotta have his beer." Goose raises his glass in salute, and the doctor does the same, remembering how his own father used to guzzle beer, his head thrown back, eyes closed, as if the first shock of coldness was a pure sexual thrill. As a boy, he stood in the kitchen on Sunday nights—the only night his father didn't have to work—while the old man brought the beer up from the basement, holding the bottles aloft as if in ceremonial tribute. Then his father began to drink in earnest, leaning against the kitchen counter, talking, teasing, happy in the ease of his own house, the mischief of free time. And yet the drink hurt his gut, tore him apart so that, the next morning, he staggered around the kitchen in tattered undershirt and drawers, groaning, heaving, one hand clutched to his belly. It was almost comic, this lurching figure who grimaced, then grinned. As a child he never thought much about it, never thought about the way events in a life stack up to surprise and undo you. He thought you just kept climbing step by step to a higher place like moving from sixth grade to seventh, no intervention required.

He watches his daughter flutter her toes, the twitching reduced to this one rebellious act: feet wiggling in the air. He wants to tell her about his father—but how can he explain that his father left for work one day and never came back, the racket in his stomach a deeper, more insidious curse than anyone had imagined. At the time he was a senior in high school, already working afternoons, putting one foot in front of the other, set on forward motion, no lags in between. Then, as suddenly, all movement stopped. He stood at the cemetery and watched the light die behind the old oak tree, his body frozen in time, dusk falling like a veil. Now *he* had to support *them,* he, the oldest boy, his own dreams tucked under the rug. And of course, it didn't matter that he was smart, salutatorian of his class, a kid with ambitions. Even the principal said stubbornly, "Go on to work at the papermill, boy. Don't try to get above yourself." And so off he went, dutifully to work, begging for a job in the chemical processing division so he could make more money, working daily, weekends, time-and-a-half until his mama could manage on her own. Then, a year later in college, he understood. When you're poor, you're nothing. A squashed paper bag. A flimsy stick. Lucky for him he turned a nothing into a something, but that something's a demanding son-of-a-bitch.

"I can tell you things," Daddy says in 1995 as we sit at the kitchen table, his back to the phone as if he can ignore its insistent rings. He talks over the noise, starting off with a story from childhood, a time when he was eight or nine and his family had moved from Mobile to Pascagoula, where his father, a baker, had found work.

"One night Mama was sure she heard prowlers, the sound of feet moving in the yard just beyond the kitchen window where the yard led to a ditch." They'd settled in a small house, hardly more than a shack on the edge of a nice neighborhood, one of those side streets that lead nowhere but into swamps full of kudzu and mosquitoes, weeds cluttering the side of a dirt road. The air, thick with humidity, would be close and hot, at night a horde of bugs crawling in from the swamp, fluttering against screens, creeping through the cracks. His mother made the children quiet down and Daddy said he listened to the crunch of leaves as something crept closer and closer to the house. "You could hear this swish-swish in the bushes, and then a sudden silence would tear your heart out." What they imagined, he said, were hoodlums, tramps, men passing through town looking for work on the shrimp boats, in the bag factories, or men so far gone, they'd sleep in the swamps. "I was quiet and still," Daddy said, "busy listening, but once the footsteps stopped, there was that stillness like when you first step outside, with only the shrill of crickets in your ears. 'Go on up to that house, son, at the end of the street,' Mama told me, 'and call your Uncle Johnny.' She pushed me forward because I didn't want to go. 'Hurry,' she whispered, 'Ask nice but be quick.'"

Then Daddy told how he snuck out the front door, hardly breathing, struggling not to think, not to open the closets of his imagination, afraid of what they'd heard prowling in their yard. It could be a black man with a knife, an escaped convict from the penitentiary at Leakesville come down here to shoot them all dead. He was almost sure he heard a rifle click, then something in the bushes, footsteps near the back steps. He ran fast, heading for the first house where a porch light beamed. Summer dark spread all around him, magnifying his fear. If he could get hold of his Uncle Johnny on the police force, he'd save them.

He ran through the dark green grass, up onto the white porch with the smooth round columns and brass lanterns on either side of the door. He'd barely knocked on the door, a rat-a-tat-tat with his fist, when the door swung open to a tall, elegant man in a vest and silk handkerchief. Daddy said he was taken aback by this figure, a man fixed up in a white shirt and vest on Friday night while his own daddy at the bakery dressed in jeans and a plaid shirt, a baker's apron pulled over him like a sheet.

"Yes?" the man spoke from the stiffness of his shirt, his face a bright slab of marble. He had peevish eyes, a florid face. A judge, Daddy would learn later.

"My mama says can I please use your phone to call Uncle Johnny." He spoke quickly, the fear pumping wild inside his chest. "We've got prowlers outside our house and my daddy's at work." He heard the plea of urgency in his voice, though he'd asked nicely and politely as if he'd walked across the street from the white columned house instead of running down the alley where the poor people lived. He was so sure of his performance, his entire body was poised to be let inside.

But the man didn't move from the door. "Well, sonny," he said with that tight, carnivorous smile. "I don't let just *anybody* use my phone."

It was the word *anybody* that stunned him, froze him in place. It was the first time he'd been told he was no one in the world, a pebble, an ant, a piece of driftwood left carelessly on the shore.

Like my mother, my father crawled out of his past, shed its skin like a snake, leaving only the dry husk behind. Daddy came from the ranks of the working poor, the disinherited, laundresses, bakers, factory workers, fishermen. His own family had shucked oysters for sale, brewed homemade beer to hawk by the glass. Only his Aunt Dot expected anything more ambitious of him. "You'll be a doctor," she said, her chin tilted as she uttered this decree. She had fancy ideas about improvement, about "getting on with things," and he intended to prove her right. A year later he went to the University of Alabama, saving money from the papermill. When he was accepted, he entered college with such naieveté, he thought he'd already been admitted to medical school.

I would never have thought much about my grandfather, a man I never knew and saw only as a short, bald-headed figure in a faded family portrait, his face serious, almost severe, if my father hadn't asked me to go to Pascagoula, Mississippi, with him to find his daddy's grave.

I am surprised but pleased. We leave in the early morning hours when the light is pale as milk, the only people on the highway being fishermen and truckers and a tired-looking woman who passes us, a can of beer perched like a beacon on her dash. Daddy sits hunched, squinting into the glare of the sun. His thinning hair is the color of milkweed. It curls around his collar, little twists of it tucked behind his ear. His face is smooth—no lines at all—only a flurry of broken capillaries that lace the skin of his cheeks. He's silent today, but when he grins his entire face opens up, lets you see the glitter inside.

Pascagoula looks seedy, the houses and businesses run-down, paint peeling off the buildings, yards overgrown with weeds and wildflowers. A town familiar with poverty and crime, I think, a banished second cousin to the swank renewal of the Sunbelt.

"That cemetery's near the water," Daddy says. "I know that much. If we can find Pascagoula Street, we're in business." He straightens, looks alert, eyes scanning the scenery.

"Recognize anything?"

He shakes his head. "Not much." But his eyes search the landscape, and I wonder if he remembers this town as a blue-collar town with fishermen and papermill workers, shrimp boats coming in, barges going by, pigeons scavenging on whatever humans leave behind, a town with none of the elegant customs and manners of places like Mobile and Biloxi. Today the town looks like a dump. Trash on the street. Houses falling down. Wildflowers growing in their foundations. A couple of fast food stores—Krispy Kreme, Hardees, McDonalds—but nothing that comes close to the old bustle of men getting off at 5:00, boys off to softball, to paper-routes, to the shrimp house to peel shrimp.

We drive down Sunset Street, looking on both sides for any sign of a graveyard. Off Sunset, there are pathetic little streets, the houses unpainted behind the sealed darkness of trees. Must be poor blacks and poor whites living together now, the porch steps decked with turpentine cans full of red and yellow gladiolas. Chipped birdbaths sit idle in the yards. A child's plastic windmill turns rhythmically on a stick in the dirt. We come upon it suddenly, two rectangular patches of ground surrounded by a rusted chain link fence, weeds growing right up to the curb.

"I remember standing near a tree at the funeral," Daddy says, fitting a golf hat on his head. And so it's in the north corner that we begin, each taking a row, bending down to read names and dedications, brushing off grass to decipher the fuzzy inscriptions. Dead flowers, withered and old, lie on a few graves. No fresh flowers anywhere. Only the dead for the dead. Occasionally, we hear cars go by, the sharp rev of an engine or the thin yelp of a dog, but mostly there's nothing but the hot sun beating down like a heater on our necks, the trickle of sweat down our backs. The sudden quiet is enormous. We cover one side of the cemetery, walking from top to bottom, calling out names and dates, then cross the narrow street to the other side, walking over stunted grass. On this side, there is no tree.

Two hours later I feel wilted, defeated, uncertain of the point. There's a sadness here, a particular loneliness I haven't felt before. My father is still looking, diligent, patient, faithfully going down each row. This is unusual for him. He's known for his impatience, his fretful badgering. "Meeting adjourned," he calls out whenever he's bored. Yet today he hasn't stopped. Bending over the graves, he looks intent, brooding, and in that brooding is a sweetness, a gentleness I've seldom seen. I stand by the gate, resting, fidgeting, waiting while my father, his legs moving stiffly through the brown grass, searches for his past.

As he walks further into the field, bending to check other graves, I remember one night during the Christmas holidays when he talked openly about his early life, his face flushed, his body slumped in some long-denied defeat.

"We lived right next door to the coloreds," he said, his voice hollow, eyes stunned by this admission as if he'd just been condemned. His body remained inert, not moving, only his eyes jumping around, nervous, uncertain. "Nobody knows this about me because I could never tell it. It was the worst thing in my life." I stared at him, embarrassed, frightened of the direction of his fear. I always thought he'd be like Atticus Finch in *To Kill a Mockingbird,* on the side of justice and morality, a friend to the oppressed. I didn't know what to do with this story because it affected me so differently than it affected him.

When I look at him now, I think how gentle and troubled he looks, how much he wants to find his father's grave. He leans closer to a gravestone, straightens, goes to the next, takes a tentative step onto the mound, not sure how to negotiate the small dirt paths between the graves. All his life he's tried so hard not to be lumped with the outcasts, the shamed.

Now Daddy's bending over, reading an inscription, his attention unwavering, almost rapt, and suddenly I see myself in his quest. I too am trying to make peace with the past, trying to find the graves, the markings, to settle unfinished business. I too want to rid myself of shame.

a different kind of woman

Gnats float in balls of motion, swimming in the recess of our eyes, circling our heads. At dusk, dragonflies, big as our thumbs, zoom past our shoulders, their buzz like the sizzle of a fried electric cord. Behind our house, the river runs like a lazy blue street, curving in an innocent path towards Devil's Hole. On the very first day we hear about Devil's Hole, the river's deepest spot, where people have drowned, their bodies dragged up as limp and pale as dead fish.

We've moved from the red-clay hick town in northern Alabama to this river community with its dusty bait and grocery store, its white Presbyterian Church, its sprawling houses alongside the river, so that my father can go into practice in a warmer climate. In northern Alabama "he was working himself to death," Mother said, "getting sick each winter, always coughing, unable to breathe, a cold forever brewing in his chest. But he couldn't stop. There were always more patients and he couldn't stand for people to be sick." Mother didn't want to move; she liked our life in northern Alabama, liked driving to Anniston and Birmingham, to the places where she had roots. But she was worried about Daddy, so dutifully she packed up the furniture and in June we drove towards our new home in southern Alabama.

It's a monster of a house, two-story, with an odd and delightful assortment of rooms: a huge bedroom we step down into from a turn in the stairs, other bedrooms with screen porches attached where my sister and I pretend to be ladies, sipping iced tea. A sun porch, all windows, leads from the living room, a small glass palace. "So many windows!" my mother says wearily, her mind filled with the task of cleaning. But when the sun sweeps through the dirt-streaked panes, bathing the rooms in luminous softness, she whispers, "Well—" and smiles helplessly.

Yet the house is old, dirty. Trash has been heaped on the front porch, dead roaches—lying on their backs, feelers extended—carpet the kitchen floor, making it harder to worry about the stove, its eyes ringed with grease. "How will I ever get this together before school starts?" Mother asks when we settle in, the strain of moving showing on her face. Her thick black hair is damp with sweat and a streak of dust highlights one cheek.

"You could get some help," my sister says, putting down her load of toys. And we all agree, though no one has any idea where help can be gotten, whom we should call.

She steps up on our porch out of the white hot glare of August. She neither rings the bell nor knocks on the oak rimmed glass door, but pauses as if gathering energy or making up her mind. I happen to be downstairs in the big open space of the living room, twirling a day-glow hula hoop around my waist. It whips around my waist in a whiz of motion. My concentration is complete, earnest. I'm learning to walk back and forth across the room, keeping the hoop whirling like one of Saturn's rings. I don't know what makes me glance up. Perhaps it's her shadow blocking the light or a slight movement, the touch of her dress against the screen. But when I look up, the hoop wobbles crazily and falls in a clatter to my ankles. I give her a scowl as I open the front door, the screen between us.

"Your mama needing some help," she says without introduction. It's a statement, not a question, and I nod. There are mounds of ironing—"four feet high," Mother says, exhaustion in her voice—in the dining room where the ironing board is set up each night. During the day my mother cooks meals, cleans up different sections of the house, takes us to the beach at 11:00, and in the afternoons, she sits on the sun porch reviewing magnets and electricity for the science classes she'll teach at a nearby junior high in two weeks. She's upstairs now making up beds, getting ready for our morning trip to the beach.

I stare at the woman. She's tall, with coffee-colored skin and kinky hair pulled back in a knot so small it looks like a bubble growing from her neck. She looks alternately scared and furious, her square jawbone assertive, yet her eyes flickering like those of a horse sensing danger, all nervous and jumpy.

"I'll get her," I say politely, nodding. I run upstairs and tell my mother a woman's at the door, a woman who's come to help her.

"At last," Mother says. She drops the sheet she's been fluffing and rushes down stairs, opening the screen door.

"Can I help you," Mother says as if the woman might be in distress. Mother must look like a woman of privilege in her pretty green skirt and blouse, white sling-back heels on her feet. She's always dressed up, never in sloppy shorts or shapeless house dresses; later I'll understand that clothes and pretty things are a necessary front, a tide of faith against "that awful past." Slovenliness means damnation, failure, an excuse for defeat.

"I thought you might be looking for somebody," the woman says, no emotion in her voice. They stand just inside the doorway, the woman a head taller than Mother even in her heels.

Mother quickly reaches behind the woman and closes the door so the cool air won't escape. She gives a little apologetic smile when she does this and murmurs, "the heat," pushing a lock of jet black hair from her forehead. "Do you do ironing?" Mother asks, glancing fretfully at the dining room where Daddy's dress shirts lie in a heap. From here the mound of clothes is shielded from view, but I know Mother can see through walls. She often knows when my sister and I are reading under the covers at night even when the door is shut. "Men's dress shirts and underwear and large tablecloths."

"Yes'm." Her eyes settle down, though she doesn't smile. She doesn't look at the white linen sofa or the lamps whose bases are brass pineapples, but keeps her eyes trained keenly on Mother.

"Cooking?"

"Yes'm. Cooked over at Barnhall for that brick quarry for awhile. Hot-water cornbread, country fried steak, every kind of green there is."

"Well." Mother looks around her as if a decision might be floating in the air. "There's an awful lot to do here. I'll be teaching in two weeks and there'll be the kids home in the afternoons." Then she shakes her head, not decisively, but with resignation. "All right then. I'll need you three days a week to start."

"Yes'm. I've got my uniforms ready. I could come tomorrow."

"Fine," Mother says, nodding. I watch a drop of sweat trickle down her neck and then get lost in the collar of her blouse.

That's how Ida entered our lives, Ida who is never talkative, who seldom lets down her guard. Even when there are only us children in the house—children whom she feeds and picks up after—Ida remains closed-mouthed, secretive. Her past is a private door and only she has the key.

"Do you have any kids, Ida?" I ask one day, idly stirring my fork in the crowder peas on my plate, making lines, then X's and fancy circles. Mother has a teachers' meeting this afternoon and afterwards P.T.A., so Ida has to feed my sister, brother and me an early night meal.

Ignoring me, Ida plops a pork chop onto my plate. It's thin as paper and fried hard like a piece of cardboard, not the way Mother usually cooks them. "Eat your meat now," Ida says, staring her bone-hard stare at me as if daring me to complain.

"But *do* you? Do you have any my age?"

After delivering the pork chops, Ida turns away, stirring the apple sauce she is heating in a pot. She puts a fork of peas in her mouth, eating her own food standing up at the counter. "What?" she says curtly, as if I've been talking to myself. She heaps more peas onto her fork and absently puts it into her mouth.

"Any kids, Ida. I told you—"

The fork clatters to her plate. "You think your mama's paying me to talk about myself? You think I don't have dishes still to do and you lollygagging with your food just to make me late? Now eat your meat like I said to."

I cut a piece of pork chop, being careful to trim off the fat, which Mother says is just empty calories, grease that can clog up your system, ruin your arteries, but when I look at Ida, she's eating hers fat and all. I wonder if I should tell her it is bad for her body so she can warn her kids, if she has any.

"Ida doesn't have any kids because she doesn't have a husband," my sister pipes up. "Isn't that right, Ida?"

Ida laughs, showing her upper gums. They're blue-black like the skin of a plum. "There ain't mens enough in this world for me to want a husband," Ida says, still laughing. "No sir, I don't want one of them problems hanging around my neck, sucking me dry. There's enough to do as it is, and all mens wants—" Then she stiffens, her whole body seeming to freeze as if she's tightening up something that has loosened involuntarily. "Watch your milk now," she says, pointing at me, back to being snappy. "You're about to spill it and I'm not mopping up no kitchen floor one more time, I don't care what your mother pays me."

"What do they want?" my sister asks, her mouth open, the crowder peas squashed inside. When she's curious, all other functions seem to stop. "Do men want your money?"

"Can't be that," Ida says, taking the apple sauce off the stove. "I ain't got none of that."

"Doesn't Mother pay you?" my sister asks, concerned. She'll always be concerned about the have-nots.

"Course she does. Who said she didn't? Now close your mouth and eat your food."

But my sister refuses to close her mouth, to chew. "But if it's not money—" She wants an explanation. Ida looks at her as if she wishes her away, wishes her floating downstream in the river. Then she shakes her head, nodding to herself as she leans towards us, her face suddenly intimate, but oddly sinister.

"Mens see a little honey on you and what they want is *that.* And if you're so stupid to let them take it, you ain't got a knuckle's worth of brains inside your wood head because once that honey's gone, there ain't nothing else they want." Then Ida bends down over her plate and lifts a heaping fork of peas into her mouth.

My sister and I look at each other, not satisfied, but frankly relieved by this answer. Mother's much too careful to let honey drip on her, and my father has never seemed to desire anything close to honey or syrup smeared on her hands or arms. What Ida's telling us, we assure ourselves, is merely something peculiar to her, a black woman's story beyond our ken. It means that Ida's just a little clumsier than she ought to be. With renewed determination, we cut into the crisp, stiff pork chops and eat our soft, mushy peas.

I think for a long time that Ida just doesn't like us, and most particularly doesn't like me, her most silent competitor, her most watchful spy. I don't understand the complexities of race as a child, particularly the southern tradition that keeps blacks and whites separate except in the domestic cloister of a white family's home. I don't understand that blacks live not only in a physical ghetto but a psychological and political one as well. I've never met a black child my own age, never talked with a black man other than the occasional ones who cut our grass. Sometimes I bring them a glass of water or a Coca Cola that my mother sends out. They smile and say thanks. Ida never says thanks unless it's "thanks for nothing" when we finish our meals and hand her our plates.

There's a certain afternoon when I watch her making cornbread, an ordinary ritual she performs several times a week. She gets out cornmeal, sugar, soda, shortening, salt and a measuring cup of water and begins mixing the ingredients together into a mush. It looks awful, but I know the delicious taste of hot cornbread straight out of the oven, a slab of butter melting in the center of a slice.

"I want corn sticks," I say, looking up from my second grade reader. I'm sitting at the kitchen table, my books and school supplies spread out all around me. Mother doesn't get home from her school—which is seventeen miles away—until after four so we kids are home each afternoon with Ida, who fixes us a snack and lets us do whatever we want, even swim in the river, something Mother is hesitant to do. "Corn sticks," I repeat in case she hasn't heard.

"Well, you ain't gonna get any," is Ida's curt reply. "Your mama said make regular cornbread and cut it in squares."

"She won't care," I say, flipping the pages of my book. I like the way the corn sticks look, like bread sausages, skinny and smooth, but crusty on the outside. Ida ignores me, still stirring the mix. "She likes for me to have what I want," I say, looking around the kitchen at the neat white counters, the old refrigerator with its ankle of rust which Mother says we'll soon have to replace.

"She left me this note here," Ida motions to that same refrigerator where a note with my mother's writing is held fast by a magnet. "Said how she wanted them done."

Furious at Ida's refusal to grant my request, I look out the door at the river. It's late September, almost October, but one of those Indian summer days when the sky is a heater, sending down hot, stifling rays. I can't think of any way to retaliate against my mother's instructions, so I say the most wicked thing I can think of. "If you don't make corn sticks, I'm going to pray to God tonight and every night this week that you'll drown in Devil's Hole."

Ida gives me a quick, stinging look. "Where you say?" She looks particularly fierce.

I point out the back door to where the Magnolia River winds like a silent trap, ready to tease your body into its depths, then hold it there in a smothering embrace. "The river," I say. "The deepest part. Devil's Hole doesn't even have a bottom. They'll never find you." Though, of course, this last is folklore, I want to impress Ida with the seriousness of my charge.

Ida looks out the screen door to where the barest hint of blue suggests the river. I think she's contemplating her fate and reconsidering my demand, her face betraying no emotion except for the hardening of her jaw. "I ain't never drowning out there," she says quietly, stirring the mush with her strong, mixing arm. I concentrate on the white bowl against her coffee-colored hand, but what

I see in my mind is Ida going down into the water, resigned, not struggling, her hands knotted in fists by her side.

"If I pray hard, you might," I say. "And it's *real* deep."

She's greasing up the square pan now, giving it long sweeps with Crisco. "How you think you're gonna get me in that water?" she asks as she throws the greasy paper towel away and inspects the pan to see that there are no bare spots.

"I'll drag you," I say. "I'll get my brother and sister to help."

Ida ignores me, busy with pouring the cornbread mix into the pan, settling it out evenly and thrusting it right into the center of the oven. Heat blasts out when the oven door opens. I feel it on my legs under the table. But as she closes the oven door, Ida turns around quickly and bends over the table, surprising me, her eyes on a level with mine. I see the whites threaded with tiny red veins, her eyelashes so straight and short they're like the bristles on a blackened toothbrush. She doesn't blink. "Don't you know, child," she says in a tense, slow voice beaded with anger, "that black people can't swim in that river out yonder. So you can pray all you wants, but old Ida ain't never drowning in no Devil's Hole."

I'm so shocked, I lose my place in my reading and the book flips closed. If what she says is true, and I have every reason to believe it is given her hard stare, then only white people can drown in Devil's Hole. I feel so chastened, so surprised I ask softly, "Then where do black people drown?"

"In our own bathtubs," she says in a cool, even tone, "where we don't even have to know how to swim." Then she takes off her apron, flings it on the table and leaves the room as if she's had enough of stupid children like me.

I sit on the steps perplexed. I feel like a sinner and yet what I vividly understand isn't just a lesson about race—there are so few blacks in our town, it's the absence of race that's defined my childhood—but the surprising threat of Ida's anger. Anger, I believe, is forbidden; it must be hidden in the deep crevices of the self. I intuit this because Mother's never angry, because she's a lady and a lady must never show her negative feelings, must always transcend them, protecting everyone around her from the messiness of emotions. "Don't go showing what you feel!" is the law of the land. "For godsakes, don't let things bother you!" Southern life seems dependent on this premise: women have the patience of Job and the placidity of the Virgin Mary. But Ida is angry, her eyes spitting fire, and I can see how useful anger is. It's what started this business in the first place: me taunting Ida. Though it's Mother's path I must follow, I'd rather be like Ida—slapping sheets in the air and flinging my apron on the table. And this, I know is a first class dilemma.

I can see the water at Devil's Hole, blue-black, a bottomless pit. Yet from the surface it looks innocent, so smooth, a flat rug of water, tiny silver fish swimming underneath. "Deep down, they're blind," Mr. Crenshaw, a neighbor, tells me. "It's too dark to see, too dark to do anything but feel, I guess." When he says it, shivers run up and down my spine, shivers of ecstasy, the tiny fish touching me, touching me, touching me. Each day I beg Mother to row us out to Devil's Hole, to let me stare at it, to put my finger in and test the water— warm? cold?—but she doesn't know how to swim and won't let us go until Mr. Crenshaw volunteers to take us himself. That day I run towards the pier, my sister running slower, anxious and fearful, behind me. "If you fall in," she says, "you can drown. Or snakes can swim out and bite you." But I don't listen to her. I keep running. I know I won't fall in. I'm exuberant, crashing through the high weeds, stickers leeching to my tennis shoes, brambles scratching my ankles. I'm thrilled by the idea of swimming into the shadowy pit, that heart of darkness, Devil's Hole. Down there, in the very depths, I can feel anything I want.

The next Tuesday, Ida doesn't come. It's not one of her "days." Now it's my mother at the ironing board, the stove, the sink. But for us kids, it's like any other day of our childhood—hot, sticky, with nothing to do but beg Mother to take us swimming in the river—until the veterinarian, Dr. Max, calls about the dogs.

"I've got two Beagle puppies just waiting for you," he says, without any introduction. "A surprise for the kids from your friend up north."

Mother groans. She doesn't like pets, especially dogs or cats who bring all their rude visitors uninvited into the house: fleas, ticks, beggar's lice, worms. Her idea of a pet is a caged bird or a school of black mollies inside a fish tank, something contained, predictable, untouchable. And besides, she's never met the veterinarian, though this stunt sounds just like her friend from "up north," which is really only northern Alabama. "I've just put an Angel Food cake in the oven," she explains, resisting the gift, the drive into town. As she talks she brushes her hair off her forehead with her hand, though it falls back again as if drawn close to her head by the heat.

"Mrs. Foster, it won't take more than fifteen minutes to pick up the pups," he says kindly as if directing a school girl. "Just leave that cake cooking." We kids are astonished at this, listening in on the living room extension, watching my mother through the open kitchen door.

When Mother's shoulders slump we know she's grudgingly agreed. Yet because of the Angel Food cake—rising steadily, its air-lightened folds swelling inside the pan—we hurry, not changing our clothes or even brushing our hair as we're usually instructed to do because we're new in town and have to make a good impression. It's July 1955 and we've lived in Magnolia Springs only a month, just long enough for Daddy to settle into his medical practice in town and for us kids to attend one week of Vacation Bible School at the First Methodist Church. It's the hottest summer in our history, in the hottest part of Alabama, which suits us fine as long as we're in motion. The house, especially the kitchen, is a swamp. Even with all the windows and doors open, with a fan on the counter, the air doesn't move. At most it shivers, making the sweat slide quickly through our hairlines, leaking in separate streams down our necks.

In the car with the windows all open, the breeze blowing our hair into tangles, we're all anticipation, trying to imagine the puppies. *Spotted with big ears and a skinny tail. No a bushy tail, a flag-waving tail.* "But I want a hunting dog," my brother shouts, forgetting perhaps what our last dog hunted, and how it was run over right in front of our house, leaving him inconsolable for days. But it doesn't really matter what the puppies look like as long as they'll roll around on the floor with us, sleep at the foot of our beds in the lump of covers we leave there. We slump back into our private imaginings as we drive past Mrs. Purvis' house with its big black iron gate, the initial "P" delicately wrought in its iron web, past Moore's Store where Pete and Moody are sitting down to a lunch of sardines and Tabasco, past the Creole school, and on to the flat ribbon of highway.

Once in town we go directly to Dr. Max's clinic, a cement block affair, completely unadorned by scrubs or trees or grass as if it's been dropped from the sky, plunked down and then forgotten. It looks like an unpromising place for a gift, but when we walk in, Dr. Max has the puppies in a box on his desk where he teases and pets them. "The best darn puppies in God's creation," he says, smiling at us with his bold Christian grin. Dr. Max is an evangelical veterinarian who believes all animals are personally blessed by God and should never be allowed to suffer.

On the way home, my sister, my brother and I pet and stroke the terrorized animals, shifting them from hand to hand, from person to person—sometimes making them straddle two laps—as Mother drives the seven mile trip home, anxious to retrieve her cake. She has a sweet tooth and makes a cake at least once a week, despite the extra heat in the kitchen. When we arrive at our two story white house, my sister and I both cuddling a puppy, Mother puts the key in the lock and jiggles, but to our surprise, the door refuses to budge. The door is warped from the humid weather, the sides swollen, the key rusty on the tip. "Goddammit," my father would have said, and my brother as if taking his cue, kicks at the door and yells "Stupid!" which makes the puppies squeal. When that doesn't work, he bangs on the windows as if a mysterious stranger will suddenly appear and let us inside, then runs around to the back door to see if we've left it unlocked while Mother tries the front lock again, wiggling the key back and forth. "I knew this would happen!" she whispers, but the jiggling is futile. There's nothing left to do but head back into town where we can stop at the hardware store and get another key.

"It's a plain skeleton key," Mother explains, more to herself than to us, as she starts the engine. "I'm sure they can replace it with another." What this says about the validity of locking the door in the first place is never questioned. "I just hope they'll take a check," she continues, "because all our cash is on my dresser." But her worry is plainly rhetorical for we're the new doctor's family in a small town where the doctor, the banker, and the high school principal are the most prominent people in the area.

As we drive down the hot skillet of a road, I watch my mother, who now seems agitated, her brow furrowed as she concentrates on the drive, the speedometer inching towards 60, while the speed limit is 40. Sitting beside her, I think she looks beautiful even though her hairdo has begun to droop in the humid air. "No one can have a hairdo here," I've heard her say to anyone who'll listen. "You just have to pretend you have one and keep going." But I know she's self-conscious about her looks, the word "pretty" hovering just beyond her reach. "My teeth aren't right," she always says with a kind of perplexed resentment as if somehow she's been gypped. "I don't have a nice smile and it shows up in photographs." And this is true. Her pictures look forced, self-conscious, for she's always trying to hide her teeth, which have been corrected with a bridge, a word we're never allowed to say. Now, hunched over the wheel, her mind on the Angel Food cake, she isn't worried about her mouth, her lack of a hairdo.

Yet at night when she's getting ready to go out with my father, the story thickens, distorts, complicates itself. My father, she says while putting on lipstick, has always wanted her to be beautiful. *To be a different kind of woman.* Later I understand my father's desire doesn't necessarily relate to beauty but to *style,* something less tangible and infinitely more complex. I imagine my father growing out of the Hemingwayesque tradition, a man who wants a sociable woman, a superior hostess, someone to drink with and spar with, someone who'll lose gracefully and then clean up the mess. But the truth is that my father has no idea who Hemingway is. He's essentially a good man who likes to laugh and party with other men on football Saturdays. Mother says he wanted a wife who would immediately fix drinks for a bunch of sweaty men coming in from a golf game. This fantasy woman would encourage his pals to hang around the house, to put their sweaty backs against her Queen Anne chairs, not minding mud stains on the carpet, cigarette ashes on the sofa, spilled drinks on the end tables. It always seems to me my mother's lucky not to be that kind of woman, one who blows cigarette rings, who wears a French twist and sandals, who shops all morning, then takes naps in the afternoon, forgetting to fix dinner for us kids. As for beauty, I think my mother *is* beautiful, though not in a conventional way. Instead she has the beauty of contrast: coal black hair and milk-white skin, a small pug nose and high cheekbones, a short but voluptuous figure, "with good legs." In contrast, my dad's getting bald—still a patchwork affair—and gaining weight in the middle, while Mother's young and trim, her black hair falling dramatically across her face when she looks intently into the oven as if a cake's perfection is a holy affair. Yet in her mind the incredible subtlety of beauty—with all its possible combinations—has been sacrificed to her ideal of perfection. I understand this. Even as a child I see that each of us carries another person inside, someone we've been told we can become, "if only we'll change," someone preferred, desired, a potential heroine who lies quite still, somnolent, ready to be awakened behind the mist of our personalities. Of course, the reality is that we can never become this person, for to become her would be to eradicate our very selves.

"I just hope it's not ruined," Mother says repeatedly, eyes straight ahead as she drives into town for the second time that day. She frowns at the road as if looking inside the oven. I can see the Angel Food cake steadily rising, but that image makes me nervous, makes me think of the cake turning black and charred, the oven emitting puffs of billowing smoke and even fire like the kind I've seen on TV. What if the house burns down? What if I lose my dolls, which are scattered like clothes across my second floor bedroom? I know it's dangerous to go away and leave the oven on, to expect anything other than catastrophe.

And yet the diversion of the puppies keeps us busy: they're crawling around our laps, snipping and mewling. It's now afternoon, and since we've rushed out of the house without lunch, we're getting hungry and cranky. We don't want to be still, to wait in the car. "I'll just run in," Mother says as she pulls into a parking space in front of the hardware store. "You kids stay in the car." But I'm not holding a puppy at the moment, so I follow her inside, staying close to her as we move into the dusty interior of the store where shiny implements are stacked inside boxes and tools hung like steel carcasses on the walls. Mother finds the skeleton key the clerk says will fit our lock and reaches quickly into her purse for the money. "I only have a check," she explains almost coyly to the clerk, "because we rushed out so quickly to pick up the beagles from Dr. Max."

The clerk, who is tall and reedy, a character Faulkner would have been proud to have cast, looks strained, slightly embarrassed. "I'm sorry ma'am, but I can't take no checks," he stutters, staring at the cash register.

"It's only a dollar," Mother counters. I see her face contract, something between anger and surprise hiding inside her eyes. So far, this new place hasn't been friendly. She straightens inside her dress and I know she wishes she'd worn high heels. "You see, I'm the new doctor's wife and I'm sure—"

"You can go right down the street to the bank," he says, pointing through the wooden wall in the direction of the bank.

"But I've got a cake in the oven, an Angel Food—"

The clerk won't budge. He stares right through her as if he's counting the toggle bolts on the shelf directly behind her.

Mother snaps her pocketbook closed and marches outside, squinting up at the bank clock which says 1:05. The bank closes at 12:00. Doesn't open again until 2:00. A financial siesta. Mother who always stands erect, whose breasts point so optimistically forward, sags as if she's been hit in the solar plexus. "Well, for the love of Tarzan!" she whispers with the first hint of defeat, then she turns around and sees the drugstore. Of course! Surely *they* will cash her check for a measly dollar.

The drugstore is a familiar place. I have been in drugstores all my life, have gone through their stacks of barrettes and comic books and Hershey bars. As we enter, there's an astringent fragrance in the air, as if lemon juice has been swabbed in the corners of each shelf. A packed tightness surrounds us as we walk through the aisles, gold tags on the merchandise. Glittery hair ornaments sparkle in the light in the beauty section; hairnets in wrapped plastic swing from tiny hooks. Mother's hair has fallen even further into her face, and she keeps pushing it out of her eyes with her hand. "How's my hair?" she asks, turning to me. "Do I have a hairdo?" I nod yes, it's fine, though in truth, it droops, a fringe of dark hair covering her eyebrows, which are finely arched.

Yet she goes forward confidently, and when we get to the counter, she asks politely to speak to the pharmacist. There will be no more bother with clerks.

The pharmacist, Mr. Phelps, comes out from a back room, a slow decisive gait, a bush of grey hair surrounding his florid face, but he stands straight and looks at us with the staid authority of a professional man. He wears a white shirt and tie under his white jacket and I know Mother finds this reassuring. When he asks what he can do for us, Mother begins her story, staring not into Mr. Phelps' eyes, but over his shoulder at the rows of medicine as if she's gaining confidence from the familiarity of all those pills. Mr. Phelps listens to my mother's story about the cake and the beagles, the rusty key, the swollen lock and finally the problems at the hardware store. As she talks I think how much he looks like one of those men getting out of my daddy's car after a golf game, one of those men my mother's supposed to laugh with and tease. He looks perplexed, even impatient with my mother's involved explanation as if all he needs to cash a check is a smile and a wink. But Mother is so serious, so intent on rescuing her cake, she doesn't see this side of him. She barrels through her descriptions of what has happened, how surprising and frustrating it's been, and then almost defiantly she holds out her check for $1.00.

But Mr. Phelps doesn't automatically reach for it. Instead he stares at Mother almost rudely as if he's trying to put something together. And then suddenly he leans towards her and says quite seriously, "I thought Mrs. Foster was a blonde."

My mother looks up at him now as if she's just understood who he is, a man like my father wanting a different kind of woman. A blonde! He thinks the doctor's wife is a blonde! And without any warning, she bursts into tears. Everything that's beautiful in her face become squashed, balled up, her lips quivering over her imperfect teeth.

Of course, Mr. Phelps is instantly solicitous. He cashes the check and tries to reassure my mother that he meant no harm—it's only a rumor—though surely he has no idea of the damage he has done. He's released that other woman in my mother's mind.

When we get home from the drugstore and open the door, the cake is a charred crust, the kitchen stuffy with heat and the acrid smell of burned sugar. Mother's so exhausted from the trip to town, so embarrassed by her tears that she takes the cake out of the oven and throws it—pan and all—into the garbage can outside. She looks pleased with this one act of defiance. My sister and brother go upstairs with the puppies, making a bed for them in the velvet pouches of my brother's violin case. But I stay close to my mother, aware that she's the one I want to watch.

We've been home no more than fifteen minutes when the doorbell rings.

"How's my hair?" Mother asks, her question almost perfunctory now.

"Push it back from your forehead," I say, "and then it will be fine."

She fingercombs it as she walks to the door. She looks distracted, pale, but to me this makes her more beautiful, her dark hair darker against the whiteness of her skin, her eyes glazed as if her thoughts are turned inward, weighing the cost of another treacherous surprise. Once again she seems unconcerned with meeting the world, with becoming a hostess, but caught inside herself like a honeybee attentive to a flower, sucking up its sweetness.

When she opens the door, there stands before us (I'm right behind her) a man who looks like a vagrant, dressed in dirty khaki with thick work boots and a felt hat crushed flat on his head. He's pale, with a rusty red beard, a scabby affair, and faded grey eyes. And yet, unlike a vagrant, he looks right at us and smiles. Then he does something unusual. He makes a grand bow, removing his hat, sweeping it in front of him as if he's an antebellum gentleman or a knight in Chaucer's world, one engaged on a romantic errand.

"I have been wanting to meet you," he says in a soft masculine voice, the dirty hat held close to his chest. "I am Mr. Smits of the telephone company, and I've heard the wonderful news that you and your husband have settled in. I want to offer my friendship and my services." He looks up shyly at my mother and smiles a tentative smile. "I tell fabulous ghost stories and fix the best gumbo in the county." His eyes hold hers and I realize, with surprise, that he's flirting with her.

Oddly, my mother is charmed. I can see it in the ease with which she tosses her head, invites Mr. Smits inside for a cup of coffee and some reheated pie. I know that she thinks longingly of the cake in the garbage can, but there's nothing to do but cut the cold pecan pie. Mr. Smits sits at our kitchen table and tells my mother and me—and then my sister and brother who creep downstairs with the violin case of sleeping puppies—about the history of this house we live in, how the owners (who moved here from Mobile, "a fine family, to be sure, who stocked the gold fish pond beneath the magnolia tree with parrot fish and lily pads") lived and died. As I watch my mother's face, I can see the other woman become muted, drifting slowly into the background, a wavering presence, and then finally, a ghost. My mother feels comfortable with Mr. Smits, who is dirty, but not rowdy, who surely never plays golf and takes a real interest in the conversation of a woman.

"It's so kind of you to receive me," he says in his formal, almost stilted voice before he leaves. "It's not every day that I get to talk to such an intelligent, pretty woman."

Mother sits up straighter, inhabiting herself. She looks self-possessed and attentive. She even looks fondly at the two beagle puppies nestled in the violin case, asleep from exhaustion.

Of course, it's a few weeks later when we find out the real oddity of Mr. Smits, who hires only women, dresses them in black, and makes them learn how to shoot a gun. A year later, several of these women come to my Vacation Bible School class dressed in black pants, black shirts, black boots, even black capes like witches wear on Halloween. They look as fierce as Amazons, their capes rustling as they rush out the door. Occasionally driving into town we see one of them perched precariously at the top of a telephone pole. Here, they look strong, invincible, totally separate from the housewives and teachers we're familiar with, and for us, this makes them more unusual, and hopelessly bizarre. Mr. Smits not only demands that these women do all the physical labor with the telephone company—setting the poles, laying cable, climbing and adjusting the wires—but he's so convinced the Russians are coming, he teaches the women to shoot at his private firing range.

Although these practices seem bizarre in the extreme, no one in our town says a word about Mr. Smits and his women, except maybe Daddy when he sees them having waffles and coffee at the Foley Cafe. "Look at all these pretty girls," my father will call out and six black-sleeved arms will rise in a simultaneous salute.

And yet I know now that Mr. Smits—who rarely changed his

clothes—was an eccentric, a character I wish I'd paid more attention to. From my writer's life, he feels like a missed opportunity, someone who might have helped me to understand not only my region and its oddities, but my sense of loss, of losing it. I don't doubt that Mr. Smits was a romantic, that he had another man inside his head who was dashing and elegant, a man who wore a tux as easily as Mr. Smits wore dirty khaki, a man who talked about Beethoven and Proust as smoothly as Mr. Smits talked about local history. This man would have been unfathomable to my father, who longed—I realize now—to be manly and athletic, to perform as Hemingway performed: in the arena of the hunt, the sporting field, the star carrying the ball, shooting the lion, the man whose body functioned with grace and ease under pressure, for my father, you see, is small and, like me, terrified of conflict.

Sometimes I imagine that late at night, all of these fantasy people who live inside our heads meet in secret to complain about us. They're faithful gossips, thrilled only by drama and the complications of pain. They say how dull-witted we are, how stubbornly we refuse them, suppress them, how nervous and unsure of ourselves we seem, and most importantly, how forlornly sad we become when they rise up to taunt us in their inevitable moments of triumph. I wish that I could talk to them, or at least talk more honestly to mine. I don't know exactly what I would say, but I think it would be more invitation than rebuke. Perhaps I'd suggest that she sit down with me before a hopscotch game. "Watch closely," I'd say, "the voice of the stone as it leaves the girl's hand, how it shivers through the air before falling with a flat thud to the ground, dust flying up in tiny clouds. See how attentive the girl is, see how much she longs to jump."

daddy's town

1957. FOLEY, ALABAMA

"It's as flat as your palm," Mother sighs when we move the seven miles from Magnolia Springs into Foley. The land looks as if it's been ironed, the streets straight seams bisecting each other at ninety degree angles. It's so bereft of beauty it looks like God just closed His eyes for a little nap before moving on to other creations. Only thickets of jack pine and occasional sprawling oaks relieve the land, sprinkled leisurely here and there to absorb your vision. Already I miss the piers that jut into Magnolia River, the roughness of the pilings, the smell of dampness, of fish and rot, and something sweet that comes up from the water. Magnolia Springs is sleepy, secretive, a single eye of beauty with roads curving around magnolias and oaks, ending in crushed oyster shell drives, and beyond, the river sleeping between the trees. In Foley there are only potato sheds, tin-roofed and ugly, lined up like blocks beside the railroad tracks and a tiny one-room library catty-corner from Wright's Drugs.

As we drive to school in the grey morning light of winter, the potato sheds are closed up and empty, the roofs shiny with last night's moisture. There's no movement inside, only dust floating around and the flapping of the tattered signs that say KAISER, HAGENDORF, HESSE. In summer, the whole place is hopping, teenage boys, their shirts off, their shoulders and backs a soft, honeyed brown, haul and load sacks alongside Mexican migrant workers who arrive every summer and live in vacant houses out in the county, or if they're bachelors, sleep under the sheds. No one thinks much about this in the 50s, migrant workers considered necessary but inferior, tolerated as long as they keep to themselves and don't cause trouble. It's usually women who work the graders, who gossip over the whirr of the conveyer belt, their hands full of potato dust and dirt, their hair covered with bandanas, their bodies dressed in shorts or skirts. No one wears blue jeans in the 50s except farmers who work the fields. In summer the lawn of the library overflows with workers sitting on the grass, eating their lunch, salami sandwiches and RC colas or sugar sandwiches and iced tea. Even the traffic heats up, vacationers breezing through on their way to the beach, people from Birmingham and Huntsville, and the social set from Selma and Cullman who own cottages on the Gulf of Mexico. But in winter, the town thins out to a trickle of cars passing through the three stoplights, families taking kids to school, going to the hospital, the drugstore, the football stadium, the Dairy Queen. Daddy knows everyone in town and we roll down our windows when we see people, "Hey, Mrs. Turner, how is Fighty Man?" "Hello, Mr. Schneeflock, did you find your canary?"

Moving to Foley means moving closer to Daddy's world, the world of the hospital, the clinic, the practice fields where my brother will play football, basketball and baseball, the Kiwanis Club, the Rotary Club, the golf course, the dens and patios of his friends who meet at each other's houses for an evening drink. But it's also here in Foley that I first really notice my father, as if he's been an apparition, an occasional addition to the primary relationship between my mother and me, a man who rushes home for supper, is interrupted, called back to the hospital, and then returns late at night after I'm in bed.

Now that we've moved, we all have breakfast together, Daddy shaved and dressed, never in casual clothes, but in a suit and tie, the coat of his suit draped over the back of the chair. He's often quiet in the mornings, almost studious, a cup of coffee at his elbow as he devotes himself to the sports page, reading with total concentration, the only sound the clearing of his throat, a hissing, shuddering noise as if he's unlodging a mountain of mucus, then delivering that glob of phlegm into one of his white linen handkerchiefs. It's a post-nasal drip that's plagued him all of his life. I can't think of my father without remembering those handkerchiefs wadded up on the table, snotty cloths my mother so disliked. "Daddy, move your handkerchief," my sister and I nag on the mornings he drives us to school and we see one stuffed in the crack of the front seat. We think them disgusting, and yet oddly humanizing, this flaw in the midst of a man the whole town loves.

Now Daddy comes home for lunch, for supper, and sometimes has doctor friends visiting, Dr. Jones or Dr. McAlister, who sit with him in the den discussing the vagaries of hypertension or some of the new procedures in heart surgery or hysterectomies. "Thank you, sugar," they say when we bring them bowls of boiled shrimp or salted nuts. Other afternoons Dr. Max bursts through the back door, laughing, his arms tanned up to the length of his shirt, his face slightly sunburned, which makes the flash of his teeth even whiter. He carries some delicacy he swears everybody should try. He'll pull out newspaper and start peeling shrimp as if he's in his own kitchen, then pile up plates for himself and Daddy so they can watch the football games on TV, yelling and laughing as if they're rowdy boys on the golf course.

They call themselves the Morning Glories, Daddy and Max huddled together on the ninth hole, setting off cherry bombs, blowing police whistles, laughing wildly when the bombs explode. They laugh even louder when someone screams.

"It's Saturday morning, goddammit, come out and smell the roses!" one of them yells. They're raising hell, waking everyone up one early morning in September, the air so hot and thick it's like walking through syrup. The grass is wet with dew, the sculpted hills and valleys laid out like paradise on this flat plain of sand near the Gulf of Mexico. Later, a group of five men will play eighteen holes, but Max and Daddy arrive early, careening into the parking lot with cherry bombs and booze. They put a firecracker in a paper cup, then fling it towards the trees. I imagine the laughter on Daddy's face when it explodes, all his teeth showing, his Buddy Holly glasses sliding down his nose. Max, who grew up in the back of a mortuary, is a perfect partner.

When we first moved to southern Alabama, my father called Max from his office one day, telling him he'd heard all about him at Rotary and would like to meet him. "I'm heading out the door right now," Max said, patting one of his dogs. Since their offices were only a few blocks apart, they walked towards each other, two small-town professional men meeting in the sunlight, shaking hands, grinning, knowing in that moment they'd probably be best friends. When I think of Max, he's the kid sitting behind me in third grade making paper airplanes and shooting them towards the teacher's desk each time her back is turned. My dad's the one who distracts the teacher, raising his hand, asking if he can go to the bathroom before she can harp on the paper planes scattered all around her.

Together they seem deliriously happy, dressed up in rival colors for university football games, Daddy in red and white like a barber pole: white shirt, red pants, red hat, white buck shoes with red laces and a red windbreaker while Max, loyal to a rival school, wears contrasting orange and blue.

"Would you like a cocktail, DeJohn, with a little napkin and a cracker?" Max asks, holding out his pinky.

"Why sure, Maxine," Daddy says, acting haughty, severe (his role). "You serve me that drink right now or I won't eat the damn cracker."

And Max will get up and fix them a stiff one, laughing when the ice spills over the top of the glass, laughing because they're pretending to be French personalities in the back country of Alabama.

When she looks at them, Mother rolls her eyes, then prims her mouth like a schoolmarm. She turns away to the silver she's polishing, rubbing hard on the tines of the forks, her face concentrated, fierce, the forks shining in the sunlight.

"Jesus, one time there was this party out at old Sam Styron's place," Max tells me years later when I ask about the good times they had, "where things sorta got out of hand, some barbeque going on, lots of food and booze, and some man always willing to take a dare. Sometimes making one up himself. It's a gentleman's farm, you see, with lots of hound dogs and cattle, even a donkey."

"I can ride that thing," Sullivan says, jutting out his chin. "Hell, I can ride that donkey backwards."

The other men chide him about this, saying he's had so much to drink he can probably ride the chickens too. "Go on, get on," somebody yells. "If you're gonna ride that ass backwards, then get up there and get going."

They help the man onto the donkey, but once he's astride it, looking at its tail, with nothing to hold onto, new ghosts swirl inside his head; someone laughs and the donkey takes off, then stops abruptly, bucking him not just to the ground but into the side of a disk parked beside the fence. The man's head grazes it, blushing with blood. The blood's so quick, they wrap his head in a towel then rush him to the hospital. One of the men calls Daddy at home, tells him to meet them at the Emergency Room "because old Sullivan's got himself into a fix." Of course, Max just happens to be there, hearing it all, how this doofus has grazed his head, sitting ass backwards on a donkey. And that's when they play the trick: at the E.R., it's Max, the veterinarian, who goes in first, carrying Daddy's black bag, plopping it down on the table while he stares at Sullivan whose head is wrapped in a bloody towel. "Listen, Johnny got caught up with another patient," he says, opening the bag, "so he sent me to take care of you. Hell, I've worked on cattle worse off than you."

"You goddamn sonabitch two-legged horse fixer," he cusses until Daddy slips into the room, a big grin on his face. "Don't you worry, Sullivan, I wouldn't let Max touch my dog, much less a good man's head." And they all have a big laugh as Daddy gets to work, cleaning and sewing up the cut.

When I asked Max much later if he and my father talked about serious things, if they shared important parts of their lives, he said, "Oh, yes, we were very close." But when I asked if they talked about their families, their children, the difficulties of their pasts, he said, "Never!" with such obvious relief I felt my throat constrict.

Something's changing, pressing deep into the marrow of our family life. It's not just Daddy's sudden appearance at lunch for grilled cheese, at supper for roast beef, but something that's been devouring Mother since we moved to southern Alabama, my father larger, more forceful while she's squeezed into a smaller, less potent sphere. "Your father used to be so affectionate," she says one day as she's airing sheets in the back yard. I'm running in circle eights, pretending not to pay attention, and she continues to talk, to tell me it's what she loved about him. "He could tease me into relaxing. He thought I was special." But now he seems too busy, too distracted by making a living, advancing himself. He's caught the scent of bigger things, a more powerful life. "He used to be so jealous . . . why he even slapped me once when he thought I was flirting." She blushes, remembering, then pulls the sheets from the line. But now the tables have turned; now she's jealous, waiting on him more extravagantly than ever, changing the channels on the TV when he asks her to, bringing him trays of food, ironing his underwear, doing the volunteer work he thinks necessary for her to do.

And yet privately, she resists, insisting on teaching and lecturing rather than playing bridge and going to lunches as many of the middle class wives in the town prefer, even though we're solidly middle class now, with a house and two cars, even a beach house on the bay—no hint of Praco in our lives. Of course, it's only much later that I understand how she's caught in a corner, fenced in, fighting her way out in the only way she knows how. She's far too complex for the constraints of a traditional southern lady in a small southern town, the kind of woman who plays bridge every week, who has cocktails in the middle of the day while chatting up other women at luncheons of chicken salad and key lime pie, the talk coy and snide, often snippy about whomever is absent, as if women are bred for manic enthrallment with the gossip of the town. Once after a meeting at the First Methodist Church, Mother is stopped by a fellow parishioner. "You know," the woman says, perplexed, "I just don't understand why you haven't taken your rightful place of leadership in the social life of our town."

Stunned, Mother replies truthfully, "But I don't intend to live a life of parties. I have other things on my mind." I imagine my mother startled by this suggestion, having moved from the rural culture of northern Alabama where there's little society to speak of at all, at least nothing so organized, so saturated with parties and events, it can obscure your family life.

In Lineville, Mother's friend Bessie was a career woman, what my sister and I called a "lady," full of gold jewelry and hair spray and perfume. She owned a lady's department store where women from the pants factory bought their Sunday clothes: pale linen dresses and flowered pleated skirts and heels so high that on Sunday all the women looked as if they'd grown three inches. Bessie made her own money, defined her day's routine; she never asked favors of her husband Hill, who liked to sit at his roll-top desk and concern himself with his cattle and his horses, managing his gentleman's farm. She taught my mother about everything from furniture to clothes, about the preferred hors d'oeuvres for parties, the right wine to order, and how to instruct a maid in the cleaning of a house. I remember sitting at Bessie's table while Gertha brought the platters of fruit, the pitcher of orange juice, then the baskets of homemade biscuits, the bacon, the jellies and jams to the table. Coffee was served from a silver urn, ornate napkin rings at each place, and when Bessie was ready to leave for her office or retire to the living room, we crumpled up our linen napkins and left the remains for Gertha to clean up.

But we haven't replicated Bessie's life, and something shudders inside our house as Mother struggles to keep everything afloat, calming and sustaining the difficult creature that is our family. It seems that after our move from Lineville, doors are shut, emotions banked, thoughts cut off. Mother is quieter as she stands at the sink looking out at the wide, leafy blooms of the magnolia tree, wondering, I imagine, where the Golden One has gone.

"We're going to the dog tracks Saturday night," Daddy says, coming in on Thursday night, a stack of mail balanced in his hands. The "we" means the Morning Glories and their wives. Daddy says this casually, back turned, eyes darting to the phone for messages, things still to be done before the news and sleep. The dog tracks will be a release, a satisfying snap from the constant edge of other people's pain. Dogs running down the tracks need nothing, not even watching if you prefer to drop back and let the air out of your brain.

Mother stiffens, an unspoken disappointment glinting behind her eyes. "Saturday?" she says, noncommital, putting away the silver from the dishwasher, rubbing gently on the tines of the forks. "Well, that depends on whether I can get someone for the children."

My father turns. "Oh, for heaven's sake, they can stay with the Mixon's kids."

"I'd rather they stayed here," Mother continues, not looking at him, an edge to her voice. She hates the dog tracks—"such a waste of time!"—but she never says this directly to my father. If she did, he'd probably "blow up," and go without her, revealing the caste system that so defines their lives, and she perfects the tactic of delay, ostensibly putting our welfare before his, the only leverage she has.

He pours himself a drink, listening to the savage crackle of the ice. When he speaks, it's with deadly calm. "Be ready at six," he says, and walks into the den, picking up the paper and unfurling it with a slap.

And on Saturday night she's dressed in a dazzling dress, anxious but ready to go.

ambition

Is our family spinning out of control? Shifting its balance? Leaning disastrously towards destruction? I don't know. We get up every morning to an American breakfast of eggs and bacon and toast and orange juice—sometimes pancakes and grits and muffins. We watch Ed Sullivan on Sunday nights, do our homework, go to ball games, have firecrackers on the Fourth of July. But I'm too absorbed with the microcosm of my mother and me to see anything larger, more dramatic. Something's changing between the two of us, an inevitable split but one that shows bright red on my radar screen. In Magnolia Springs I was still the baby, pampered and petted, allowed to cuddle, but in Foley I'm expected to grow up, to stand alone and enter the world of achievement. You've gotta be smart, smart, smart. "You wanna grow up, doncha pooch?" Daddy asks me, and though I nod, secretly I yearn for closeness, surrounding my mother like Jello, congealing to her form. But no longer do I sit beside Mother in the early light of morning, the grass wet with dew, the humming-birds fluttering near the windowsill; no longer do I feel certain that I can claim her attention. "You gotta be a credit to the community," Daddy says, looking furtive but determined, putting on his black glasses, yanking up his black bag, and striding out the door to his car.

"I want you girls to develop talents," Mother says as she scans the phone book for teachers, "so you can feel comfortable in the world."

Of course I nod, but already it feels like a pressure pulling at the roots of my hair. Now I must win Mother's approval not by affection but by acts of performance, soaring like a banner in the air.

"First position," Miss Roberta calls out as we begin the *relevé* at the bar. "Now lift slowly, girls, slowly, holding your turn out. Tummy in, Priscilla. Back straight, Delores. That's it, now slowly to *demi-pointe*. Feel as if you're gathering yourself up, girls, feel the lightness, the body no more weight than a leaf." My legs quiver, but I summon the picture of a leaf dangling from a tree, ready to fall. I am a leaf, almost transparent, surely weightless. I'll fall when Miss Roberta tells me to fall. "Feel your center of balance. And now slowly, lower your heels and breathe out. Breathe out, girls. Let your breath exhale with the release." The leaf scuds away from me with my breath. I see it blown into the corner of the room, crowded by other leaves, crushed to death.

When we turn to Miss Roberta we're fifteen girls in black leotards, black tights, and black ballet slippers, elastic bands across the top. Most of the girls have their hair pulled back into neat, shiny buns, chaste, almost nun-like, but my hair won't behave for such things. I push curls behind my ears, but with the first *jeté*, they spring towards my face. I envy the other girls, for more than anything I want to *look* like a ballerina. I think this will help me in the Ambition Department: if I can assume the posture, I'll become it. Otherwise, how will I ever be Miss America?

Since we moved to southern Alabama, Mother's been teaching seventh and ninth grade science—first at Elberta and then Foley—giving lectures on health and nutrition at night at the church, the civic club, the library, and on weekends, going to parties with my father. She's always in a hurry, throwing on clothes, running a brush through her hair, rushing out to the grocery store, the dry cleaners, the drugstore, the playground to pick one of us up. She's escaped, leaving me in a whirlwind of loneliness, and I must find a way to get her back.

This is my second year of dancing classes, but the first year Mother has driven us to Fairhope, a town twenty-three miles from Foley, to take lessons. Fairhope, my birthplace, is legendary, born of socialist origins and progressive ideas, a place where art and the intellectual life still matter, a place where independent, talented women flourished in the early 20th century, establishing suffrage clubs and holding political office. Though much of the political clout is gone, in the early 60s, Fairhope women still maintain artistic respect, often sending their students to Julliard or to the Joffrey Ballet.

At Miss Roberta's we have a mirrored wall, a built-in barre, a change room and separate bath. In Foley, we were stuck in the band room, moving the trombones and trumpets and saxophones over to one side, hauling out the mats, then looking at a blank yellow wall while we learned to *plié,* to do *arabesques* and *battement fondu.* Every time we had to go to the bathroom, we rushed across the playground to the elementary school, tugged off our leotards, tugged them back on, then rushed back, always at pains to keep our ballet shoes dry. In Fairhope, we're expected to become dancers, to learn grace and coordination, the discipline of the body, that subtext for achievement.

More than anything else, my body is limber, as supple as a reed leaning in the wind. There's something astonishing, almost reverent, about bending the body into a knot, leaning backwards from the waist, trusting gravity, your hands brushing the floor as you arch into a perfect comma, your bones no longer bones, but elastic branches that follow the mind's bidding. I press my hands deeper into soft spikes of grass, lower myself onto my elbows and crawl my hands towards my feet. I'm now upside down, hands clasping ankles, head looking through feet.

But it's not perfect. My legs are too close together and I feel myself wobble. I have to flip over and start again. I look first at the sky, the sun a big spotlight glowing red in the evening light; I breathe deeply, relax, and try again: the backbend, then the alligator crawl through grass towards my legs. This time I can't quite grasp my ankles. The grass tickles my chin, and I fall over. *Stand up and try again.* While I'm upside down I see my sister going across the yard to play piano with Susie Provost, her feet rushing away from me along the path. When she opens the door to Susie's house, Sheba, the Great Dane, comes bounding out. Immediately Sheba charges towards me, sniffing my crotch until I laugh and fall over yet again, lying flat on the grass, my face to the bleeding sun, my breath in little short jabs as if I've been running up hill. I lie in the sun and feel a perverse desire to do nothing. Nothing at all. I'll sit and dream my life away, swim the Amazon, trek through the woods from Alabama to Georgia, live on top of a mountain with dogs and books and a cold winter wind that shakes the roof of my house. But, of course, I can't. Already I've learned the fateful lesson of approval, an aching need for the complimentary remark, the applauding gesture, the favorable nod. *Isn't she smart? Isn't she cute?* As always I hear that voice in my head, *try again,* a voice like a scapel, a switch.

"Go away, Sheba. Go away now. I've got to practice."

Try again. And again. And again.

And yet dancing isn't enough. We're in pursuit of *talent,* and more lessons are required. While Jean and I are in dance class doing our *pliés* and *relevés,* our splits and front walk-overs, Mother, our missionary, seeks help from the legendary piano teacher, Mama Dot. The first time they meet, Mama Dot's lying on a reclining lawn chair in her back yard, staring up at the pine trees and the empty stage of the sky. Her back yard is a sprawling garden of azaleas and dogwood, a place where ivy crawls up the brick wall outside the kitchen window, where a forest of trees bank two sides of their house. Inside, the grand piano occupies the central space in the living room, sleek and stern in its silence.

I can see Mother standing on Mama Dot's lawn, the grass brilliantly green in late September, the white cotton sheets Mama Dot always dries on the clothesline whipping in a southeasterly breeze. Mother looks down at Mama Dot, who is prematurely gray, her short thick hair cut in a ducktail, her blue eyes piercing, scrutinizing as she takes in Mother's well-cut dress, her high heels, her intelligent hazel eyes, and I imagine an immediate recognition: they are women who define themselves by the acuity of their minds.

"I've got to find a music teacher for these girls," Mother says, picking at the lint on her skirt. She likes to look neat but she's barely had time to run a comb through her hair, to hike up her slip. "They started in Lineville, but I can't find anyone in Foley who can take them."

"What about Mrs. Humphreys?" Mama Dot asks, her eyes sharpening, her shoulders like pointed wings.

Mother shakes her head. "She's filled."

"Letty Wallace?"

Mother shakes her head again.

Mama Dot doesn't seem to respond. She stares like a hawk at

the grove of trees as if she can see something no one else can see. Mother takes a deep breath. "I'm already bringing the girls to dancing twice a week, and I could bring them here to music as well."

"No," Mama Dot says, a simple sound, her eyes locked to the trees. "I'm recovering. I can't teach anyone right now." What she doesn't tell Mother until much later is that she's come back from shock treatments only to discover that she's lost the ability to memorize music. Instead, she lies in a chaise lounge, remembering thirteen days without sleep, her mind accelerated, running like a startled deer, then numbed by exhaustion, her vision diminished to that beautiful shade of gray like the silvery lining of trees at dusk. And yet music is her life, her own beauty deferred to its fierce, elemental demands. Now she can play only what's in front of her, the sheet music she's collected over the years, not the Bach or Beethoven or Grieg she's been used to performing.

But Mother is persistent, and weeks later she brings us to visit, to run across the lawn to where Mama Dot sits in her chair, staring beyond her at the trees, waiting perhaps for that silvery moment of dusk. The first thing I see are long thin legs ending in strange, man-like shoes laced up the front. "Why do you wear those ugly shoes?" my sister asks. They *are* ugly shoes, but Mama Dot only laughs.

"I have to wear them because I ruined my arches," she says, and there's sudden life to her eyes. It's her eyes I watch now, eyes that transform her face from somberness to a surprising, irresistible joy as if the shoes are both a shocking taboo and a gift. "But they *are* ugly." She wrinkles her brow, then laughs as she runs her hands through that thick pelt of hair.

"We're going to be Miss America," Jean says, as if we can do this jointly. At night we model in the bathroom, taking turns standing on the closed toilet lid, first Jean with one hand on her right hip, then me, arm bent seductively behind my head. We smile crooked-teeth smiles into the fluorescent lights, pretending radiance, our heads balanced to wear the crown. My sister, I think, is only a pretender, but I am in earnest.

"Well, that's fine," Mama Dot says, then she and Mother talk about lessons, about pianos, while my sister and I fidget, tired and hungry, anxious to go to Ben's Bar-b-que on the way home.

"Let's go, let's go," we beg in that silent way, pulling on Mother's skirt, yanking on her purse, digging at the grass with our shoes.

"Well, I'll drive the girls to Mobile for lessons if you can't take them," Mother says finally. You can tell she's serious; this is no idle thought. Mobile is more than an hour away but she'll drive to the moon if necessary to pursue our talents, to make us well-rounded and smart, to have a leg-up in the world.

"Mrs. Foster, you can't take those little girls all the way to *Mobile.*" Mama Dot sits straight up in her chair, her face alive with indignation. "That would be criminal. They need to play, to tell stories and dream. When would they have time?"

Mother looks stricken. She glances at us, biting her bottom lip. She's never even *thought* about dreams. And stories? Who has time for stories? Our household's chock full of distractions, a platoon of people coming and going, and my mother's younger brother, Bobby, having come to live with us, dropped into our lives through the unhappy circumstances of my grandmother's death. For months, Mother received calls from her sisters, begging her to take him, telling tales of his beatings, the stories always ending with Granddaddy using his miner's belt, a thick, heavy strap that cut the skin to ribbons. "It was done in the tub," her sister said, "where he couldn't even defend himself." Born after my mother left Praco, Bobby came, at age twelve, into our household having nothing but blood ties to establish any rights. "This is your uncle," Mother said, but he was too young to be an uncle, and it was clear he'd been neglected, and as he stood in our kitchen, a kid of twelve, a shock of black hair and pale skin, looking shyly down at the floor, uncomfortable and frightened, having learned to see the world as a great punishing force. He'll live with us for six years, but never really become a part of us, forever circling like a lone, orbiting moon.

Mama Dot is no longer sitting in her chair, but standing beside us, staring at my sister and me, lured into saving us from our urgent, straight-forward lives. *We must not go to Mobile.* It's in just this quixotic way that it's decided. In another month, we'll begin taking piano and music theory three times a week, coordinating music and dancing so that while one is at dancing, the other will be at the piano with Mama Dot. While we go to lessons, Mother studies catalogues, talks to teachers, trying to see if there isn't something else we can learn to do.

Two years later I stand numb in the dusty wings of the stage, feeling for gum wadded up in the hem of the curtain. While the Blackwell sisters sing "Over the Rainbow" with something sleepy in their voices, I fall into the bottom of darkness, my mind closed up and dumb. "You gonna *be* Miss America," Bernice whispered to me right before we left for the talent show. She was stringing celery, pulling the strings off like tiny filaments of thread, then chopping the stalks up into little pieces for tuna salad. Bernice was our maid, the only person who knew how frightened I was. While I worried and fretted aloud she stood at the ironing board, listening, her mouth bunched up with snuff while she made smooth glides down the length of Daddy's white shirt. Sometimes she seemed not to be listening at all, humming "Amazing Grace, how sweeeeeet the sound," but then she'd put down the iron. "You don't wanna do this," she said. "You gonna tell your mama?"

I hung my head. I couldn't say no to Mother. I could see her waving to me from the audience, a smile that said, *you'll be fine.*

"Well, then you gotta think of somebody else to be. You tell yourself up there you Miss America, then you go out smiling like a queen."

I laughed when Bernice said that and she laughed too, showing purple gums, her teeth old and yellow, the snuff making dark stains on her bottom lip. "It be our little secret," she said. "Just you and me." I nodded, *our secret,* and yet despite my terror, I really did want to walk out on stage with a crown, everyone clapping, tears of happiness brimming in my eyes.

Now there's clapping, the Blackwell sisters bowing, smiling big, flashy smiles, then running off the stage. For a moment I stop breathing, listening so hard to the first strains of music, waiting for the cluster of chords that signals my entrance, and then I'm dancing, *jeté, jeté,* my arms floating out like swans, my body remembering what my mind's forgotten. I'm smiling at the audience, catching a glittery eye, the scrap of a sleeve as I turn and turn. And yet for the first time it occurs to me that my mother might not be watching, that she might have gone outside to the water fountain to take an aspirin for her headache, and for a moment I lose my place, standing stock still on stage, staring petrified at the audience, until something jolts inside me and I pick up the thread of music and leap through the air.

That night I lie in bed, my sister next to me, her hair spilled onto the pillow, its brown the shade of bark and trees. Jean inherited Mother's thick, dark hair while mine is blonde and fine, a nest of frizzy curls. Her mouth is slightly open, her lip as pink as the roses on our sheets. One arm is flung behind her head, the other cups the ends of the covers. She's turned slightly towards me as if she fell asleep in the midst of telling a secret. I inch closer to her. Then turn over on my side so we're like bodies holding something between us. Very carefully, I hook my finger around a lock of her hair and hold on. Thus anchored, I lie in bed eavesdropping on the sounds of the house, the shudders and aches of its breath, its snorts and expirations. When the air-conditioning comes on, there's the whoosh of power as if the entire house is taking a huge gulp of air. As I wait for sleep, I imagine the house talking to me, telling me what I must do: *You must be wonderful,* it whispers. *You must surprise everyone with your triumphs and talent.* And in my mind I see my mother coming closer to me until she's trapped like a spider in my web.

mama dot

1959. FAIRHOPE, ALABAMA

At last! I'm riding in the back of a large pick-up truck with twelve other music students after Mama Dot's summer recital. Standing up, I'm a bold spring willow swaying with the bumps, the moist salt air ruffling my hair, coating my face with a film of salt. 1959, the era before seatbelts, before environmental safety controls, before complications to childhood fun. No one seems to care that most of us are leaning against the side of the truck, licking at the rush of wind, reaching up to grab at leaves, at hanging moss. We aren't driving fast, just going down a curvy twist of road to the beach. Beside me Lizzie Sheridan lets her cotton shirt crawl up her chest when she lifts her arms to twirl Spanish moss as we glide beneath a tree. Under her shirt I see her old faded bathing suit, the color of a Piggly Wiggly paper bag. Her arms are skinny, freckled, her hair a limp palomino blond. But her mind is clear music. A high octave treble. I know she's in her own world and I associate her with Fairhope, with Organic School, with the mind turned inward, meditative, dreamy, like shadows on water. Like Lizzie, the other kids from Organic seem different, as if they know they can make themselves up, can start from inside and work their way out. They dress badly, wearing leotards under their skirts, baggy shorts, tennis shoes without socks; they never tuck in their blouses. I'm wearing a new bathing suit, carrying a special towel I bought just for this trip. It's the code of my family: everything has to be *new*! But no one seems to notice. I think of Mama Dot (who's riding in the truck's cab with her husband Uncle Kenny) setting the metronome and saying, "Again now, girls," looking at us with her intense hawk gaze as if given the right attention, we might become prodigies.

And yet this particular afternoon, I'm not thinking about music, about the future, about becoming wonderful. I'm simply delirious with joy at the thought of sleeping on sand, waking up in the morning in the open air, the musk odor of the sea at my back, the whish sound of wind through the pines. I imagine opening my eyes in the darkness of night, smelling water, its smell like the smell of the female body, as ripe and damp as wet seaweed; then, when my eyes adjust, the slice of pearl-white beach against the water's black liquid movement. The tides are soothing, safe. Sleeping on the beach is so foreign to my family, the very fact of this trip feels rebellious, forbidden. I'm sure that many of the other kids have camped out, have been "beachcombers" in other places, but in my family a real vacation means TraveLodges, restaurants, and brand-new coordinated outfits, not blue jeans and tennis shoes. "I grew up with nature," Mother says, frowning at the thought of the outdoors with its dark bushes, its dirty undergrowth, its snakes and nasty bother of bugs. "I'll take the inside of an air-conditioned house, thank you very much!"

Nature, like leisure, won't get us anywhere in the world, won't improve our SAT scores or embellish our performance on stage. The outdoors is only for kids in summer, for lazy rides out into the country on our bikes, the sun burning our scalps, the gnats and mosquitoes flying blindly into our eyes.

When the truck stops, we tumble out—eight girls and three boys—dropping our packs where Mama Dot directs us and racing for the water. It's shallow and we splash a quarter mile out before we can drop into its blue-grey wetness, water the color of steel. Sometimes the water's so shallow you have to wade out a half a mile before you have dunking potential. But today the tide's in, the waves crest gently against our chins.

When Lizzie shoves me under, I swallow a mouthful of salt water. But even with the surprise, I hold on, pulling her under too. I push deeper, lying spreadeagled on the bottom, coming up for air when my lungs almost burst. Here, with the world of water all around me, I sense that this odd crew of kids, artist kids with stringy hair and crooked teeth, will be the only world I'll ever need to know. But simultaneously, I see them with my mother's eyes: Lizzie's ugly bathing suit sags against her skinny body; Lucy's vague, squinty eyes will always seem petty; even Shay's overlapping front teeth are the color of chicken bones. I know these worlds are mutually exclusive, and yet I'm attached to both, a membrane held by ragged strings.

We snuggle into blankets on the sand, fluffy pillows brought from home, our feet wiggling, our bodies tired. We sleep, the waves breaking, slapping against the shore, the smell of rain in the air. I fold my head inside my pillow, dazed and happy, needing nothing but the smell of the sea. Above me a black sky, a smoky moon. The sound of a motor somewhere out in the bay. All the restlessness leaves my body and I see something clearly: it does not matter about Lizzie Sheridan's ugly bathing suit. It does not matter. Beauty in the mind. The deep swimming throb of the soul. I sigh with pleasure and relief and fall effortlessly to sleep.

At the center of this world is Mama Dot, whose boldness astonishes me. She wears only shorts or pants, and faded knit shirts or sweaters under which her bosom is collected into two prominent cones, suggestive to me of some private maternal strength. I can imagine her children once nursing there, cuddled under one breast while she sits on the wooden bench in the yard watching a woodpecker at his task or a white lily blooming, solitary, in the woods. I remember being very impressed by her breasts, most often a prop for her bifocals which hang around her neck on a chain. More important, she wears that short, almost mannish haircut and those ugly brown orthopedic shoes from which her long thin legs emerge like stalks. And yet with all of this unfashionable weight, she's incredibly beautiful, not in the typical Southern way of soft voluptuousness, but in the clarity of her bones, in the clear gray of her eyes, and in the ease of her movement, the way she runs her hands decisively through her hair or holds her face in a pose of intense concentration while listening to a Beethoven sonata. I can see her looking up suddenly from my lesson, staring across the great expanse of the grand piano with that instinct for interruption, like a dog smelling a scent. "Uncle Kenny?" she says, and there will be the slightest strain around her eyes as if she's checking on a restless child. I see him pass through the door, bespectacled, wiry, with his bristle-brush flat top, some piece of wood in his hands. "He's working," she says, her face relaxing. She nods for me to play the Grieg again.

But it's not really music I learn at Mama Dot's, but the pleasure of solitude.

"Where have you been?" Mother asks when I rush in for my lesson, banging the screen door.

"Out there," I say and nod towards the woods, thick and empty beside Mama Dot's house.

I can't miss her frown, but how can I say that I've been shedding weight. In the woods I'm not besieged with worry about what I know and don't know, what I should pay attention to, what I've not accomplished. In the woods, I'm shrouded in silence—the rustle of a blade of grass, the whiplash of a bird's wings, the scuttling of a squirrel, a chipmunk, the microscopic crashing of a frog leaping repeatedly at the trunk of a tree— sounds so different from the mix-master, the TV, voices on the telephone, at the back door, all circling the air with a demanding buzz as I walk through the kitchen and den of our house. In the woods, I smooth out, my mind loose, lightened, a delight I know no way to express in the company of others, their voices stretching me into invisible thinness. I stand very quiet and watch the squirrels nervously scratching the trees. Cardinals fly into the glade and balance on impossibly small branches, their beauty so stunning something solemn and incredulous bursts inside my heart. I don't know how to explain this and would never try. It's my secret. I think that I'm like a leaf changing color, something no one will ever know because it's all happening on the inside.

After my solitude in the woods, I sit at the piano while Mama Dot listens and watches, one bare leg crossed over the other, her gaze concentrated on the pouncing of my fingers. Now I associate Fairhope—and within it, Mama Dot—with the right to an artistic life, or if not that right exclusively, then at least the right to deny distraction, to string yourself along a fine vein of certainty. To deny distraction is no small thing when you come from such a busy household, Grand Central Station for the neighborhood, kids rushing in and out, Max with a sack of oysters slung over his back ready to be shucked, the telephone ringing, the back door slamming, the TV playing, my father dropping ice on the floor, the ping-ping of tiny crashes obscured by Max spreading the oysters on the counter, his talk a mania that ricochets around the room, my sister telling my mother about her homework as Mother wipes up the mess Max is making. But isn't this the stuff of life, this talk, this laughter, these events? I feel like Virginia Woolf's Lily Briscoe longing to remove herself from the social orbit of Mrs. Ramsay while simultaneously craving the stories of the tribe. To pull yourself back into the quiet escape of your own brittle thoughts, to say no to gossip, to the sweet friendship of that world takes enormous, selfish energy. It's like pulling yourself away from a hurricane, refusing to be sucked into its high winds, caught in the force of its tides. To be alone is to be soft, vegetable-like, resilient only for yourself. In Foley I can seldom do this, can't quite pull away, carve out a territory of my own. But in Fairhope, the world falls away while another world unfolds, fleeting but startlingly real.

"Uncle Kenny was raised by Marietta Johnson," Mama Dot tells me after my lesson, her voice reverent, as we walk through the back yard between the azaleas, the bougainvillea, the wisteria, to the cottages Uncle Kenny is building "for young couples." Marietta Johnson, I know, was a brilliant reformer, the founder of Organic School, one of the first progressive schools to flourish in the U.S. under her radical ideas, believing children should grow up "unforced and unwarped by external pressures." Mama Dot and Uncle Kenny both graduated from Organic, and their boys go there now. "She absolutely saved him," Mama Dot says, twisting a branch of wisteria, the blossoms trembling with each yank. "Brought him up and gave him a home and showed him the importance of working with his hands." I know almost nothing about Marietta Johnson except what Mama Dot tells me, but I long to be under the sway of her overflowing personality, her belief in storytelling and nature study. I wish suddenly that I could be an orphan, could do more than play scales and cut out paper dolls and fight with my sister. I wish that I could wear shorts and forget to brush my hair. For a moment I stop—*who can possibly save me*—then we walk on past the borders of the yard, through goldenrod and milkweed, Mama Dot striding swiftly through the tall grass until she sees a monarch, its gold and black wings fluttering just beyond the maple tree. "Look," she whispers and I pause beside her, staring at its glittering wings while a summer breeze ruffles the legs of my shorts.

Then Mama Dot walks on, talking about Uncle Kenny and bending down to pick a wildflower. But I remain dead still, looking back at the woods where trees and vines grow so thick they're a wall of green. Insects drowse in lazy circles. The heat throbs against the earth and it sprouts lush grass and spiky weeds. Several blocks away the blue-green sea slaps against the pilings of the piers and floats tangled driftwood to the shore. This is my world, the place I love . . . but how can this be when it's the very world my mother avoids?

I stare up at the sky at birds, at clouds, some shadow darkening my horizon.

PART TWO

1998. NOTASULGA, ALABAMA

"You talk too much!" An elderly man glares angrily at me in the middle of my presentation to an adult writing class. "You're not giving any of us a chance to say a thing."

I'm stunned by his remark and feel such sudden quivering rage, I have to bite my lip. But I'm rescued by another student who says insistently to him, "Why, look here, she's the teacher. She's supposed to talk."

That night when I phone my mother, I light into the man, calling him an old geezer, a crusty sonofabitch who can't listen to women.

There's a pause on the other end of the line. "Oh, honey you have to let that anger go," Mother says, and for a moment I want to light into her too.

"Jesus, Mother, don't you ever get angry. I mean, look at your childhood. Weren't you just mad as hell about what happened to you?"

There's silence on the other end of the phone, and I wait impatiently, slouched on the bed, taking off my shoes, waiting for the motel room to cool down. "You don't understand," Mother says quietly, and it's the tenor of her voice I listen to. "I didn't know if I was angry or not."

Suddenly interested, I sit upright, staring at the phone. "You mean, you didn't know what your feelings were?"

"That's right," she says. "I don't remember feeling furious or frightened. I didn't think I had a right to *feel* anything so I didn't."

I'm surprised that Mother's saying this, and I'm not sure if my surprise comes from her admitting it or her actually knowing it. I take a deep breath; I'm no longer worried about the old man, about my own fury as I'm drawn back to stories of her past. "Did you know that when you lived in Praco?" I ask. "I mean, did you know you'd gone numb?"

The air-conditioner surges on in my motel room and I listen as it whooshes through the vents, coming at me in a steady stream of frosty air. "No," Mother says softly, and I imagine her standing in the kitchen, a spatula in her hand, the phone cupped close to her ear. "I didn't realize it until I read *Man's Search for Meaning,* that book about concentration camp survivors. You know when they first came out of the camps, a lot of prisoners felt nothing at all. They'd lived such desperate lives, they'd lost the ability to relate, to feel pleased at liberation. I was reading that book and it hit me: that's what happened to me too."

I sit very still, barely breathing. There's heat between us now. I feel myself slipping away from the bed, the room, the motel, floating out into the air. It's as if I'm standing right beside her, looking into her face while she looks back into mine.

"What about now?" I ask.

There's silence on the other end of the line.

"I never learned to feel anger," Mother says. "But I recognize sadness."

escape

1959. Foley, Alabama

"I wish they'd hurry up and get going," Mother says as we watch Daddy load his golf clubs into the back of Max's truck. It's spring-time, the smell of summer in the air. Outside in the driveway, Daddy and Max are horsing around, Max telling a tale, and Daddy bending towards the truck, shaking with hilarity, his mouth wide open, showing all his upper teeth. Max snickers, then slams the door shut tight and we hear the toot-toot-toot of the horn as they careen out of the driveway.

Mother frowns. She's been watching them too, holding a colander of peas in her hands. "Thank god, I don't want any friends," she says, sitting down beside me, picking through the peas. Lids lowered, she snaps one fiercely.

"Why not?" I look up with sudden worry.

"Family's enough," she says, reaching across me, rearranging the apples in the fruit bowl, throwing out one that's gone soft. "I've never needed anybody else." And then she begins to shell the peas, the green flesh shooting out of the pods like angry marbles. "I don't want anybody taking up my time, knowing my business. All that fuss about what you did all day." She grimaces, snapping another pea. "Your father needs friends, but I don't."

That night, lying in my bed, I feel queasy, disloyal; my stomach hurts. Like my father, I love my friends, especially my best friend Lisa who whispers to me when we lean over to get our arithmetic books out from under our desks. Lisa's already getting breasts and dark curly pubic hair, but I forgive her with the private assumption that next year I'll catch up. And yet Mother says friends are unnecessary, that we're enough.

Much later in my life, I understand that my mother did have friends, though they weren't like the traditional friendships of the other women in our town, women who met for coffee and gossip, who went shopping together in Mobile and ate lunch at the Battleship Hotel, white gloves folded neatly beside their purses while they ate chicken salad or shrimp remoulade with tall glasses of iced tea. Mother never ate lunch with anyone. She liked nothing better than to eat peanut butter crackers in the car while she drove, the windows rolled up, the air-conditioning on, her mind pinned to some revelatory thought about child development, the field she wished she'd pursued. Sometimes she'd eat a banana and a coke at the kitchen counter, her sleeves rolled up, one high heel off, but she never sat down at the table after breakfast and hated to have people watch her eat. "I'm just not hungry," she'd murmur, though she was always picking up a half slice of cake or tasting a cookie "just to see if it's any good." Unlike Mother, the neighborhood women spent hours in each other's kitchens, laughing and whispering together, trading recipes and borrowing each other's clothes, shopping in Mobile or—for a fling—going all the way to Atlanta. They were mostly housewives and mothers who planned dinner parties and trips together, who sewed special dresses for their daughters and bought sweet-smelling sachets to put in their underwear drawers, while the women my mother talked to were working women who'd lived under the pressure of darkness, overcoming some great trauma in their lives. It was this trauma that bound them together, the miracle of tragedy and survival they seemed to sniff out of each other and hold infinitely close.

Often I'd see a look of intense curiosity cross Mother's face as she stood on Mrs. Schreiber's porch or Mama Dot's steps, listening to a story. "And after the surgery?" she'd ask, her voice lowered to a whisper, her body loosened, her face enraptured by what the other woman was saying. But if I tried to eavesdrop, bending down to tie my shoe, the story faded, drowning into commonplaces about food and assignments. And yet there was one story Mother revealed, a story about the German seamstress who lived just across the park from us and altered our clothes.

"In Germany, she was very brave," Mother tells us one December night as we drive the two blocks to Mrs. Schreiber's small house, our Christmas dresses of green velvet and white chiffon pinned up with paperclips and bobby pins because we never manage to find the pin cushion or needles and thread. "You see, she lived quite another life than the one she lives here." I'm surprised at this, having known Mrs. Schreiber only as an ordinary seamstress, a refugee who emigrated with her family to Alabama, knowing no more about our flat farmland with its potato fields and gladiola sheds than that it was a haven from the camps of Europe. Besides, Mrs. Schreiber is stout, with frowsy hair the color of lint and a large, comforting bosom that feels like pillows tucked inside her dress. She wears what I call "old lady" dresses and no make-up, a woman as different from my mother—who always dresses in stockings and heels and lipstick—as anyone in town. "She actually *saved* her family from the Communists," Mother continues and I see the pictures from our *Weekly Reader,* how the Communists sent their enemies to labor camps in Siberia, letting them freeze to death or starve, lining them up before firing squads at the slightest infringement of rules. "Just imagine, without her, her children might have died."

When she sees us, Mrs. Schreiber always looks surprised as if she's forgotten who we are until she recognizes Mother behind us, rattling her car keys as she puts them in her purse. Then Mrs. Schreiber smiles, beckoning, and we descend into her fitting room, a tiny front room with a mirror, a dress dummy, an upholstered chair layered with clothes to be altered, full of pins and chalk marks and white basting thread.

As I undress, Mrs. Schreiber brings out from behind the curtain a footstool made out of fuzzy rug material so my feet won't slip as I climb up and down to be fitted. While she gazes at the new dress, the room tightens around me, smelling of sauerkraut and strudel, the chords of a Beethoven sonata coming from the record player in another part of the house. "Oh, my, my, my," Mrs. Schreiber says, touching the fabric, caressing it with her fingers. "Very pretty," she smiles. "You be belle of the ball soon," and her dark eyes brighten with inky desire.

But I'm too anxious for compliments and ask impertinently, "Please tell us about your escape."

Mrs. Schreiber drops the fabric and for a moment stands silent, the heavy bulk of her body stilled. Horrified, I think I've made a mistake, embarrassed or alienated her and now I'll never get the story. "It was *terrible,*" she murmurs finally as she bends over to pick up the pins. When she rises, her face is tight and stern. "The Russians"—she hisses—"were *beasts!*"

Mother, behind her, nods in agreement, then elaborates as if she's a self-appointed interpreter. "Girls, Mrs. Schreiber and her family had to escape because they were stuck in East Berlin when the Russians came in and walled off the city." Mother sits crouched on the chair, her knees pinched together to avoid a dress full of pins. "You see, the Russians put up all that barbed wire and guarded the checkpoints." I know exactly what she means for I've seen the pictures of The Wall, a thick, ugly structure with soldiers in grey uniforms and red armbands patrolling its border. "And she had Russian soldiers living right in her house," Mother continues, "soldiers she had to kowtow to, didn't you, Mrs. Schreiber, keeping your boys away from them, what with the bacon sizzling and the smell of fresh-baked bread." As Mother talks, I think of Joerne and Franz, Mrs. Schreiber's two brilliant sons who seem only slightly different from us because of their accents and their thick, heavy eyebrows, things which make me shy of them. I try to imagine them hungry as Mother tells us the terrible things that could have happened to them when Mr. Schreiber refused to name names from his army platoon which had invaded Russia during the war. Neither Mother nor Mrs. Schreiber ever mention the Nazis, the Jews, or the horror of the concentration camps. That part of the war is off-limits, omitted, for this is a story centered around our new enemies, the Russians.

When Mrs. Schreiber turns me around she looks solemn and worried as if she's reliving the experience of terror right here in her sewing room. She sighs loudly and looks out the window at the darkening night as she tells us about her escape from Berlin. "We had no choice," she whispers, "we had to leave." As she talks of the intricacies of concealment, of leaving in the dead of night, I imagine that I too am hiding in the woods outside of Berlin, the trees just beginning to silver with the coming of fall. Light shimmers through dense leaves, the forest growing darker as I make a path through the wilderness, me and my husband trying to find food for our boys, trying to keep the possums and raccoons away, the occasional fox darting through the shadows. Of course, we have to travel at night, walking quickly and quietly through the forest, always alert for soldiers, for camps of men prowling the woods. In the day, blessed with the thought of sleep, we hide behind a clump of bushes, the boys covered in coats, each of us taking turns with the watch. Sitting in camouflage, my heart clamors with fear.

While I've been daydreaming, the story has moved from the forest back into another part of the city where, in order to complete their escape, the Schreibers have to catch a train out of East Berlin. "It was our only hope," Mrs. Schreiber says, "to buy tickets and move out with the Polish immigrants into West Berlin."

"Oh, it was uncanny," Mother says as Mrs. Schreiber bends down to mark the hem, "the way you fooled them." Mrs. Schreiber smiles, the pins now held firmly between her teeth. "She and her husband split up," Mother tells us, leaning forward, a brightness to her eyes, "each taking a child into a separate car, sitting with the Polish immigrants, workers who'd come to East Berlin for factory jobs and were returning to their homes. You had a ticket, didn't you, Mrs. Schreiber, but not the correct identification?"

Mrs. Schreiber nods, looking up from my hem. "You must have identification."

"Or be sent back and punished," Mother finishes.

"We were *so* frightened," Mrs. Schreiber says. "We didn't know what would happen."

I listen more consciously now as Mother tells how the armed Russian soldiers patrol the station, marching through the trains with food stains on their clothes, heavy mustaches shadowing their faces. They wore thick coats and spit right on the floor. "And her little boy is so still," Mother says, "he's too afraid to move."

For a moment I can see him, his muscles taut, the hairs on his arms standing up, his tongue moving silently inside his mouth as he remembers the bacon they cooked in his basement. "We were so hungry by then, so weak." Mrs. Schreiber smiles. "Who can forget the smell of bacon when you're hungry?"

I see them sitting on the train, numb with panic. It doesn't matter where they look, there's danger. The soldiers are crude, peeling fingernails, blowing their noses, wiping the snot on their sleeves. They stare with contempt at the passengers, smirking because they're the conquerors. Peasant conquerors. The other passengers look blank, unfocused. A little girl twirls woolen thread through her fingers, making a lattice, unraveling it, starting again. An old man nibbles at a crust of bread, his lips barely moving. "At the front, a conductor calls for tickets and the Polish immigrants pull out yellow slips of paper folded in half," Mrs. Schreiber says. "I watch him moving forward, marking them, his fingers dirty, nails bitten to the quick. He's Russian, and I remember they don't always read German, so I rummage in my purse and find a yellow laundry slip and I fold it in half, like this"—she folds up a piece of fabric—"and wait for him to move up the aisle." Her boy, she says, doesn't take his face from the officer's sleeve as it nears his cheek and reaches across for the slip. "The conductor stares at my laundry slip, looks down at Franz, looks at me, squints at the paper, says something to another officer. And then," Mrs. Schreiber beams, "he marks it! He marks my yellow laundry slip!" For a moment we're all quiet, relieved and excited; I find myself smiling at this artful deception as if I too have been saved.

"Turn now," Mrs. Schreiber says to me and she gets up off her knees, moving to another place on the floor. "But my husband and Joerne are in the other car," she continues, marking with her chalk. "What can they know about the slip?" She calls for the conductor, tries to translate, pointing and motioning to her boy, holding up her fingers, *two*. And to her surprise, he smiles, indicating she can fetch them, never knowing he's been royally duped.

"Isn't that a wonderful story?" Mother says, turning to us, her face pale in the dim winter light. She seems happy, pleased with its European terror, its female cunning, the nimbleness of Mrs. Schreiber's escape.

We nod, convinced it's more dramatic than Mother's escape from Praco and yet confirmed in our hope that women can be heroines, can step out of the ordinary into the extraordinary, can trick the authorities, can leap over the boundaries of good behavior. And for a moment, we four women sit together, warm in this knowledge as if we've been released from propriety, saved from obscurity. In my secret heart I wish for a tragedy to overcome, something dramatic and big, something that will pit my life against the forces of evil so that I too can be brave. Of course, I have no idea that life will bring me sorrow enough, that small moments of terror will become huge, terrifying, that every day will be a stumbling into the unknown.

After such lofty passions, it's hard to return to our benign world, to a house with daily routines and no panicked flights into the woods. On the way home I'm still immersed in this story and say quietly to myself, "Maybe Mrs. Schreiber would be a good friend."

"Oh, no, I don't want any friends," Mother says quickly, glancing at me in the rearview mirror. "Family's enough."

"But what about Bessie? *She* was your friend." I think of Bessie leaning over in her leopard skin coat to pick up her purse, hiking up her dress to re-attach her stocking to her garter. With Bessie, my mother seemed girlish, the younger sister awed by glamorous clothes and matching luggage. Bessie liked mink and fox tails, and high narrow shoes with heels like stilettoes and beads on the toes. She never wore anything as demure as pearls, but favored diamonds and topazes and blazing sapphires. With Mother she'd talk about her store, about a new design that had just come in, and listening, my sister and I would feel relieved, seduced by the continuous thread of their talk.

"Of course, we were friends but we didn't bother with a lot of foolishness about ourselves."

Hearing this, I feel gloomy, defeated. I know she means intimacy, girl-talk, those gossipy revelations that distract us from the boredom of each day. I tell myself this is because of that Maypole dance, a single instance in Mother's young life. She must have been six, the very last day of her first year at school. She said she loved the smell of chalk, the press of a pencil, the crackle of wood in the stove, the way the windows glazed with sweat. Best of all, she loved the Maypole dance with its colorful ribbons, the smell of new grass beneath her feet. That day she held tight to her ribbon, the youngest kid twirling around and around, everyone twining themselves closer and closer to its ruby-red heart. At least, until someone messed up, someone hurried and restless and stupid, someone who stopped the dance. "You!" they all yelled at Mother. "But I didn't do it," she cried in startled anguish. "I held onto my ribbon. I did!" But it was no use. She was banished from the circle, made to stand all alone and watch.

At home Daddy and Max are in the kitchen talking politics and laughing, drinking vodka and bourbon; they seem completely satisfied with themselves, tearing into bags of potato chips and pork rinds, things Mother doesn't usually buy. For months, Max has been trying to get his widowed father to marry Daddy's widowed mother so that he and Daddy can be brothers, but so far this plan has failed miserably. At the very least, he hopes to detach Daddy from the faithful grip of the Democrats.

Looking at them, Mother sighs and picks up a magazine. There's the smell of liquor on their breath, the hint of danger. Not violence, but danger to the family, to the singular loyalty Mother believes family is about. She sits under the blue light of a lamp, her head tilted as if engrossed, eyes lowered to the print. For moments she reads in complete stillness, shoulders hunched, neck bent, arms loose, but at the first hoot of laughter, her head bobs up like a cork.

Nights later we're surprised when Mother comes into our room to sit on our bed, her nightgown draped over her breasts, over the tops of her black velvet bedroom slippers, her face drawn and blotchy. She seems lonely, forsaken. What days before has been stable and indestructible is now slippery and frail. Sitting down on my bed, she looks younger, more desperate. I see her breasts floating beneath her nightgown, breasts that are full and white and that excite me in a strange, erotic way. She slouches on the bed and seems for a moment like an older sister who's wandered into our room to confess secret thoughts.

"Your father never thinks about me," she says, her voice tight and sharp like the point of a hat pin. "He's never once thought about me as a person." My sister and I lie still under the covers, unable to move. I see them walking home from a neighborhood party a few nights back, their bodies as awkward as third graders marching in from recess. A coldness seemed to brush their elbows and knees so that they stiffened in walking. Daddy bit a fingernail. Mother gripped her purse against her waist. "I want to go to Birmingham," Mother says, tears clouding her words. "I want to leave." Then she asks if we'll go with her, and we know she means will we leave our father, our safe middle class life to go deeper into the wild night of cities and lights.

"Of course we will, Mommy," we say. We'll go. Wherever you go. In my dreams, she's always driving, rushing forward while the landscape recedes, trees drifting backwards, houses dissolving, bridges evaporating as she stares straight ahead, thinking of where she would like to go.

But the next morning she's at the kitchen counter making shrimp salad and a lemon meringue pie. By noon, she's polished the candelabra and put glorious pots of violets in the windowsill. She decides she wants to teach school again, to get up at 5:00 in the morning and prepare lessons in seventh grade science, to buy a new awning for the patio, one with pink and white stripes, something festive and charming you can look up into and imagine a happy life.

When she leaves our room at night, my sister and I grow very quiet. We know we are her work, her future, that we must never disappoint her but fill the gap of experience and perfection which has somehow eluded her. We turn out the light and lie still in the dark. Our future seems luminous, but full of hazard. What will happen, I wonder, if we don't turn out the way she's planned, if our lives aren't the least bit miraculous, but ordinary, as commonplace as a penny? What then will she do?

exploding triangles

What if only *I* turn out to be ordinary? A girl slaving in bakeries, dusting hot brownies with confectioners' sugar and winding ropes of buttery batter around the sides of birthday cakes, or sitting patiently beside Miss Mannick in the gym, punching out tickets for the high school basketball games? But I don't believe it. In my mind I'm inextricably linked to my sister and as I watch her sleep, she looks settled, secure, one arm tucked under the pillow, her body curled towards me in such girlish trust, I sink back with a sigh of relief. We're anchors to each other, bound by the force of Mother's ambition. At night when the three of us drive home from Mama Dot's, a heavy darkness shuts everything out, sealing us in as if there's nothing in the world but the skittering of animals in the bushes, the loneliness of a country road, and the odd contentment of finishing a lesson. When I look at the dark shape of Mother's head, the profile of my sister, I know I'm the third leg of an equilateral triangle, balanced and firm. More than anything else it's this sense of destiny I carry inside me.

I don't know when I first hear the word "New York," but when Mother says it, I know instantly it's a sword, chopping me in half, dropping me to the floor. It's a Saturday morning in October and I'm at the kitchen counter, pouring lemonade, opening a bag of chocolate chip cookies. "New York City?" I repeat, my voice rising anxiously with the words. "You mean you're really *going* there?" To me, it's as far away as the North Pole, as foreign as the moon. I think of the film we saw in Miss Williams' class, heroin addicts lying moaning and wasted in cold water flats. They're chalky-lipped, pale, writhing beneath grey-weathered sheets.

Mother glances at Jean; the look on their faces is conspiratorial, secretive, and as I turn from one to the other, surprise flows through me like an electric shock. They've decided something without me.

"Well, your sister needs to look at boarding schools," Mother says quickly, not actually looking at me, but writing something down on a pad by the phone, "and this will be a good opportunity to see what's there." A rush of fear sweeps through me. I had no idea my sister wanted to leave, to be separate from us, to live so far away. To me, it's unthinkable, unimaginable, and when I look at her I expect to see a traitor's mask, but she's sitting on the bar stool as usual, blowing her nose, then eating the last of the angel food cake. "Then Mrs. Gaston asked us to stay in her sister's brownstone across from Central Park," Mother continues, "where we'll see women in beautiful furs and fine clothes—"

"Walking their dogs," my sister interrupts, "and going to the Empire State Building."

"To Carnegie Hall," Mother adds.

But what I see is a triangle exploding, three perfect sides collapsing, splintering, my ideal structure crashing down. "What about me"? I start to ask, but before these words rush out, the phone rings its annoying sound, and somebody pushes open the back door, calling, "Yoohoo, anybody home?" Mother smiles at the Egg Lady who comes grinning into the room, then picks up the phone while looking directly at me as if to say, *what can I do?* Jean's already walking out of the room, never lifting her eyes from the pages of her book.

I tell myself to wait, snuggling close to Mother, demanding to be taken, whatever the price. But some new pride rises inside me, and I slink away from the kitchen towards the backyard where a gray mist trembles above the grass, dissolving like smoke in the air. Let them go. What do I care? I'll never go to boarding school, never leave my favorite teacher or best friends for some stuck-up people in New York. And yet secretly I know I've been deserted. *My mother gone. My sister gone.* Had I been a normal child, I might have ranted, bullied, shocked everyone with my fury, but already I'm learning that pain can be a wedge, a secret pleasure like a bad word smudged inside your brain. And without another thought, I walk out into the backyard grass and empty my bladder, letting the pee run down my legs into my socks and the soles of my shoes. I slosh and squish. I stare hard at the clean white sun. I can think of no other way to admit my fury.

As an adult I know too well that anger in disguise creeps underground, seeping below the surface towards depression, loneliness, a nerveless passivity, but in childhood I turned this anger into a constant vigilance. Where is Mother? Is she in the kitchen? the bedroom? the bathroom? "*Mo-ther!*" I call from the cloistered darkness of the hall. Without a response, I go looking until I find her powdering her nose or picking up a pile of laundry. "What?" she asks, glancing up, her face as luminous as a polished spoon.

"Nothing," I say. "I just wondered where you were." Then I

moon around, peeling back a hangnail, pulling lint from the air, making furtive glances to make sure she's still there. To ease my mind, I think of Mother as a young girl waiting for the bus out of Praco: her hair, thick and black, has been curled the night before; her skirt falls gently just below her knee. Behind her, there's the ugliness of the hills, treeless, carved out by dynamite, then the company store, squat and dilapidated, a new NEHI sign already splattered with flies. She's craning her neck, looking for that bus, saying *hurry, hurry,* like a mantra in her head. I'm relieved by this memory, for this is the mother I know: lost and struggling, anxious to punch her way out into the world.

Not another word is said about the trip, but in the kitchen Mother looks happy, consumed. She's never so focused as when there's too much to do, a project to complete, work to accomplish. Suddenly there's a flurry of activity, plans to be made for someone to pick me up after school, to fix my supper and take me to lessons. And then on Wednesday I watch in nervous embarrassment as Mother and Jean lug their suitcases out to the car, Jean's slip hanging down, Mother with her fur stole in her arms.

"Goodbye," I wave, my books clutched tight against my chest.

They wave furiously back, their faces bright, expectant, but I'm already distracted by numbness; the single thread of feeling is the clenching of my hands around my books. I don't know when I notice my father behind me, but I'm startled to see him dressed as always in a suit and tie, ready for work as if the earth's still turning on its axis.

I've never been alone with Daddy and Don before. As I move towards Daddy's car, I wonder if this is some sort of test, a cockeyed experiment to see if I can stand all this maleness unrelieved by female diversion. But I'm too sad to worry about that. Instead, I sit silently in the front seat while Daddy hums Peter Cottontail, accompanying himself with loud bursts of whistling. I think of Mother and Jean sitting in the plane, buckling their seatbelts, then the plane rising higher and higher until it's no bigger than a speck of dust. Only distantly, as if from another planet, do I hear Daddy's raspy voice, "Hippety, Hoppety, Peter's on his waaaaay."

For the next three days I hide in my bedroom, the living room, the dining room. I can lie on the living room couch and stare at the mirrored sconce, imagining the curtains opening on Broadway while Mother and Jean sit in the audience in silent wonder. I try not to think of their defection. I think instead about my sister going away to school, leaving me alone to brush my teeth at night, to stare at the nightlight in the hall, to eat fried liver and baked custard at Morrison's, but I can't imagine my life without her. She's the only one who makes noise on a regular basis, who leaves in the middle of a conversation to read her book. She's in her pre-beautiful days, chubby and awkward and desperately afraid of sharks. "I can't go in the water," she yells when we go to the beach. "There might be sharks out there. If they're there, they'll find me," while I plunge through the waves, delirious with joy. She sits on a striped towel and devours books about Christianity, the covers lurid with a swooning Christ, bright red blood dripping from his wounds. I've never thought about her as separate from me, but suddenly she's taking on significance, becoming a threat.

"They asked me if I liked G.B.S.," she whispers over the phone the next night, "and I didn't know who the *heck* they were talking about." I'm sitting in the kitchen on one of the bar stools, the phone clutched tight to my ear. I desperately want to know what they're doing, if they've seen any heroin addicts, any pale, shivering people lying on doorsteps, but I don't dare admit my curiosity. "I told them I *didn't* like him," Jean says louder, "but then we saw his play and I had to admit I did. It's Shaw. George Bernard Shaw."

I laugh because she hates to be wrong, because her confession makes me like her again.

The days creep by so slowly I don't feel like the earth is moving at all. I eat silent suppers with Daddy and Don, all of us sitting before the TV watching Walter Cronkite and Harry Reasoner, then Matt Dillon on *Gunsmoke* until finally it's the night before Mother and Jean are due back home. Every night I've slept alone, surprising myself by my dreamless sleep. But in the middle of this night, I sit straight up in bed, sweating, panting, my pajama top stuck like glue to my chest. More than anything I need to call my mother, to make absolutely sure she's coming home, but of course, that's impossible. She's staying in a brownstone with maids and butlers and fancy-dressed doormen who swoop out into the street to hail you a cab. As I stare into the darkness, I see the shadow of my dress hanging like a shroud from the closet door. That's all it takes. I jump up from bed and rush out into the hall. My father's a light sleeper, a snorer, but the only way I'll ever go back to sleep is to crawl into their bed and sleep in my mother's place.

Like a thief, I creep into their room, listening to Daddy's regular breathing, the hiss of clogged breath, a snore, then finally a settled rhythm. In an instant, I'm cradled in my mother's place, my head on her pillow, my arms tucked close as I snuggle deeper under the covers. I don't dare move, stretch my legs, or untangle my twisted pajama legs. At night Daddy opens a window and I watch the curtains billow, floating out then drifting back until the space between waking and sleeping vanishes and I'm flying around the outside of our house, my nightgown fluttering around me like wings. The air feels cools and damp to my face, but I can't see in the darkness. Trees loom up so suddenly I bump against them, the branches scratching my face, pine needles brushing softly against my skin. The only thing I can see is the outside of our house, its angle and curves, but I can't find my way in. Flying close to the walls, I look for doors, windows, cracks I might squeeze myself through, but there's nothing but roof and walls, bricks and shingles. In terror, I feel my nightgown tangling around my legs, binding me up. Somewhere nearby an owl hoots its screeching cry. Milky clouds shadow the moon. More than anything I want to see my family, to float down to my bedroom and sleep beside my sister. But a feeling sweeps through me like the assault of a thousand pins. *For you, there is no inside to the house.*

In my bones, I feel a sharp turn in the story. My parents are casting lots, choosing sides. In order for the tribe to move forward, it must select its leaders, groom them meticulously, then prepare for the journey. And yet on the surface nothing much has changed. Mother and Jean return from New York and to my relief, boarding school is never mentioned again. Instead, my sister sinks back into our double bed with chocolate chip cookies and fig newtons, and we take up our lives as before, going to school, to dancing and music lessons, adding clarinet and saxophone, playing in Mama Dot's woods, eating in the back seat of the car as we drive through the frost-laden fields of winter in Alabama. I would have forgotten my night dream if soon after the trip to New York, Jean hadn't come home one day with an award.

"Mom, I won this thing," she says nonchalantly, holding out an envelope like it's a mysterious mistake. It's a 1961 summer scholarship from the National Science Foundation for junior high students, a prize that will sprint her into the ivied halls of a well-known college for a month. Though pleased with the award, Jean's not thrilled about giving up her summer until Mother and Daddy get in on the act, praising and coaching her about what to expect.

"This will put you so far ahead," Mother says, sitting down on our bed, her high-arched brows drawn together as if she's lost in deep thought. Mother never slouches but sits erect as if she might be called to the door or asked quite suddenly to perform. Only her head tilts slightly in sympathy and there's a new eagerness to her voice. "You'll learn so much you couldn't learn from staying here," she says. "And you'll be much more prepared for biology, understanding mitosis and meiosis." As she talks, I stare at myself in the bevel of the mirror; my face slides sideways, becoming distorted, unreal, the face of a freak until with sudden clarity, I realize that now I'll be the only daughter in the house, the one sitting at the breakfast table with funny stories to tell. I imagine Mother and me driving up the azalea-lined lane to the Grand Hotel for a late, intimate lunch; we'll be met by a fashionable doorman suited in black with bright shiny brass buttons and knife-creased pants. Bowing, he opens our door and ushers us inside a room of Oriental rugs and floor-to-ceiling windows with a view of gardens of irises and roses plunging towards the sea. I feast in the smell of orchids and perfume, of the tiny rosebuds in a vase on our table as we order shrimp creole and rice. Even thinking about this, my mind fills with all the stuff I'll tell Mother, how the walls of my junior high smell like rain, the floors dusty and damp, my brain clammy as the chalkboards waiting to be filled. But even as I imagine this, I know that Mother hates to eat lunch, hates to sit down in restaurants, to dawdle over talk and food, indulging the senses, the body released from duty and work. "Eating such meals," she says, "is a big waste of time."

Still, I hold onto this fantasy while Mother and Jean speculate on Tulane and Emory, prestigious schools within driving distance of Foley. I imagine Jean far away, in Pennsylvania, in Spain, out of my life so I can pick at the remains.

It must have been in late May when two surprising things happen, events seemingly unrelated to each other, but overlapping in my mind. First, my sister rushes in one Tuesday with another letter. "It's here," she says breathlessly. "My assignment."

Mother and Daddy crowd around her, intoxicated, anxious. "North Carolina," she yells, her eyes jumping across the page.

"Where in North Carolina?" Daddy asks, his hand already reaching for the letter. He likes to see things in writing.

"North Carolina Central University," she says. "In Durham."

"Well, let's find it on the map," Daddy says and we get out the old atlas, dog-eared from wear. We know that Duke University is in Durham and Mother says that Jean can visit there too, can see what that campus is really like.

Now Mother and Jean talk endlessly about her scholarship, about what kinds of clothes she'll need for North Carolina, the sweaters, shorts, and summer dresses. Scads of underpants and training bras. Sitting beside them, I begin to have bad thoughts, having no choice but to kill Jean off, imagining something quick and merciful, her body flying through the windshield like a torpedo headed for a tree. I don't know why I think of this as merciful, but in my mind she's alive and then dead, like the snap of your fingers, a wish fulfilled. After this symbolic death, I feel freer, happier, and sit eating chili at the kitchen table while they discuss which long sleeve shirts she'll need for the cool North Carolina nights.

Now that Jean's residency is known there's a sense of relief in the family, the hope that everything might turn out all right. Maybe that's why there's a second important thing, a sudden loosening of the reins when Mama Dot's boys, Kenny and Geoffrey, ask us to go sailing in the middle of Mobile Bay.

I'm ecstatic. This sounds dangerous enough to stop my bad thoughts, to make us equal again. On the day of the trip, while my mind's trapeze-jumping with excitement, Jean sits in a peculiar knot, arms crossed over her stomach, legs double-crossed, hooked at the ankles. She gazes out the window as if she sees nothing except what's blooming in her head. I think only that she's scared. I know she's afraid of water and has come only to please Kenny and Geoffrey, who are gorgeous teenage boys, living reckless masculine lives. "Hurry, hurry, hurry," I urge Mother as we dawdle towards Fairhope, barely hitting fifty. But Mother is sunk in a silent funk as we pass the Creole women selling watermelons in Magnolia Springs, the aluminum trailers squatting together like chickens ready to roost, Mr. Tremble's brindle cows bunched up beneath a shade tree.

At the country club dock, Kenny and Geoffrey are waiting, tall and tanned and fabulous, coiling and uncoiling rope, the boat ready to go. It takes almost no time to tack out of the harbor into the bay, and as we glide through the water, wind ruffles my hair and I relax to a new sense of freedom. I forget about awards, about this odd tension in my life. I love only the water and the soft, fragrant air, the seagulls shadowing the sky, squawking and dipping into a blue-green sea. Beside me, Jean looks frightened, hunched over in her green leaf print suit, the beige lining edging up over the seam of the bust line. She seems inverted, locked into a daydream, one arm clasped around her knees, the other holding the side of the boat. At the other end, Kenny and Geoffrey are bronzed and beautiful, shouting to each other as they tack, and when I look at the shore it appears no larger than a sandwich heel of bread. It's now that Kenny drops anchor, leaning into the spray of a wave. "Okay, girls, ready for a swim?" He grins his wide-mouth grin as if taunting us to jump into fire.

"Here?" Jean's eyes widen. "In the middle of the bay?" The lining of her bathing suit is creeping across her chest like an invisible skin suddenly become visible.

"Nowhere else," he laughs.

Animals jump inside my chest. I feel their clawing against my skin, a purring deep down at the base of my navel.

"Sure," Geoffrey says, standing up in the boat, balancing himself. The boat rocks gently as he dives in a smooth, clean line, splitting the water like a knife. When the sea closes over him, knitting itself back together in a froth of white, there's nothing but the wind rushing against the sails, the cloth whumping and slapping against itself. Geoffrey's head emerges ten feet from the boat, bobbing like a cork. "Can't get any better, girls," he calls, turning over on his back. He floats contentedly like a man in a bathtub.

I stand up, a surge of energy snaking up my spine. I put one foot on the rim, breathe deeply, leaning into the wind.

"Wait." Jean's hand tightens on my swim suit, holding me back. I think she's just scared and I want to shake her loose, but when I turn, her eyes show a sadness I don't know how to explain. The yellow flecks in her green irises shine in the sun.

"I can't accept the scholarship," she whispers, the wind blowing the words from her mouth. She's still huddled against herself, one arm around her knees.

"Why?" Her words stop my breath. In my mind, her body reassembles itself from the tree and soars back inside the car, leaving her whole and safe, ready to read another book while inside me, a seed of disappointment grows huge, monstrous. Embarrassed, I turn away from her, staring at water that sparkles like taffeta, silky and smooth.

"Because," she says, emotion creeping into her voice, "it's . . . it's . . . a *Negro* college."

I don't dare look at her. I can't. Instead, I'm jumping, rising up in the air and then hurtling down in slow motion, feeling for the first time all the loss and shame of my childhood knot like a fist inside my lungs. I don't think about the racism involved—I haven't yet understood the horror of that, though the very next week, one of the Freedom buses carrying black and white CORE members will be firebombed and destroyed by a white crowd near Anniston. Freedom Riders will be beaten by white mobs in Birmingham and Montgomery, leading Governor John Patterson to state he won't guarantee their safe passage through Alabama. But I won't read about this for years. No, I mourn the loss of my time alone with my parents, my chance to shine, to do something remarkable, imprinting myself on their lives. As my body shoots down into the deep blue sea, the bubbles all around me like fizzy champagne, I know that my sister and I are locked in an ancient struggle, armed with the crudest of weapons, the most fundamental desires. This is the season of danger, the darkness at noon: One of us will be chosen and one of us will have to lose.

"I don't want to talk about the past," Mother says as she stands at the sink peeling hard boiled eggs for a salad. "It's over and done with. I came from Praco but I left as soon as I could."

"What about your mother. Do you just want to *forget* her?"

Mother squints at the sunlight coming through the window. A big red sun hangs above the trees, catching in the feathery branches, spreading flat sheets of light. "She had a hard life," Mother says. "I understand it now, but I didn't as a child."

I fret because I'm getting nowhere; I can't pull any more information out of her head. I love to hear about the past, the meanness of that place, a sordidness that makes *Jane Eyre* seem pastoral. Hearing it makes me feel special, endowed with a mission, but Mother openly resists. "What about your grandfather," I say. "The one who was supposed to be a mathematician."

In my child's way I know that I've got her. She loves too much the fact of his intelligence, his position, to deny him completely.

I know, of course, how the story goes, how he immigrated from Scotland, leaving a professorship at the University of Glasgow, and became involved in the labor struggles of the 1890s, moving to Alabama as a union organizer in the mining wars of '93. According to rumor he blew up a bridge somewhere in northern Alabama, trying to stop scabs from moving coal out on the trains, and was forced into hiding, shuttling from household to household at all hours of the night to avoid arrest.

"He's not worth talking about," Mother says. "He got all involved in politics and left the family. You should never leave your family," she continues. "Your family's the only thing you can count on."

"But what did you *think* of him?" I know that he went back to Scotland, leaving my great-grandmother pregnant and alone in the backwaters of Alabama.

"He was a rascal," Mother says with certainty, throwing the eggshells away, then washing and drying her hands.

"What about your grandmother, that woman named Barbara? What happened to her?"

Mother looks thoughtful, the cloth now limp in her hands. "Well, she became mean," she says, looking directly at me. "But then, she was left all alone. I guess that's what bitterness does."

Now I can't look at her. I slink away, back to my room where I sit on my bed, my hands clenched between my knees. For the first time I'm worried that this might happen to me. Mean. Bitter and mean like Barbara. "That woman had eyes like flint! She'd whip a dead horse just to see if it would flinch!" *She was left all alone.* I see myself in my dream, staring at the house, trying to find my way in. I hear their laughter, their talk, the great chaotic noise of family life. An overwhelming numbness fills my throat and I curl around myself on the bed, folding my knees to my chest. I think of my sister, how I need to hurt her, a desire that leaves me baffled and ashamed. Though I can't find words to say it, I wonder if there's something rotting inside me, something alien and hateful that will soon begin to smell.

miracle boys

"It stinks," my brother says, sniffing the air.

The acidic odor of Perma-Straight stings our nostrils, reddens our eyes, but my sister and I giggle as we comb the straightener through his curly blonde hair. Our sixteen-year-old brother sits trapped before us, fidgeting on the side of the tub. His hands knot and unknot against football-muscled thighs. We know that what he's doing—straightening his hair—is somehow shameful, secretive, his vanity shifting from its tough masculine detachment to this feminine desire. If his buddies find out, they'll stuff brassieres in his locker, write BABE, SISSY or LITTLE MISS MUFFIN across the back of his jersey. It's because of this that my sister and I laugh, relieved that he's vulnerable, ridiculous, not all muscle and bone. For thirteen years I haven't thought about him; he seems to live on an island apart, our family split down the middle: boys on one side, girls on the other. In my mind, he's my father's property, just as my sister and I are my mother's, our lives honed by the same vigil, only separated by sex. Now, quite suddenly, he's come into focus.

"I don't know what's so funny," he says. His razor straight mouth twitches at the corner; he's trying not to grin. If he laughs, it will be an admission, an alliance with us. My sister and I watch closely, waiting for the soft, unbending of his will. But he only closes his eyes and tightens his lips as if swallowing something tart. "Hurry up," he says, flexing his shoulders so that muscles bunch beneath the skin. He leans towards us, grimacing, his chest a thick slab of force.

Pragmatically my sister sets the timer while I slide a plastic shower cap over his head. "How long?" he whispers, squinting at us. With the shower cap on, his features are too blunt, too ordinary, to arouse much interest. I think with satisfaction that he wouldn't make a pretty girl.

"Thirty minutes," my sister says, suppressing a grin.

My brother groans.

At the opposite end of the room, I stare into the full length mirror at this image of him: in the plastic shower cap, he looks undignified, absurd. Yet my imagination resists such a thought as if it can't comprehend the male's purgatorial descent. I don't allow myself to *see* him as a human form; to me he's already something preserved, unchangeable, like a dinosaur in a display case at the museum. After all, he has a history, an image in the world.

It all began that second game of the season, a hot September night, the southern breeze blowing its humid breath down our throats. Cheerleaders sweated in their gold wool sweaters while the water boy ran ceaselessly to the surge of players coming in off the field. I sat with Louise, one of my best friends, who ate Reese's Cups and peanuts constantly, screaming, "Kill 'em," her mouth full of mush. The whole town was watching, even Charlie Petry, the one-armed taxi driver, who sat on the fifty-yard line, and Mr.

Ulitzsch, the watch repairman, who barely spoke English and made guttural grunts of outrage when the other team scored.

"Go on. Get 'em. Take 'em apart," the crowd yelled as if they were watching a live war zone, each advance or loss bringing jubilation or despair. Football was the only sacred ritual in this town, our communal way of shaking loose the boredom of everyday routine. In the stadium you could yell and hiss. You could see and be seen. You could work off a week's worth of humiliation and fury. In the stands, romance and repentance sat side by side.

"Here, have a Reese's," Louise said, dropping one in my lap. "Save it for the next touchdown."

That night, my brother (in ninth grade, but on the varsity squad), sat silently on the bench as Lou Riggens, the senior fullback, ran the ball down the center, then faked to the right, gaining five yards, not seeing the runaway opponent who would in the next minute, snap him to the ground. When he fell, it was almost private, secretive, a chance meeting with the grass. Others fell on top, a human mound, arms and legs thrust out like planks from a falling building. When they emerged from the pile, Lou didn't move. He lay moaning, writhing, and his agony struck terror in our lungs. Silence rattled the stands, but when they carried him off the field, we stood up and cheered.

No one noticed my brother, #33, run out to take Lou's place. Instead, there was a sense of mourning, defeat. For the first quarter, Lou had steadily plunged through the defensive line, beating pathways between elbows and knees, more lion than agile tiger, inching his way forward with deliberate force. The second string senior had a pulled hamstring and sat moaning on the bench. Now it was my brother's turn. The crowd, seated again, was nervous, edgy. They knew Lou Riggens, knew his square, hefty body, had followed him religiously for the last three years. My brother was a newcomer, a youngster without any past, just a kid really who'd been pushed to the front of the line. In the stands we waited, expectant, our heads bunched together like trees in a forest. Remembering how he looked at the breakfast table—sulky and still—I took the Reese's Cup and squashed it in my fist. Yet when the ball was snapped, my brother shot forward, dodging and faking his way across the field while arms reached out to stop him, tugging at his jersey. Each time he wrestled free and ran on, a tornado of speed, while the wind ruffled the streamers clasped in our hands. The lights beamed out heat, and sweat trickled down our collars. Flushed with pride, I forgot that my palms oozed a chocolate mess as I thrust them high in the air. Then the stands went wild as he covered sixty yards, a human dot emerging like a god between those spikey goal posts. In that moment his fate was sealed. For the rest of the game he was electric, a mythic figure of speed and dancelike dodging, escaping as deftly as Houdini from his opponents' traps. He played first string for the rest of the season, made All County, All State. By the end of ninth grade there was no question where he stood: he was the leader of the pack.

"Get this stuff off," he says now, jerking at the cap.

"Ten more minutes," my sister replies, her eyes on the timer.

"Ten more my butt." He yanks the shower cap off of his head and leans over the sink, his large frame jutting out before us, demanding attention. "Just wash it," he says.

"You'll ruin it," my sister says, "and it won't be our fault." But already she's lathering his hair. We both know better than to openly defy him. I watch, holding the towel, as her hands soap with suds. My brother leans over the sink; his strength seems atrophied, still.

After the neutralizer's applied, he refuses to remain in the bathroom. He says he'll wash it out himself after the required five minutes. Dismissed, my sister and I brush our teeth and slip quietly into bed. Yet in the dark, some twin of my brother appears before me: in his football uniform, he trembles and shakes, losing control. He undresses, throwing off his helmet, his jersey, and finally his pads as if he's an animal shedding its skin. Weight and muscle collapse with the costume until he's skinny as a scarecrow stuck in the dirt. In this condition I'm not afraid of him. Like me, he's a prisoner of masks, a mimic, an imposter. I watch as he becomes aware of himself—his body so vulnerable, so small, it embarrasses him. When he looks as if he might cry, my world tilts violently. I hide under the covers until a black velvety sleep takes me in its grasp.

At the breakfast table the next morning, my brother's hair is straight. Not fly-away straight or poker straight, but the curl relaxed, with just the hint of a wave so that it dips in front. He doesn't look at us, but stares sullenly at the three strips of bacon, two eggs and two pieces of toast Mother's put on his plate. Three different colored vitamin pills sit like worry beads beside his ten ounce glass of milk.

"Don't forget your protein drink," Daddy says, looking over the sports page at my brother, not noticing his hair. Don nods, but his expression doesn't change. In the morning, he's silent, sulky, staring moodily at the food he has to eat. Daddy, beside him, is small and red-headed, his feet tidy in black lace-up shoes. "What was your time yesterday?" Daddy asks, dragging the corner of his paper through his scrambled eggs. A small yellow clump attaches itself like a snail.

"Nothing to brag about," Don mutters, gazing up under sleep-hooded lids. But there's pride in his motion as nimbly he flicks the egg back onto my father's plate.

"Well, take another vitamin," Daddy says as he crunches on toast, crumbs drifting like dust across his lap.

During the ride home from school, I watch my brother from the back seat, wondering if anyone in his class noticed the difference in his hair. Boys, I believe, notice nothing but big breasts—hooters, jugs, gazongas, they call them, their eyes lit up like pinball machines—while girls, always on the prowl, scan everything. If this is true, my brother's lucky. Girls won't reveal his secret; they know better than to tell, know better than to gossip openly about a star. Instead they'll titter in the bathroom between cigarettes, then crush the giggles down their throats when my brother comes into view. I watch as he hangs his elbow out the window, careless, assured. The car eats up pavement, the wind whipping at the sleeve of his shirt where blonde hairs wander down to the whiteness of his wrist. I stare beyond him at the grey sheet of sky where nothing moves. Not a cloud. Not even a branch. I wonder if he feels like that, a grey sheet of emotions, football the only way to vent his fury at the world.

That evening after I change into a t-shirt and shorts and come to the kitchen for a snack, my brother's best friend, Charlie, is there. With Charlie my brother comes alive, makes music alongside Charlie's teasing grin. Unlike my brother, Charlie pays attention to us. He's a wicked flirt with a roving eye. He notes my shorts without saying a word, only pursing his lips as if he's about to whistle. Unlike my brother, he makes me feel like a girl, or what I imagine a girl to be: someone admired by men, noticed for her sex, a 20th century Ginevra Fanshawe in short shorts and a teased bubble hairdo. With my brother, I'm passing, mimicking what I've seen others perform. I hug, I kiss, I squeal when the Beatles appear, but privately I'm too serious for the seductress' role.

Out of the corner of my eye, I notice the laundry door left open, my brother's jock strap hanging like a limp rag over the pencil sharpener just inside the door. Charlie's gaze follows mine.

He grins. "What's *that?*" he asks in mock surprise. He's a year older than my brother, shorter, darker, a beautiful tenseness to his body when he moves, like a cat stalking prey. He loves to tease, loves to catch my sister and me in a loop of lies about bodies and sex. He feeds us misinformation—calling football "fartball" while winking at us, then laughs with my brother about "that enema-bag guard." We love him for this, for including us in the game.

"What *is* it?" he repeats.

"A hat for your crotch," I say, though I know this is stupid. It's the stupidity of embarrassment, of circumstance. He's making me undress my brother, and my brain responds with small arms fire. Of course I already know that boys wear this strange object when they play football, but I don't know why. I don't know much about male anatomy, only that the penis is wrinkled and dangling, a useful spigot. To me, a jock strap is the equivalent of a brassiere, some kind of harness to keep you from jiggling. I wonder idly who teaches boys about such things, who fits them, shows them how the body should look. Do they get fitted as girls do for bras, staring at themselves in the mirror or is it more regimented, sterile, almost generic, one size fits all?

"It's a hat, all right," Charlie says, his gaze like a pulse. "But not for a Sunday School picnic."

By the time my brother's a junior in high school, college recruiters come regularly to our house dressed in tweed sport coats, dark pants, their college pamphlets and maps spread out on our dining room table like 4-color travel brochures. *Where do you want to go? Who do you want to be, be, be?* The younger ones bring wives as if this is a social call, the men talking football as if it's world affairs while the women serve pickled shrimp and dip, moving quietly in the background like Oriental shadow dancers. Occasionally, a recruiter stays for dinner, his big knuckled hand carving into

Mother's roast beef. The air at dinner becomes formal, serious. The vegetables are passed to the right, the butter cut into little pats. On such nights, the men discuss films of the Vigor game, the Satsuma game, the Grand Bay game, the Escambia game while they pull open their Brown-and-Serve rolls and smile dimly at my sister and me. The time I remember best is the October night the scout from the University of Alabama comes to town, a young, nice-looking man, dark and barrel chested, a faint smell of peanuts on his breath. Behind him at the door stands his pretty wife, dressed in emerald green wool, her chestnut hair short and perfectly coifed, sweeping away from her ears like wings.

Coach Johnston, the Alabama recruiter, arrives on Thursday in time for afternoon practice. Immediately afterwards, he talks with my brother, the two of them huddled together over the dining room table as if there isn't enough room to spread out. My father's ecstatic, fevered by hope that his son will play for the almighty Bear Bryant. It's his dream that my brother will be "at the top of the heap."

Yet it's the wife I'm interested in, this statuesque brunette who looks like a Miss America contestant with her painted red nails, her cinch-waist dress, her talk of shopping in Tulsa, Memphis and Baton Rouge. While the recruiter pumps my brother full of football lore from the University of Alabama, my sister and I watch the wife, who sits perched on one of our kitchen stools, talking easily and briskly with my mother about the cities she's visited while married to "the Coach."

"You know they have ducks in the fountains at the Peabody," she says to us, "and they walk every night to the elevators on red carpet just like royalty. Imagine that!"

I know intuitively that what she has is style. She seems charmed by all that's around her, even our small, flat, motionless town. Of course, she's from the city where they have trained beauticians and department stores, not out-of-work factory women who send off for a hair products catalogue, then go to work at the order department at Sears.

At the end of this night, my brother glows as if a magic carpet has been thrown at his feet. We can all feel the excitement in the air, the way the coach has complimented him, has played to his desires. "You just let me know when you think you're ready," I imagine him saying, "and I'll have you up there before you can blink."

What's said in private I'll never know. All I see are the outside tests: the increased vitamin intake, longer practices, less home visibility. It's all serious business: heat and know-how.

During his eleventh grade year, my brother and Charlie function as a team, the "miracle boys," impervious to danger, nourished by the hot lick of speed. At home, their legs tremble with impatience, pumping up and down as they eat their steaks with ketchup squirted out from a plastic tube. But on the field, my brother runs the ball through impossible gridlocks while Charlie catches a pass so low he bends like a ballerina in a sweeping pas de deux. They're always together, magnets to each other. Elvis' "Hound Dog" blasts from my brother's room on weekends, echoed by their laughter, their hoots of defiant surprise.

Suddenly it's springtime, almost summer. The azaleas have bloomed and died. The heat wraps around us all like a glove, tightening its grasp. Everybody sweats though it's only late April. Charlie's upper lip sprouts moisture; my brother's hair has relaxed back into crinkly curls. My sister and I have thrown away our crisp white shirts for bright colored loose knit tops with stretch band waists. We all sit at the dining room table, a watermelon before us, one of the first of the season, its cold, red fruit making us pant with anticipation. Mother's getting knives and plates, but Charlie and my brother don't wait; they pull off hunks with their fingers, the juice dripping freely from their mouths to the table.

"Mother said *wait*," my sister says, watching the juice puddle then disappear into the wood.

Charlie grins. "No shit," he whispers, pointing a finger at her. "But you won't tell."

We love it when they curse, including us in their lives. Usually they're all jock talk, all insider jokes, girlfriends and rolling eyes.

"No shit," my sister says louder as Mother enters the room.

Mother pretends not to hear as she distributes knives and plates. Newspaper—which most of our friends use for watermelon—is too primitive for Mother, even though it might have saved the table from our mess. Instead she asks Charlie what we all suspect to be true. "I guess you're getting excited about going to Georgia Tech next year?"

"Yes, ma'am," he says, all white teeth and handsome summer tan.

But it's my brother's face I watch. Enjoyment retreats behind a scowl so furious, so brief, I wonder that no one seems to notice. That scowl is the beginning of a punishing stare, but who gets punished? Not Charlie. He's happy-go-lucky, football's Peter Pan. It's only later that I understand, later that I see the connection between Charlie and my brother. Together, the game's more than competition, more than a means to an end. Without the interference of adults, it's still a game, a ritual of danger and discovery. But now Charlie's defecting, leaving my brother to the lions and tigers, leaving my brother alone with my father's ambition. Alone he must push. Alone, he has no choice but to succeed.

But there are moments when he's released. In the summer my parents travel to New Orleans for a convention, and my brother and Charlie plan a party, not just an average party, but a three-county jamboree with women from the beach, from the Junior College, from the city schools in Mobile. The house throbs with people, girls giggling in our bedroom as they drop cigarettes on the floor and re-tease their hair; muscle-bound football players cruise the halls, squat awkwardly on Mother's Queen Anne chairs as they pop open beers. Music from Chubby Checker, Elvis, Lou Rawls, the Beach Boys hangs in the air. My sister and I float through this crowd invisible as spies. We're in heaven, thrilled at the hairdos of the girls, hair which doesn't even move when they throw up in the toilet.

"Their hair is so per-fect," I whisper to my sister, my voice gurgling with enthusiasm as if I have fish bubbles in my brain. I see a woman lying on my bed, her skirt hiked up to reveal the thick band of a girdle. Yet even passed out, the shape of her hairdo is intact. It surrounds her snoring face like a helmet, the two sleek side curls plastered to her cheek, the bangs shifting only slightly to reveal a smooth, untroubled brow. I wonder if she wraps it in toilet paper at night.

When the party's over, the house looks deflated, like the leftover skin of an animal. My brother makes attempts to clean up, and though he re-arranges furniture, washes dishes and vacuums rugs, he can't seem to rid the house of odors, of spilled beer and perfume. But my parents are not furious, at least not in the way we expect. My mother sighs at the stained places on the rug and my father says in a short, jerky voice, "You can't afford to *ruin* your chances." That word hangs like punishment in the air.

During my brother's senior year, more recruiters come. From Georgia Tech, Tulane, Florida State, University of Florida, Georgia, Tennessee, even Harvard and Yale. Their desires and pledges scream above us like ambushes, hoarse cheers of fate. *Come to us. Play for us,* the voices demand. The air crackles with excitement. My brother's pursued, seduced. I wonder if he feels like a woman tantalized by offers, each one seeming better than the last until they're all irrelevant, trivial, too many beats away from his heart. Who is to say that too much is better, is less frightening than too little? When I look at the hardness of his face, I know there's nothing light or airy about becoming a star. Most often I see him after practice, slumped and exhausted in the reclining chair, his face puzzled, then empty as if he can no longer remember the point.

Maybe what he sees is a long dark tunnel of fear. A Halloween trap. Blood mixed with laughter, a wicked wind howling above his head. Maybe his life doesn't feel blessed as everyone suspects. Maybe becoming a star is more than hard work and talent; maybe it cuts off a lifeline somewhere deep within so that as you expand, you also contract: a creature flattened against the wall of your shell. I don't know that any of this is true. I only know that there are moments when his face shouts resistance, a fury too large to hold. I know that no one talks to him about what he *wants* to do, about what frightens him, challenges him, about the miracles of his mind. Instead, he's pulled along like a tree in a hurricane, a primal struggle without any choice. No one in the South assumes, in the early 60's, that a young talented male might not want to be a college football star, that there might be other means of success. Nor does anyone question the limitations of such a role. It's expected that after college, a football player naturally develops his connections, collecting favors, monopolizing on the power of his name, reminiscing about his body in motion as if that is his badge of honor to redeem.

When I see my brother withdrawing from this trap, I love him with a fierce curiosity, as if he's a geographical mass I've explored with hands and feet, but have never seen. In the dark for the first time I see him: bruised and weeping. His hands dangle uselessly at his side as he moves towards me. But it's his eyes that have changed, eyes that can out-glare my meanest stare. Those eyes, I think, have seen ugliness and memorized its spite. Now they're wide with terror, with the approach of nakedness and collapse. Yet he walks by me, unseeing, mute.

By the end of spring the recruiters are putting on pressure, flying him to campuses all over the South. One weekend, he's in Tallahassee, the next in Knoxville, a third in Tuscaloosa, then over to Atlanta to see Charlie. Yet there seems little choice in his decision since at every turn the house whispers, "Bear Bryant! Bear Bryant!" It's at the height of Bear Bryant's career when Alabama players streak triumphantly across TV screens all over America. My brother, it's believed, can become one of those prancing giants. With such an investment, my parents will become more rooted in the world, a star shining above their heads while they lie back, grateful, transfixed, the light from my brother illuminating us all. "Bear Bryant," the air whispers. "Bear Bryant."

One spring morning in March when the sky looks split open, grey giving way to blue as if better times are surely coming, my brother emerges from his room looking tense, truculent. What I imagine is this: My brother twists the curls of his hair in a nervous gesture as he stops beside my father's chair. My father's drinking a tall glass of ice water, a cloud of eggs spread across his plate. "I'm not going to Alabama," my brother says quickly, as if he's trespassing on sacred ground. A hush follows these words. My father stops drinking and stares attentively at his glass. An ice cube breaks, crashing with the force of an avalanche in the Arctic Sea. "I'm going to Georgia Tech," my brother says more forcefully, his gaze zooming beyond my father to the outside world. It's an astonishing choice. I imagine in his room, he's happy, ecstatic. In his dreams, he'll pick up with Charlie where they left off, the two of them racing like fleet-footed warriors across a smooth green plane, becoming boys again, playing cowboys and Indians, the stakes no bigger than daring each other to escape. With Charlie he'll survive. He'll surely win. There's nothing to stop them, nothing but a guilty tremor that beats somewhere deep inside his skin.

"That's fine," my father says as he spears his cumulus clump of eggs.

Two months later I watch as my brother stands at his window, gazing out at the park across from our house. A child swings back and forth, hurtling herself through the air with the repetitive faith of childhood. Birds fly up from a nearby bush, a wall of screeching sound. It's May, the beginning of summer, the last summer of his youth near the lazy shores of the Gulf of Mexico. In his hands he holds a letter, his latest from Charlie at Georgia Tech. He holds it tentatively as if it might scorch his fingers. *Hey, kiddo,* it says in a tightly scrawled hand. *Things are coming up bad all over. I can't quite believe it yet, but I just talked to the dean and, well, it looks like I just flunked out.*

My brother's motionless, quiet. I think, watching him, that he needs to straighten his hair again. It's knotted and furious. It kinks like tiny fists springing up from inside his head.

the big pond

1962. MOBILE, ALABAMA

Once my brother's gone to Georgia Tech, there's a hole in our life. We don't know much about him except what we hear after Daddy's trips to Atlanta for football games: *He made a good run. I mean he got in there and really hustled.* Now it's back to my sister and me at the kitchen table, vying for attention, trying to make it to the Big Pond.

"It's easy to be a big fish in a small pond," Daddy says, sitting beside us, his coffee cup full to the brim, a handkerchief wadded up in a snarl by his plate. Mother listens as she does dishes at the sink. "The difficult thing is to be a big fish in a big pond," Daddy continues, looking into the depths of his cup as if there might be a prophecy floating there. "That's another thing entirely." And he gazes out the window at the pine trees knotted together, bordering our yard. Squirrels sprint frantically across the lawn, digging at leaves, then standing stock still to eat until Sheba, the neighbor's dog, rushes out from the bushes, lunging towards them, scaring them away. For a moment I think Daddy seems sad as if, like Sheba, the prize has just been frightened off.

As he talks, I see myself walking in Mama Dot's woods in the blueness of evening, running through a thicket of oaks and pines until I'm lost in a maze of leaves. The Big Pond must be like this, without boundaries or constraints, a place of nervous mystery. The Big Pond, I believe, demands the logic of the heart.

"The Big Pond is in a *city*," Mother says, turning from the dishes she's rinsing in the sink. "I've never wanted to live in a small town, but your father—"

"I'm going to live in New York," my sister pipes up, grabbing a muffin Mother's left out on the table for us to eat. But I sit very still, trying to imagine such a place, a city with lights and noise and hordes of people where the indefinable Big Pond exists. All I see is a girl standing on the edge of the highway, ignored and vulnerable, while a stream of cars rush by. The only person I know who might have another opinion about the Big Pond is Mama Dot, and I plan to ask her at my next lesson.

But that never happens. No longer do we go to Fairhope, bumping across Fish River bridge where the river fans out in a watery harp, to the woods and solitude. No longer do we sleep after recitals on the beach, our hair sun-dried and stiff from salt water, our toes coated with sand, little piles of shells near our pillows so we can see them first thing when we wake up. We've lost this paradise to the sudden, unsettling diagnosis of Uncle Kenny's tuberculosis. "He's got to go to a sanatorium," Mama Dot announces, running her hands through her thick grey hair, her eyes tense with worry as she looks out at the rose garden where tea roses bloom in flames of scarlet and mauve. "He's got to have his rest and treatment, and though I don't know how we'll ever afford it, the boys and I will just have to make do on what we have."

Stunned by this fearful knowledge, we're herded into daddy's office for skin tests, for clearance, then herded as quickly into the backseat of Mother's car, in pursuit of another teacher, more lessons. Mama Dot will no longer take pupils, will spend her time helping Uncle Kenny get well. For two years we've been driving once a week to Mobile for dancing lessons at Mrs. McDonald's Dance Studio on Government Street, and now we're introduced to Mrs. Bair, who's landed in Mobile from Connecticut, a fact that makes me wary of her. Because she comes from Connecticut—so close to New York—I know she's cultured, which means the possibility of malice towards us, for the South is *behind* in everything, especially the arts. "Why do you need all that fancy fooling around on the piano?" someone in our town will ask, and Mother's face grows hard with impatience. "They're taking lessons so they can *appreciate* good music," she'll say, but we know it's an uphill fight, for culture in our town summons up water ballets, accordion solos, and the asafetida bags the doctors joke about on the records my father orders. In the evenings we listen to these recordings with my father, my sister and I giggling at the comments on piles and sores and misbehaved colons, my father laughing so much he seems touched with madness. Beside us, Mother looks distracted, her gaze focused beyond us into the glove of darkness that is our front yard.

"I want you girls to have talents," Mother repeats as we drive the endless miles to Mobile, past flooded farmland and the swampy creeks where catfish burrow in the mud and mosquitoes breed in drowsy pockets. "I don't want you to be ashamed the way I was, going to college without the least bit of refinement." Refinement means music and dancing, something to put down on my college applications under the heading OTHER INTERESTS. It's a requirement, I know, for the Big Pond.

When we arrive at Mrs. Bair's driveway, three kids in torn, raggedy clothing circle the yard, leaping and squatting, playing a childhood game. As we get out of the car, the oldest girl, who seems about eight, straightens, then turns an absurd scowling face to us as if we're interrupting the most important moment of her life. "Who are *you*?" she asks with a fierce grimace, her lips pinched together at the sides. "And what do you *want*?" She has a slash of dirt across her cheek and stares at us with the fierce pride of an oldest child. She carries a stick, and points it at the baby who waddles around, gurgling happily, then squats on the concrete. His diaper smells. "Pick him up," she says to her sister, who's no more than five or six years old. Inside the red brick house—which is surprisingly ordinary with overgrown shrubs and plain screen doors—we hear the sounds of a piano, the arpeggios of a scale, the muted voices of people talking, then the beginning of a sonata, soft and suddenly beautiful.

"We've come to take music lessons," Mother says as if she's talking to an adult. The baby, seeing us, toddles towards us, then plumps back down on the concrete and grins, waving his arms. Behind us traffic churns. The new leaves on the trees flutter in the breeze.

"With my mother?" the girl asks, unrelenting in her stare. She points her stick at us.

"Yes," we say in chorus. For a moment I think we might curtsey.

"Well, you can't see her yet. She's with another student." And then she turns away, tapping her stick in the air with all the authority of a conductor arousing the French horns to triumphant sound. When she twirls suddenly it's with that same grim, patronizing glare. "Do you have any *cookies*?" Mother looks at us, but we shake our heads, having eaten all of our animal crackers and drunk our cokes on the ride to Mobile. We eat everything very fast, barely making it to Magnolia Springs before we're digging our fingers into the crumbs, licking our palms.

"But you could go get us something," Jean says, seizing the

opportunity. "You could go to that pastry shop on Dauphin and buy us elephant ears."

"Yeah!" the little girl shouts with glee. "Yeah, yeah, buy us some elephant ears!" And now she's all smiles and happiness, jumping up and down, waving her stick in the air. She comes very close to us, almost purring with tenderness, staring at my mother with sudden adulation in her eyes. "Will you buy one for *each* of us? We need to have one of our own so we don't have to share." Behind her, the baby cries, "Mama! Dadda!" and rocks happily on the ground. The other little girl stands beside him, not smiling, silently rubbing the sides of her feet on the concrete.

Mother nods. "But you'd better take care of your little brother. He needs his diaper changed."

The little girl turns to him dispassionately. "He's hungry, aren't you Zack? You want some *el-ey-phant* ears!" Hearing her, Zack tightens his fists and sucks noisily on his grimy thumb. "But *hurry*," the little girl turns back to Mother, pointing her stick at us, "So they can eat theirs before their lesson."

At first I'm stunned by these children. How can a lady from Connecticut have such dirty children? Their dark hair is matted to their foreheads and tangled around their ears; their clothes are limp with heat and sag in the back; they're ribbed with dirt like the Butterfield kids who receive Christmas baskets from the church every year, who have lice and worms. And what's more, they don't act ashamed. They don't seem to know it's too late to go barefoot, impolite to ask for free food. Already I can tell they're greedy and impatient, demanding and insistent.

It's only when Mrs. Bair, our new teacher, steps out of the house, that the girl becomes quiet, gazing at her mother with absolute adoration. "Ma-*ma*," she calls. "Ma-*ma* . . . look. *Look*!" And she does a cartwheel on the concrete, her skinny legs opening up like rusty scissors, then crumpling as she falls in a heap to the ground. "Wait! I have to do it again." But I don't watch her anymore. I'm staring at our new teacher. After the spartan beauty of Mama Dot, with her old khaki shorts and orthopedic shoes, her prominent cheekbones and searing gray eyes, Mrs. Bair looks absurdly dramatic. Her very long blonde hair, pulled back into a loose ponytail, only heightens the pasty whiteness of her face, her cranberry lipstick, her blue eyeliner, the black sheath and clingy white pants that wrinkle around her ankles. She's wearing flip-flops and dangly earrings. Her face, keen and pockmarked, looks wintry with indoor life. Everything about her seems incongruous, misplaced. I feel the beginning of dread. What can she know of the Magnolia River, of the blind fish that swim in Devil's Hole? What can she know of lying dizzy in the sun, watching a wasp buzz back and forth in its senseless drone beneath the shadow of the eaves? Mama Dot understood these things, would jump up after your lesson, rushing outside to find the woodpecker she heard just as you were finishing the Grieg.

"Come in," Mrs. Bair says, her eyes flickering blueness, intensity, a severity I don't want to know. To avoid her gaze, I study the pockmarks on her face, the tiny indentations that embellish the slash of skin from cheek to ear. She opens the screen door, then turns to her daughter. "Sherry, you bring the kids inside. You can have milk and crackers at the kitchen table."

The little girl startles to attention, her feet planted on the ground. "We can't! We're waiting for the elephant ears."

Only then does Mrs. Bair smile. "Okay, but come inside once the elephant ears arrive." She turns to me and says quietly, "Sherry is a genius. She already plays Beethoven and Schumann, but she's fickle and wants her own way." She doesn't look at Sherry as she says this, but studies my face which I'm careful to keep expressionless as if I hear about geniuses every day.

Sherry is a genius. All the way home that thought burrows like a thorn inside my brain. I see Sherry parading around the yard, indomitable, autocratic, her smartness overriding everything else, leading her effortlessly towards the Big Pond. Already these advantages weigh heavily in my mind. To be a genius is to be allowed privileges, authority, to be born with something that nobody else has. My mother, I assume, is almost a genius, though this has never been verified and only gives her prerogative in the naming of others. Of course, we never refer to genius, only to people who are "very smart."

"Oh, she's very *smart*," Mother will say about Lucy Polk, a high school senior who won the national science award for growing her own penicillin for the science fair. "She'll do something in the world." I always see Lucy in her room, silent and secretive, growing penicillin in a test tube in her underwear drawer, getting up in the middle of the night to check on its progress. We imagine her picture splashed across the newspapers after she's made a life-saving discovery, and then our whole town will be famous. In the early part of my life, my brother's praised for having a photographic memory, though I can't remember him announcing a thing he's learned, and yet when I see him I think *memory*, as if it's a little halo surrounding his head. Genius is what mother would like for us, but I can't help thinking that all my wishing and hoping to be smart is distracting me from something I need, something that's much closer, right next to my bones. Years later, still full of longing, I stop a man in the midst of passionately undressing me. "Do you like my mind?" I ask with something close to desperation. My voice is taut, beseeching, and he pauses above a button, then smiles. "Yes," he says softly, without touching me. Relieved, I let my dress fall to the floor.

The next week Sherry's playing the piano when we arrive, sitting atop two pillows on the chair, leaning into the piano, her elbows held out like tiny wings. She looks like an urchin, her hair hanging forward, snarled in knots, but she seems absorbed, in a trance, an expression of guilty pleasure on her face. She's playing something by Schumann, and then suddenly when she messes up, she yanks her hands free and says, "That wasn't my fault," and starts over. It's only when she hears Mother come into the room—"*Oh, I'm sorry. I thought we were late*"—that she stops abruptly and turns around. "What did you bring me?" she asks, her face lighting up, her eyes zeroing in on Mother's purse for the white pastry bag. "Did you go to Dauphin and get elephant ears?"

"Sherry," Mrs. Bair interrupts. "That's enough. You're being rude. Now get up. Your lesson's over."

"But I want to do it again," Sherry says and begins playing, scooting up closer to the piano, her hands flying across the keys. Now she's banging out the piece, no longer absorbed, merely hurrying, determined to finish.

When she finishes, she gets up quickly, wiping her hands on her dress. "I wrote all the diatonic triads for major keys on my board," she says to Mother with that flush of enthusiasm of a child praised for progress reports. "Didn't you bring me *anything*?"

Mother looks embarrassed. "I'm sorry, but we had to hurry," and Sherry's face clenches up as if she might cry until her sister waltzes in.

"You're supposed to be copying the alphabet," Sherry says to the girl, hands on her hips. "Now get out of here. This is MY room," then she lurches forward with a windmill of fists.

"Girls!" Mrs. Bair catches Sherry, who then tries to climb up into her mother's lap, her legs circling her thighs, her hands grabbing at her dress.

"Ma-*ma*!"

But Mrs. Bair won't allow it. "Ma-*ma*!" She pushes Sherry away, peeling off her fingers. "Stop that. Go outside and play or go to your rooms."

Sherry's head droops and she looks at her feet. "I hate you," she whispers, but Mrs. Bair is already absorbed in some new thought, putting away Sherry's music, dropping the pillows onto the couch. And in the secret hardness of my heart, I'm overjoyed that Sherry is bereft.

That spring we go three days a week to Mobile, leaving right after school, my sister and I running to mother's car in the line-up, getting in, throwing our books to the floor, ready for whatever snack Mother's prepared. We settle into the rhythm of the car, driving through the outskirts of Foley, past Kaiser's potato fields and the tin sheds full of gladiolas, into the blood red sun of a spring afternoon.

Imagine that you are me. Riding with your mother and sister beside weed-choked ditches, through farmland and fields and into the watery swamps that lead into Mobile Bay. You feel the slight dip and leap of the car when it crosses the first of many bridges, a sense of subtle pleasure that the car is rising like a bird in the air. You are needy of such pleasures, for this trip is a familiar one, taken during rain and sleet and sun, with gulls flying over the bay, occasionally an egret or a heron swooping onto a grassy island, landing with a great flap of wings. You tell yourself not to think, not to feel, that this is just another day in a group of endless days of music and dancing and school. Your sister seems happy to be a part of it. Your mother drives with the concentrated zeal of the driven. Only you hold back, uncertain, dreading Sherry, the eight-year-old genius! You too want to prance and pout, but feel like yourself only before sleep, in that wide, clean space of drowsy trance. It's your one moment of pleasure, slipping free of your body, the sky drifting in the darkness of your eyes. More than anything you wish you could tell someone, *"this is me"* but it would sound too goofy to explain. Better to stop thinking. Better to put yourself on hold, to stare with squinting eyes at the bay, hoping that today *IT* will appear as it does in your dreams, a watery animal, half fish, half lizard, covered with shimmering scales that glitter like diamonds in the sun. *IT* came to you one night in a dream, appearing suddenly on your doorstep, droplets of water sparkling with wetness as it landed with a hiss outside your door. And when you opened the door, you knew that *IT* had come to protect you, had arrived just in time to kill your enemy, the snake, lying sleek and black and coiled on the bottom step.

Closing your eyes, you let the cloud-covered sun warm your body until slowly you become smaller, tighter, your neck elongating, your body shifting shapes. When you open your eyes, you're no longer a girl going to music lessons, but a creature crawling out of water into air, pure and bright and whole.

I'm not ready for my lesson. Sitting in the Bair's kitchen at the table with the salt and pepper and the little jars of jam, I try to finish my assignment. I'm supposed to transpose a melody from the key of C into the key of E and though the book lies in my lap, I can't think. I'm distracted, edgy, remembering the rush of spring air on my face, the staccato flash of red and pink azaleas, and suddenly all I want is a vanilla ice cream cone with chocolate syrup dripping off the top. I don't want to do my assignment. I don't want to be here. I spy Jean's bag on the table and quickly rifle it, hoping she has the same exercise as me. But I don't find anything but her school books. I see papers on the table and pick up each piece. On one chords range in all the major keys. Some have been erased and redrawn, but they're large and black and easily visible. SHERRY is written at the bottom of the page. I'm looking hard at this sheet when Sherry strides in and with a sudden swipe, yanks it out of my hand.

"Cheater," she says, wagging the paper at me.

"Am not," I glare. "I was only looking." And yet some tiny part of me feels guilty, implicated. Culture is still foreign to me, this awkward apparatus I'm supposed to carry like a house on my back. Even playing Chopin's "Fantasy Impromptu," I think only of sand and sun and dirt. More than anything, I want to walk out into the land, to hide alone in the woods and wake restless to the morning's heat. I see the piers jutting out into the bay and feel the roughness of the pilings beneath my feet, the smell of dampness, the water glassy smooth like a mirror shrouded in fog. I stare at Sherry with sudden defiance. If she quits, she'll be labeled eccentric, impetuous, a genius who didn't live up to her potential; if I quit, I'll just be a quiter, nothing more. I don't know how long I stand there staring at her until out of the corner of my eye I see the faintest glitter, the hint of brilliance. I get up, dropping my lesson to the floor.

"Where are you going?" Sherry yells. "You've got to finish your lesson." Her bright eyes follow me to the door, stabbing me with reproach. "You can't just drop it on the *floor!*"

But I don't look back as I run out the door.

To release yourself from duty is a voluptuous surprise, vetoing the sturdy promise of a shield, protection from hostile forces, furtive encroachments, insults and betrayal. Instead there's nothingness. Nothingness and the possibility of everything. Possibility holds your hand, guides you blindly through the rushing waters. This, after all, is the dream of fairytales, the benevolent mentor, the rescuing prince, the fairy godmother.

"Come back!" Sherry calls. "Come back!"

But I sit quietly on the bumper of Mother's car and kick pebbles into the street, defying the Big Pond with every whack.

heart breakers

1962. FOLEY, ALABAMA

It's months later, a late Saturday night. Jean and I have been reading in bed, our heads propped up by pillows, the covers rustled to
the floor. Mother and Daddy are out to a party. Usually we hear
them come in, Daddy's cough, Mother's keys, the rattling of the
louvered doors, but tonight we're surprised when Mother slips
into our room, wavering just inside our door. We both sit up
immediately, certain that something's wrong, for Mother's eyes
look startled, her jaw tightened against tears. Automatically, she
sinks onto our bed, her skirt bunching up all around her. But it's
her mouth I watch, the way it trembles, then settles in a hard,
clenched line. "He danced with everyone else and left me sitting
there," she says, tucking her legs modestly under her as if even in
defeat she must be ladylike. She's not looking at us, but at her
reflection in the mirror, a stunned, startled look like a deer caught
in the headlights.

I see my father waltzing around the room, holding Nettie Wright or Bobbie Jo Beech or even the Egg Lady, who's short and fat and wobbles when she walks, as he swirls to the beat of Benny Goodman or Artie Shaw, adding a step now and then, being frisky, fun, dipping and swerving, as if he's a high school Romeo.

Mother sighs and her body shifts as we hear the toilet flush in the other room. "I sat alone at that table," she whispers, "looking at those ugly red streamers. I can't believe I was left there all alone."

But oddly I can imagine my mother alone, can see how erect she sits, her beauty stiffening, hardening while all around her the night's dissolving into whiskey softness. Lipsticks smear. Collars loosen. Jackets are flung off and mascara bleeds. But Mother doesn't move. Her hair is perfect, her lipstick neat and fresh. Her legs are crossed at the knee and she stares into the party as if she's been quarantined in her seat. All around her, men slam down liquor and go for more, boozy women sway to the music, Sandy Perkins dancing in the middle of the aisle, one hand splayed across her stomach, the other fluttering behind her. Cigarette smoke paints the air. This is the American Legion and nobody stands on courtly behavior. It's part low-rent country-club, part free-for-all, a place that delights my father, who foxtrots and two-steps all around the dance floor, as dramatic and irresistible as a storm. Like most parents, they seem fundamentally mismatched: daddy ambitious but playful, declaring there's no reason to sacrifice a good laugh for a hard time while Mother says social life's a pure waste of time. Time should be spent in progress, whether that's cleaning out a messy closet or learning about DNA on a Saturday night.

Now Jean and I move closer, our books dropped behind us on our pillows. We're her hungry audience, her sympathizers, her soothsayers, her confidantes. "I bet you were the prettiest one there," I say, leaning towards her, smelling her White Shoulders and Germaine Monteil beneath a thin layer of cigarette smoke. "I know you must have gotten compliments on your dress."

Mother looks down at her dress, a drape of gauzy black that fits tight in the bodice with a wide swirl of skirt. "It was too dark really to see it," she says, as if suddenly amazed at this fact.

"You should ask someone else to dance," Jean says. "You shouldn't let yourself just sit there all night."

"I can't very well do that," Mother says, her face flushed, embarrassed. Somehow we know that this is true. Mother needs to be chosen, charmed, waltzed around the room like the Golden One who magically escaped from Praco. In the background we hear Daddy rooting around in their bedroom, dropping his shoes on the floor, coughing, blowing his nose, then nothing, the absence of sound. He must be in bed. We listen like voyeurs, pretending we're not eavesdropping, merely caught in a silent knot.

Mother sighs and sits up straighter, as if shedding weight. "Let's not talk about it anymore," she says with sharp finality, as if her mind's turning over, rescuing her from the limitations of her life. "It doesn't really matter. It's just a party and you know I don't like parties. You girls are what matter," she says emphatically. "*You girls.*"

We grow quiet with the stillness of anticipation. Will Mother suggest more lessons, more performances? Jean begins running her fingers up and down her thigh, doing arpeggios, pumping the flesh as if her fingers are springloaded, ready for work.

And yet it's now that some rebellion bursts inside me, some dam I've been afraid to let loose. "I'm not going back to Mrs. Bair's," I blurt. Saying it, I feel the rightness of it, the acute memory of Sherry's "cheater" like a stab inside my brain. And yet I'm shocked. I've only decided it this moment, and I've planned no defense, no rebuttal. I can't say why I've decided to quit music except for my annoyance at Sherry. I imagine Mother protesting,

"But honey, there's so much you can *do* with music and when you grow older, you'll be sorry you didn't keep it up." And beneath that thought, the real one, *I never got a chance to take lessons. I never had a chance at talent.* For a moment I feel guilty, unworthy; I take a deep breath, ready to defend my decision.

But to my surprise, Mother's face doesn't change. She's not staring at the mirror anymore, but looking at my sister. And to my horror she says quite calmly, as if we've been talking about Jean's progress all along, "Mrs. Bair thinks you should go to the regional competitions, honey. She says you'll do quite well." Mother sits up straighter, her body interested, diverted from sadness by this new hypothetical success.

"Yeah?" Jean says, her face curious, pleased. "What will I have to do?"

"Oh, you'll perform before a panel of judges," Mother says, a new eagerness creeping into her voice. Once again she takes possession of herself—she seems smarter, stronger—all the ugliness of the night lopped off from memory. "You'll have to play your very best."

"Did Mrs. B say what I should play?"

"Oh, no, it's too soon. But you'll have to practice."

I can't believe they're talking about this. It's as if someone has knocked me in the solar plexus and I can't catch my breath. Why aren't they bending over me, worrying about me, anxious and confused? Why aren't they arguing with me, chastising me? Frightened, I look out the window where the sky swirls with distant lightning; thunder edges closer to the window, rattling the panes. Uncertain, I pick up a hand mirror, staring at my face where I see a new pimple spreading its red worry across my nose. I bend in closer until I'm leaning into it, everything distorted, waiting for my true feelings to arrive.

It's now that Jean jumps up from the bed. "Come on," she says to Mother, holding out her hands. "Let's dance. Let's see what we can do." She pulls Mother to her feet and to my surprise, Mother lets Jean slip her arm around her waist, taking the role of the man while Mother puts her hand on Jean's shoulder, her rumpled dress spreading out like a cloud. They begin awkwardly, blind partners doing the box step, something Mother taught us in fifth and sixth grades, helping us dance around the kitchen, while we looked steadfastly at the floor, trying not to step on each other's feet. At first they're clumsy, their bodies stiff as dried grass, their elbows right angles in the room. Jean laughs as they bump into the bed, then the dresser, but as their bodies get in sync, suddenly, they're gliding and turning and strutting around the room like those dancers in Matisse, blue women floating in the air. As I watch them from my island on the bed, I know suddenly what I feel, the oldest emotion in the world, the horror of exclusion.

Sometime later in the night it begins to rain, the hard clatter of drops on the roof waking me from sleep. Listening to those rough sounds, I feel suddenly lonely and look over at Jean. She's sleeping, her body curled intricately in the sheets. I get up and walk down the hall to Mother and Daddy's room, but they too are burrowed in sleep, Daddy turned over on his side, one arm dangling towards the floor. Mother sleeps flat on her back, her arms folded neatly across her chest. Even the room smells of sleep: a musty, cloying thickness to the air as if they've been sealed off from the world. There's no reason to check on my brother. He sleeps like a log. Instead, I walk to the patio door and open it. It isn't just raining but bleeding a torrent of water, a downpour, a gut-buster, water spilling from the sky in satiny sheets, flooding the yard. The petunias are flattened. The ferns bend down, beaten with rain. When I look into the sky, it's so fierce, so voluptuous I'm filled with wonder. The sky is opening up, the world changing. My body prickles. I feel so alive I take one tour *jeté* out into the night, my feet baptized in water. The sheer force of all that rain releases me from my bad thoughts. Whatever reason I am here on this earth seems tied to this moment. There is nothing I can't do, can't be. Nothing will restrict me, bind me to this earth. I don't know how long I stay there, entranced, but once I close the door, the moment's whisked away, and bad thoughts rush in like bats swooping through a window, fluttering near my face. My mother and father have always hungered for a star, needed one so badly, they'd sacrifice their very lives for the chance; now my father's intimately tied to my brother while my mother circles my sister like an orbiting moon. For a single instant I wonder what I'll do, as if the world's my oyster, the fierceness of the storm my sensual guide. But that freedom's short-lived, for once I'm inside the house the old terror grips me, what *will* I do?

For months I'm in a funk. I feel famously betrayed but also the betrayer. I'm the maid-in-waiting holding up the queen's jeweled gown, only to realize I'll never be queen, but this impossibility seems as much my fault as anyone else's. Bitterness is seeping in, but the bitterness is mean-spirited, petty. For the first time I don't want to hear Jean's stories, all her corny opinions about Susie Bates or Linda Bordreaux, to know whether she understands exactly how to use "egregious" in a sentence. Whatever agendas she's planning for herself are irrelevant to me. As we ride to school, I turn my head away, looking out the back window of the car, watching Mr. Thiel's pecan grove fade into the distance until its only dust and light.

Maybe I could have held on to my small piece of ground, like a tadpole caught in a swift-moving stream, if Jean hadn't gone through yet another miraculous change. For the past three years a lifejacket of baby fat had plumped out her upper body and grey owl glasses obscured hazel green eyes. She seemed to ignore this plainness, this odd baggage of a body, as she whipped another ice cream sandwich out of the freezer. We all teased her about her three stomachs, the rolls of fat that fit together like stacked inner-tubes around her waist. But it was this awkwardness that endeared her to me; I'd always been easy in my body, and together we seemed to make up a whole person. At least, that is, until the summer of her ninth grade year when she shot up like a weed, let her wavy hair grow long, swaying past her shoulders, and substi-tuted contact lenses for the ugly grey glasses.

One afternoon when Jean comes home from school, her bed is piled with new clothes Mother's brought home because her old ones no longer fit. There's a jumper for me as well, a green cor-duroy with knife pleats and a wide cloth belt. The three of us set-tle together in our room to try on the new clothes, a familiar scene in which normally I hog the mirror. As usual, I tear off my school clothes and put on the green jumper, imagining myself at the upcoming football games. It fits perfectly and for at least three minutes I don't worry that I still have the body of a sixth grader—no hips, no breasts—in admiration of myself. I'm enchanted with the material, with the way the belt cinches me in half, giving me the semblence of curves. I don't know when I look over at Jean, and see her emerge in a fawn colored skirt and sweater edged with a darker suede. The skirt is the newest style, a straight skirt that hugs the body, a little knife pleat that opens coyly at back. It's as if Jean has stepped out of a magic bubble, rushing in as a chubby kid, then emerging as a teenager. Now she stands before the mir-ror, her hair brushed out, swinging down her back, her body sud-denly tall and willowy like the models in *Seventeen*. I'm so star-tled, I sit down clumsily on the bed, stunned the way you are when you're swimming in the Gulf and a wave smacks you right in the face, sending you down in a swirl of dazed motion. *How dare you?* I think, then glance at Mother who's looking at Jean with the same amazement that distorts my face. "We'll need to get you some new shoes," Mother says. "And a blazer would be nice. I don't want you to freeze going to ballgames or on those Future Doctors of America trips."

Jean gazes at herself as if she's just now catching on. She's used to ignoring the mirror, giving it only a sideways glance, but now she holds her gaze, aware of new power, new strength, the world perhaps opening its fickle arms. "I'm wearing this tomorrow," she says, then turns to Mother. "What else did you get? I want to try it *all* on."

Like everything else in our life, we're forced into comparisons. As Jean moves from gawkiness into beauty, I go straight down the tubes into ugly. Frizzy hair. Pimples. The works! I'm convinced of it one afternoon that same year when I'm picking up my books, ready to leave my 6th period algebra class, thinking about nothing more significant than the day's equations.

"Patricia," Mr. McDuffy says, looking at me with an air of earnest scrutiny. I'm still stuffing pencils in my purse as I walk slowly to his desk, distracted until I feel the intensity of his gaze. I haven't been very attentive today and I'm afraid he'll scold me, telling me I'll have to work harder if I expect a good grade. He's tall and broad-shouldered, with tufts of dark hair escaping from the open collar of his shirt. This so embarrasses me I'm glad when he crosses his arms, sets his jaw in an authoritative clench. Now he's the teacher again, aggressive, quirky, a man before whom I'm supposed to perform.

He studies me for a minute then a smile creeps slowly across his face as if he's just noticed something amusing. "You know," he says in a thick southern drawl, "your hair (pronounced hay-er) looks like a pickaninny's." And his face lights up with amusement, like the bully in the schoolyard who's just watched you fall.

Instinctively I put my hands up to my hair while a shameful

fury floods through me, nailing me to the floor. He's just told me I'm ugly. Not only that. He's meant to humiliate me, to stab me with a sharp sexual judgment. And yet all I can do is to give him a murderous look and walk out of the room until minutes later, I slam my books into Mother's car. "Sonofabitch, he's getting bald!"

"What?" Mother asks, eyeing me oddly in the rearview mirror. She doesn't even know I know such words, much less can speak them so vehemently.

I look out the window at the stream of kids emerging from the elementary school, knotting and bunching in groups of threes and fours. "Nothing," I reply, planning my revenge. Though we've never talked openly about men, it's accepted without question that a woman, though assessed constantly by her other women, is actually defined by the opposite sex. "God, what a dog!" guys in my class say freely about any girl with a pug face or too broad hips. Besides I'm used to hearing commentary from men about the women in church, as if their appearance is the ultimate reason for attendance. "Janice Hooper looked real fine," one might say, "a real pretty girl, but that Mabel Wright's sure stuck in a rut. She looks like an old dried up prune. Somebody oughta make old Dennis buy her a new hat . . . something to cover up more of her face."

That night before the national news, when I tell Mother and Daddy what happened, I imagine them calling the school first thing in the morning, vehement that an apology be given, reparations made. "I mean, he has to look up some of the answers in the back of the book," I say as if this supports my case.

But I've barely finished this recital before I'm cut to the quick. "Let's not be *controversial*," Daddy says, shaking his head, turning back to the nightly news. I shouldn't be surprised: in the early 60s it wasn't popular for parents to be advocates for their kids and the only men who did so made fools of themselves in front of coaches and teachers, embarrassing their children, who turned away, shadow-eyed, to stare at the grass growing near the bleachers.

"But he's a monster, a bully," I wail, though it's no use. I know the rules: weakness makes you vulnerable, pathetic; better to steel yourself against the bullies or plan a secret revenge. Back in my room, I sit on my bed, staring into the mirror, sticking out my tongue. My hair spreads around my face like a wiry sponge, dense and moss-like, spiraling out of control. I want to cover it with a pillowcase, a towel, anything to remove it from my sight. It's now that Mother opens my door and holds out a heaping bowl of ice cream, the hot fudge dripping down its slope.

"Why don't you lighten it," she says, studying my frizzy kinks as if they're aberrant cells you could study under a microscope. I know there's no other escape than to start destroying it: bleaching it, straightening it, rolling it so tight on orange juice cans the pins dig deep into my scalp.

1997. Iowa City, Iowa

Pale winter light steals through the office window where I'm talking with Susie, a student in my writing class. I've recently asked each student to write the secret she cannot tell, the secret at the bottom of the heart, the one every writer needs to know. I've made it clear this secret will not be shared, will be used only for imaginative work, but now Susie's in my office, lips quivering, eyes huge, hands clenched in her lap.

"I need to tell you what I wrote," she says, sitting awkwardly across from me, a stack of books beside her on the floor. "I know you said it was private, confidential, but I need—" She stops, her face white and heavy with fear. "I wrote that I've *already* decided to fail," she blurts, then bows her head, silent for a moment before she continues with a whisper. "You see, I wanted so badly to please my mother that I made everything impossible. Why do I want her approval so much?"

I'm surprised at this revelation, and look quickly out the window at smokeblue clouds in an Iowa sky. But what I see is my own mother staring at me, her head bent towards me, asking, "What's wrong, honey? What is it?" and my not being able to tell her, to explain that whatever I do it doesn't seem enough, though I'm not sure what enough really is, if it's just some fiction, some ideal that fills up the cavity in my head.

"I had to leave," Susie says. "And I got into a lot of trouble. I did *that* on my own."

That night I walk through the snowy streets of Iowa City, the bare limbs dressed in a fancy slip of snow, an icy wind blowing its harsh sting across my face. I think back to my own decision to fail, marveling that my student has said so simply what it's taken me over thirty years to reveal. In my own way I got into a lot of trouble too.

When I see the lights of my house, I walk faster through crisp, hungry air, anxious to feel the warmth of my bed, to slip out of my clothes and snuggle under the covers, to remind myself I'm not that girl anymore.

ghost girl

It's June. I'm fifteen years old. All month the sun heats the earth
until it offers up scorched, raw nerves. The rivers and bays swell,
eels undulating near the surface of brackish water, mouths open,
eyes closed like blind ballerinas. The pansies wilt in the midday
sun. The world is white, limp with heat. But at night, moisture
returns. It swells up from the ground and fills the air with its
heavy breath. As the fog rolls in, I stand at my mirror creating
myself: first I contour my face, smudges of brown streak my nose,
the hollow vases of my cheeks, the soft underlid of each eye, the
taut belly of my chin. Then the false eyelashes are applied with
tiny tubes of glue, the eyebrows drawn on, the cheeks sculpted
with blush. I stare at myself as if at a drawing, a design emerging
in the mirror completely separate from what I know of as me.
Next the hairpieces are fitted into place. Nightly I roll the fake

bangs (stick-straight synthetic hair ordered from the glossy back pages of *Mademoiselle*) on an orange juice can and when softly curled, I attach them with bobby pins to my scalp. After covering the pins with a twist of false braid, I tease, fluff and spray my own hair. I turn every which way, admiring myself until Bobby Darin comes on the radio and I sing along, fitting myself with the soft, pillowy bulk of a padded bra and the spiky ribs of a waist cinch. I stare down at legs shaved smooth as bone, at white sandals sprouting petal-pink toes. When I slip on a t-shirt and shorts and stand before my full-length mirror, I'm relieved to see I don't look like me at all.

"Hurry up," Jean yells from the door, and after a quick wave to Mother, I'm beside her in the front seat of the car on the way to the Gulf of Mexico, to an open-air pavillion known as the Hang-out. Above us, the moon's shrouded in thick, grey clouds but the lights of the Hang-out are bright, noisy. The juke-box blares. Bobby Rydell. Neil Sedaka. The Beach Boys. Otis Redding. As I weave my way through the crowd, I feel the sudden thrill of attention. It's here that I dance and dance, my hips nimble, legs strong. Nothing matters except the gyrations of my body, the heat of being watched. I dance only to fast numbers. For slow ones, you have to be touched. Sometimes we girls dance together, ignoring the boys, but it never matters to me. What matters is the heat of motion, the pleasure of a stare: I dance as if caught in a circle of fire, tilting and whirling like a dervish, eyes feverish, neck silky with sweat until at midnight we climb back into the car for the lonely drive home. At home I duck into the bathroom, never turning on the lights as I wash away this self in darkness.

It's much later in summer when I see him standing near the edge of the crowd. A tall, sunburned boy, dressed in a white t-shirt and jeans, his arms casually crossed in front of his chest. I feel the power of his shoulders, the swivel of his head, the dark inventory of his eyes. I can see he's watching me as I dance. A thrill explodes in my stomach. I turn away from him, swimming my arms through the air, but even then I feel his eyes, his shoulders, the promise of his hands. *His hands.* That thought freezes me cold and I slip through the crowd and out the back door. Alone, I listen to the ocean roar, wishing that I too could roar, could scream all this pretense away.

That night I do look in the mirror. I stare at the fringe of eyelashes now snug in their dainty tray. I stare at the fake bangs rolled on their orange juice can. I stare at the washcloth streaked with shades of rose and brown. My face, naked, confronts me. I see the pores of my nose, the faint hint of brows. I see the fluff of my hair tightened into kinks and frizz. I stare and stare until I know the awful truth: I must *never* show this self to the world.

And then, miraculously, it's late September. The heat has lifted, the air touched with the faint chill of fall. Football games nose their way into our lives. Student Council elections come and go. Now when I turn to the mirror it's to pull my hair into a tight little knot. I bend to wash my face in water so hot it brings a radiant flush. I wear loose pajamas, a long white t-shirt, fuzzy bedroom slippers. My face is utterly bare. I look sleek, clean, as tidy as a penitent, and this, I think, is who I really am: clean, hungry, full of sober thoughts.

Tonight I sit on the white couch in the living room, knees crossed, paper and pen ready to use. I open my books. I like the quiet. The settling of the night. Outside pine needles swish against the roof as a breeze moves through the trees. A car rushes by in the dark, a nervous runner, taillights glowing, then fades into nothing. Again the quiet. The papers of my book feel rough, almost pebbly to the touch, and I like the way it settles in the nest of my knees. Now I'm relaxed, engaged, ruled by the sharp claw of my mind. For hours I'm utterly content, studying American literature, Spanish, world history. It's only when I read a chapter on Catherine the Great that I sit up straighter. I understand a tyrant like her, that need to punish, to rule. I imagine her leaning out of her golden carriage, whip in hand, and what I see are the two creatures I call myself: the one plain, intense, hungry for praise cursing the artificial, repressed other. "Beat her," I say, and feel pleasure in the act. It's the female side I now want to kill. And yet even as I speak I know that summer will come again, the scent of magnolias, the moisture budding on blades of grass. I'll suck in my breath to feel my stomach's tightness, to expand the cherry nubs of my breasts. And then it will start all over again.

This division in myself seems too crazy to explain. And yet I know that something's wrong, very wrong, this arrangement like stepping off the face of the earth, without oxygen, without sunlight, dangling in the blind emptiness of space. Every day when my sister comes home from school she flops down on the bed with a library book. She's usually wearing a straight skirt and sweater, her hair arranged in what we call a "flip," lipstick and eyeshadow still highlighting her face. I stare at her with incomprehension: To read a book, it's imperative the lipstick be OFF, my hair pulled severely back and clipped to my scalp. To reach the inner world, the outer world must be shut down. It's as simple as that.

Perhaps this was the beginning of depression, but at the time I wouldn't have called it that. I thought of it as perfecting myself, making the outside attractive, filling the inside chock full of ideas. My only goal was to do it *better,* to succeed in either of these roles, to be chosen so that I too could feel the transcendent power of success. Now, more than ever, I must study other girls: their hair, their skin, their breasts, their smiles.

Walking home from the Dairy Queen, swirly cone in hand, I dawdle past the old Methodist Church and see in the alley Jenny

Lee, one of the popular high school girls known for her beauty. She's getting out of her boyfriend's car, laughing with that backflung, teasing glance, her hair thick and shiny, her body radiant with health, long legs in pedal pushers, a plaid shirt knotted at the waist. Her boyfriend grabs for her hand, but she yanks it free and laughs at him, then turns and runs down the alley, still laughing as he bolts from the car. I stop where I am, ice cream dripping, melting in the hazy sun.

I begin to work harder. One hundred sit-ups. Two hundred touch-your-toes. Hair dipped in lemon juice, washed in egg whites. I insist that Mrs. Schreiber hem my dresses shorter until they barely cover my ass. In my room I sit on the bed, trying to speak Spanish, but if it comes out all wrong, my tongue thickened, my accent messed-up and useless, I switch to math. At home I watch and wait as if there's something urgent I need to know. When Jean rushes out of our room and into the kitchen, I follow right behind her. "I'm *starving* for a pizza," she says as she comes into the kitchen. "I can't wait even a minute longer," she says to Mother, who's standing at the counter grating cheese for crab imperial. "*Starving,*" Jean repeats, as if she's devouring it before it can be made. She drums her fingers across her thigh, doing arpeggios, rocking her head from side to side to some interior beat. Mother immediately puts down the grater and bends to the shelf below, searching for the pizza pan, telling Jean to look in the pantry for some Chef Boyardee. But Jean doesn't bother. Instead, she scoops up some of the cheese Mother's been grating. "Mmh, I can use this," she says and Mother nods, going to the pantry for the mix. As I watch them, a strange animal lurches inside my stomach, thin metal arms clawing and scratching, sending a terrible ache straight to my heart.

This is so normal, a mother and daughter fixing the daughter's food, that I know I've twisted it into something odd. Does Mother look at Jean with a sudden flush of pride? Does Jean always interrupt Mother right in the middle of things? I don't know. It's as if I've been asleep and am suddenly waking up. I can't imagine rushing into the kitchen and demanding a pizza. I can't imagine words coming out of my mouth except in the familiar cliches other people want to hear.

"How's school?" a neighbor will ask, coming into the den where I'm sitting at the table with a book.

"Oh. Fine." I finger the book, smiling my pleasant smile.

"Learning anything new?"

I hold up my math book. "Just a little Advanced Math." And though I want this banal conversation to continue, I simultaneously long to flee.

In spring, I stand for hours in the stifling sun of a Saturday afternoon watching the cheerleaders practice their jumps, springing up from a squatting position, their legs widening like scissors in the air. Then, at home, I mimic them, jumping and jumping, tightening the muscles in my legs, determined to be like them, to be one of them. Suddenly it seems only natural to let my body speak, to stay quiet on the inside while my body yells, *"Here I am. Look at me."*

Mrs. Manning says if we want to try out we'll have to put our names down on a list, and as I write my name, I can feel myself lifting into the right shape of things. I know how to jump. How to flip over backwards. How to keep the rhythm going between my hands and my feet. And quietly, silently, despite myself, I begin to hope. And pray.

Of course at home I pretend I don't care. I'm just going to give it a whirl.

"You should win," Jean says while we're sitting at the supper table eating our butterfly pork chops and our fresh lima beans.

"You've always been limber and I know you jump higher than the rest."

"Don't say that," I shush her. To *admit* I want something will only set it against me, deceiving me into openly desiring it, expecting it, then blasting me with outright defeat.

Only at night, when I'm very tired, do I feel the sticky cord of longing. Even though I try to stifle it—pressing my hands against my eyes, saying, no! no! no! (my own perverted cheer)—I can already see myself in the uniform, striding out onto the field, bold and confident, as carefree as the wind whipping through the streamers. And more important, I can imagine myself rushing into the kitchen and demanding a pizza, "God, I'm hungry," I'll say. "Absolutely starving. Feed me some food!" as if that's the easiest thing in the world.

The day of the try-outs, I'm so nervous I can't eat any breakfast. I'm sure Mother insists I drink my orange juice, but I can only manage a couple of sips. Jean talks about the upcoming Future Doctor's Club trip. "I'm riding up with the Wenzels," she says, pouting. "I don't wanna be stuck with Mr. D because he's such a slow poke, we'll get there after everybody else." I excuse myself and go back to my room. There's no need pretending I have a grip on things. Anxiety leaks out, oozing from my pores. All I can do is repack my shorts and t-shirt and recheck my hair, relieved to feel the comforting stiffness of White Rain hairspray.

During third period, we line up on the field, the grass still slippery with dew, the crowd in the bleachers roaring, "Gooooooooo, LIIII-ONS, gooooooo!" They're restless, swaying side to side, glad for any reason to be let out of class. For an instant, I thrust myself out into the limelight, away from the shadows, a girl lined up with twenty-five other girls to vie for her rightful spot, and then I do our routine as if I'm saving my life.

I can never decide if hope is such a tiny room that it's easily overcrowded or if the room's quite large and hope is being held down, pressed against a wall so that it dare not breathe. I only know that I go through the rest of the day in a daze, without any buzz in my brain, answering questions in American history, reading *The Old Man and the Sea,* even playing softball in gym on the flat, treeless space beside the junior high school where everyone can see how stupid you look. After the last bell rings, I walk home alone, dragging my purse, letting it bump against the clots of grass alongside the road. I walk home because it takes more time. The list will be posted at 5:00.

At 4:45, I jerk up my purse and bang out of the house. I don't want anybody along to jinx my chances. I walk fast past Mr. and Mrs. Burns' house, past the preacher's house with its upstairs curtains blowing out the window, flapping in the air, then past the long stretch of flat fields where goldenrod is already in full bloom. When I glance back at the preacher's house, the curtain's caught in an updraft, slapped against the side of the house. I can't move. I know the curtain must be free or I won't win. I stand there for minutes, hours, decades. A breeze cools me and the curtains flutter. When I pass the junior high school, I look up at the tall windows and say my last prayer. *Let me win.* Then I walk straight to Mrs. Manning's door, where a group of girls crowd together in a knot. Nobody looks at me, a bad sign, but I have to see for myself.

It's a short list, only eight names. I scan it quickly, disbelieving, as if there's a blind spot in my sight. I go closer, feeling the names on the sheet as if reading braille, needing to decipher them letter by letter. Mine isn't there. I step away, stunned, my throat closed up, my mind numb, pain dancing just beyond me, a ratty ball of thread floating in the air. I know that soon enough it will attach itself to me, a parasite leeched to my skin.

"Shit," somebody says, and several girls laugh.

"Same old fucking team," another girl says.

But already I've turned away, moving back into the shadows, back into the cool darkness where, like a possum, I hide. I can feel myself tightening up, as if of necessity, I will be cramped. I pass the open field where the goldenrod looks bent—almost broken—in the sun, past the preacher's house, the curtains now pulled back inside. I pass the Burns' house without even looking in their direction. Then I'm home.

"Did you win?" Jean calls out as I come through the door.

"Nope," I say, walking past her into the hall.

She has a frown on her face. "You *should* have," she says. "You were the best."

But I don't answer, only head into our room. Please, no sympathy. That would only make things worse. But within minutes Mother knocks on my door, asking if she can come in. I'm sitting on my bed, facing the closet, my shorts and shirt neatly folded in the chair. I don't want to see anyone, but I know this is weakness and shame. "Come in," I say in a bored, neutral voice, then look at Mother's shoes, at the way the little alligator buckle curves over the top of her foot and the high heels dig into the carpet as she talks. She stands in front of me, telling me it's okay that I didn't win, that I can try again next year, but when I look up at her, she seems puzzled, bewildered, and I realize she doesn't know how to help me, that whatever's happening inside me is a mystery to her. Everything must be so much easier with my sister where desire isn't blind hunger but honed appetite and clean acquisition. And despite all my stoic determination, I begin to cry, huddling into myself, wanting more than anything to give her the fleshy excitement of my win.

The next week I stop wearing the waist cinch and padded bra. I don't unroll the fake bangs. I put on mascara and lipstick and leave quickly for school, raising my hand in class, answering as many questions as I can. After school I study for the first time without pulling my hair back into its tight little knot, without washing my face with water so hot my skin looks like a blistered wound. Instead, I sit at the dining room table, books scattered around me, a plate of cookies in my lap.

And yet it's during this time that I also lie unmoving on my bed.

Outside cicadas chatter. Frogs leap. Mosquitoes cloud in a frenzy of blood. Lying on my bed, I'm mute, inconsolable. I look at the ceiling where tiny holes decorate the tiles. I like the monotony of it, counting my way around one square. When Mother comes into the room, she stands quietly in the darkness. I feel her presence like a cool breath of air. In my dreams she hears me cry, barely a whimper, but rises from her bed and scoops me up from a circle of fire, carrying me safely through the sky. We fly without wings, our nightgowns fluttering, our arms held close to our chests. We're both looking straight ahead, unblinking, into the brilliance of the sun.

"What's wrong?" she asks, and an old happiness blooms inside my chest.

"I don't know," I say. "I don't care about anything."

"Is it school? Did something happen at school?"

"No."

"Are you worried about a test, something you're supposed to present?"

"No." It comes out flat, despondent. I long to say, *Mother, I don't have anything that's mine. I'm not sure what it means to be me.* But it's impossible to speak about such things, to make that tiny slice into the heart, so I look at the ceiling, staring intently at its whiteness. I feel beyond desire, beyond hope or possibility. In reality, I'm grieving, mourning for what cannot be. I'm broken and there's no one—not even my mother—who can mend me.

And I don't know how to mend myself. I feel powerless to try. Help in our family has always been sought from outside: from courses and achievement, from performance and praise, from some form of improvement. The idea that there might be other ways to initiate change would have been a revelation to me. But now, staring at the ceiling, the thought of going outside the boundaries of our family myths seems dangerous, subversive.

When I glance at Mother, her face looks soft, bewildered, full of concern. Suddenly I'm afraid that she'll offer another lesson, a new dress, the bromide that tomorrow is another day. "I'll be okay," I say quickly. "I just want to lie here and think."

But of course, I don't think. I can't. Reflection is treason, for how can I say, "Look I just don't want to be me."

The next week Mother sets up a meeting for me with the minister of our church, a man known for his counseling skills. I don't know why I agree to go. Though he's an intelligent, sensitive man—there are no psychologists in the area—I have no intention of revealing myself to him. For one thing he knows my family too well, and I've just begun to realize that my parents live difficult, burdened lives. Besides, he's a man. I'd be embarrassed to confess the nature of my distress. When he takes me into his carpeted study with the bookcases full of books, I stare only at the religious woodcuts, squinting to see them clearer.

"Why don't you try to tell me what you've been thinking about?" he says, looking at me with quiet tenderness. For a moment, I imagine telling him this need for violence to the self, this deep sense of loss as if a part of me has shriveled up and died. I imagine telling him that I've dropped in a hole and nobody notices that I'm gone. But as these thoughts grow in my mind, I become self-conscious, awkward, and burst into tears, begging to go home. "Yes," he murmurs, "Yes, of course."

As I stumble out of his office, light spills through the clouds. When I look down at my feet, I see clearly the graininess of the pebbled drive, a leaf lying absolutely flat on the ground. Beyond me there are no shadows, no mysteries, only the potato fields that reach endlessly towards the horizon, low flat land, a carpet of brown and green. While the minister calls my mother, I stand in the drive in total stillness because it's just occurred to me that whatever is wrong with me is *mine.* Something like happiness pours through my nerves.

If this were a fictional story, it's here that the conflict would erupt, the narrator waking from her troubled dream to defy her parents. I know where it would happen: in the kitchen with light flooding through the windows, splashing across the mixmaster, the toaster, the refrigerator, the stove. My mother would be at the sink, peeling carrots, my father just arrived, a load of mail in one arm.

"I don't want any more lessons," I say because lessons seem the most concrete thing I can resist. There's a truculent defiance in my voice, a snide smirk on my face. "These *lessons* aren't teaching me what I need to know. They're full of shit!"

"Don't say that word," my father says. "I don't want to hear you—"

"What do you need to know?" my mother asks, turning from the sink, the carrot peeler limp in her hand. She too looks disturbed, almost frightened, the sun gleaming just behind her, flashing against the chrome of Daddy's car.

"How to get *out* of here!" I say, taking a deep breath, a quiver in my voice, how to *think and act in the world.* And then what I don't say, *I'm going crazy, don't you see I'm going crazy?*

But it never happens. Instead, I sit in my room, slumped on the bed, unable to speak, while Jean rambles on about whether she'll be valedictorian or not. "I'm at the *top* of the class," she says, "but Mike Alveraz transferred from UMS with more credits and technically that puts him *ahead* of me."

I nod as if I'm interested while down deep, my old fear is stirring: I am ordinary, average, unremarkable. But this fear is too dangerous to reveal, and instinctively I push it away, down to the soles of my feet.

"But I *should* get the award," Jean says, and again I nod, believing that I too must push myself to new and dizzying heights. I'm like the boy in "The Rocking Horse Winner," frantically rocking myself to death. But I don't know how to stop, how to turn myself around. And so I come to a decision: I will pretend to be Pat, the silent, ambitious daughter, the girl who always does what she's supposed to do, while deep down another part of me will be watching, waiting for the moment when *I* can slip out into the world.

"I know what I'm going to do," my sister says with sudden enthusiasm. "I'm going to go call the principal about this," and she flounces out of the room.

And silently I say what I am going to do: I'm going to be a ghost. I'll slip in and out of this body and no one will be the wiser.

I'm sitting in English class, staring out the window, waiting for Mrs. Jackson to finish reading "A Rose for Emily," when I see my sister walk by with several of her friends. They're out of class, strolling along, probably on "senior" business, but when she pauses by my window, she sees me staring and stops with her friends, crooking her finger at me to come out. I shake my head no. I can't just leave class. Mrs. Jackson is droning on and on, poor Miss Emily getting her comeuppance from Homer Barron and then in the end, giving it back full force. I've already read this story several times, so I'm only half listening, my mind drifting like a lost ship at sea. My sister's friends beam happy smiles at me and I roll my eyes, thinking they're laughing because I'm stuck with the Peeper Creeper, the Elberta boy who tries to look up our skirts and sits right beside me. But when class is over, they're waiting at the door, arms open to encircle me. I don't know what's going on, why I'm being embraced as if something has happened, when absolutely nothing is happening to me. Then suddenly they're all talking at once, all laughing and joyous and to my surprise they're telling me I've been selected to the Key Club Sweetheart Court. Not the queen, of course, but even my sister isn't the queen. And it doesn't matter because my head is so light I believe I know how a snowflake must feel as it blows so whimsically, so gracefully to the ground. Then quite naturally, before I've had time to enjoy the full benefit of this pleasure, I know—though I can't remember if it's because she tells me or if I just figure it out—that I'm on the court, in this rare position of popularity, because my sister has gone privately to each boy in the club and persuaded him to vote for me. She stands beside me now, her hair a mahogany sheet that swings when she turns, her body larger but prettier than mine. At that moment my ghost-self nods and smiles, accepting all the attention, while I remind myself: I'm just looking on, watching everything as if it's a godawful play . . . and here's the character Pat acting out her undying gratitude.

In the car that afternoon when Mother picks us up after school, Jean recounts the good news as if it's the biggest coup in town, this new thing that I've just won. Mother looks appreciatively at me in the rearview mirror. "Really?" she says, and for a moment I feel her energy pulled towards me, lured into the dark maze of my fragile life. I see again how distinctly her eyebrows arch, little rivers of black trained up a steep hill. Suddenly I'm excited and terrified as if I've really won what Jean says I've won. "That's wonderful, Pat," Mother continues, nodding, a little fret mark appearing between her perfect brows. "Really wonderful. I'm so proud of you. And you can put that on your resume."

And suddenly I'm me again, the ghost self shattering like splintered glass. I look out the window at the cars lined up in rows, the cheerleaders huddled together on the auditorium steps. The road is straight as a knife blade shining beneath a penitent sun. The leaves of the magnolia trees look clenched, the blooms, sodden, fallen to the ground. Mother and Jean are still talking about my resume, about how I can use this Key Club thing to my best advantage, but I don't really hear them anymore. Instead, I'm wondering why I hate them so much.

That night, Jean and I are studying in our room. I'm flipping through the pages of my history book, skimming, staring hard at the pictures, reading the captions. Jean has an Algebra II book propped in her lap. She's been erasing a problem, blowing tiny bits of eraser into the air, when she stops and stares at me.

"What?" I say.

"I didn't ask *that* many of them to vote for you," she confesses.

I'm lying on my back, one arm propping up my book, the other fiddling with my hair. I don't say anything because there's nothing left to say, yet I see her hand reaching over to soothe me, to pat me, to let me know she's on my side—

"Don't *touch* me," I hiss. And for a moment we're both stunned as if another person is inhabiting my skin.

Jean withdraws her hand. "Well, if that's the way you wanna be," she says and picks up her book, slamming it together and making a big to-do of walking out of the room.

I stare at the closed door as adrenalin rushes through my body. This, I know, is my true voice, this hiss as hurt and angry as a coiled snake.

That summer I don't go to the Hang-out. Instead, I swim. I read novels. I look out the window, dreaming about where I might belong. I decide I want to attend a private girls' school in Mobile for my senior year where I'll learn Latin and ancient history, where the girls look plain and fierce. "I want to learn French," I tell my family, an easy lie. For some reason I still hope that Mother will see through the maze to the core as if she's looking in a microscope at the infinite dance between hope and despair.

"It won't help for only one year," Mother says when we sit down to discuss the possibility. She's always interested in education and I know she wants the best. "You can't learn French in a year. And besides you've been studying Spanish. You should work harder at that. Colleges will be more impressed with intensive work in one language rather than a superficial knowledge of two."

As she talks, I stare into the dark weave of the rug. The reds are brighter than the dark. But the dark is more substantial, more real. You don't notice it as you walk across it, and yet it's always there, inevitable, submerged within the background.

"But there's no reason you can't take a college course," Mother says, her face intent as if she's listening to the silence between us. She reaches for a bottle of hand lotion on the dresser and squirts some into her hand. "I'll check at Springhill College this week." She smoothes the lotion over the backs of her hands and says in a hopeful voice, "Maybe there's an afternoon or night class you can take."

I say neither yes nor no and yet as she turns to go, a new terror sweeps through my mind: *I am a baby, bound to a board, unable to move. I see the doctor leaning towards me, donor blood swirling inside its sleek plastic cage. I need a transfusion. Without it, they say I'll die. But tonight I don't care. I want what's inside me to fight its way out into the world. I look towards my mother. Only she can help. Only she can unwrap me from this mummied self. And yet when I look at her, I see that she too is paralyzed, unable to move, her mouth quivering with rage. She both sees me and doesn't see me as she stares silently into the night. Grief swells in the back of my throat and leaks like sap onto the pretty sheets of my bed.*

the truth in small things

1965. MOBILE, ALABAMA

He swoops into the classroom, the black sleeves of his clerical robes flapping like wings. His silver hair, curled over the white collar, silhouettes a lean, intelligent face. So *this* is a Jesuit! I think he's beautiful and sit up straighter in my desk. I'd expected him to be fat, round-faced, Irish, but instead of being disappointed, I'm ecstatic as Father McCown settles his books on the desk, then stands behind it staring meditatively at us, his scrutiny inquisitive, not unkind, as if he's breathing us in, our smells mingling with his. I glance around me, trying to see what he sees: two fat businessmen, their shirts wrinkled from the heat, probably embarrassed at finding themselves once again in student desks; they sit beside me. At the very back of the class an older woman in tennis shoes and a plaid dress clutches two notebooks in her hands. Her face seems too eager with its tilted chin and skittish eyes. She bounces one crossed leg up and down like I do. Scattered between us there are younger people, probably students who work days in

Pizza Huts and Toddle Houses and take classes at night at this small Catholic liberal arts college in Mobile. Then there's me, the youngest of the bunch, a high school student who's come here one night a week to learn how to write.

Father McCown moves to the front of his desk quietly, only his robes rustling as he walks, and leans against it, still looking at us. We sit so silently before him I can hear a moth fluttering around one of the pale, globed lights. It flits about, then lands near the rim of the globe, folding in its wings like an umbrella closed up for the night. And within that silence, Father McCown begins talking to us as if he already knows us, as if this is the second or fourth class and not the first. He talks about literature and writing as if they're ordinary things we can be part of, as if they're as common as dirt and we're worms ready to wiggle our way through. "Literature is simply an entry into the dailiness of our lives," he says, "the confusions and wonders of man's inner being." I wonder if this is part of the Catholic tradition. In high school, Mrs. Flynn, our English teacher, acts as if literature is beyond us, something we'll grasp only when we finish our education at teacher's college or have seen a "big city" production of *Hamlet.* When she talks about Shakespeare, her voice becomes precise, dramatic, and she lifts her face as if pointing it towards the sun. But Father McCown thinks that literature is right next to us, beside us in the aisles. He says he can smell it in the room. I sniff, but catch only chalk and dust smells and the sickly sweet fragrance of cheap perfume. "Literature is no more than a path, a country lane leading to another village," he continues, "or a city street which crosses more and more streets, all of which we can walk on if we like."

I imagine myself in a dark alley, creeping out onto Main Street, following behind him in his footsteps.

Father McCown talks not only about literature that first night, but also about Greece, where he was a scholar in his youth, walking not as I'd expected among the ruins of the Acropolis, but barefoot in the provinces through villages and towns. "The roads were hot and dusty, with goats in the fields," he smiles. "I was always thirsty, but the farmers were generous and when there were no farmers around, I talked right nicely to the goats."

By the end of class, I'm half in love with him, determined to impress him, hoping to use *ennui* in a sentence, my voice steady and clear. But I'm also frightened, having never tried to write myself into life. Success still sits on its elegant throne, swaddled and petted, its gaze as arrogant as an empress proclaiming her terms: instant triumph (oh, the very smart!) or inevitable failure, nothing in between. There's no room for curiosity, immersion, a second chance. Like all dictatorships, this way there's much less mess.

By the second class, we've gotten down to business—writing first drafts out in long-hand, then looking up words and syntax in the dictionaries and style books we bring each week to class. Our first two assignments, one-page descriptions of places that have made an impression on our senses—seem too easy for a college paper. Yet when I think of Father McCown walking around the countryside of Greece, glorying in the dust of the past, in the rich yellow sun in a foreign blue sky, the only place I know that seems worthy of the assignment is Bellingrath Gardens with its stately Old South sense of leisure and refinement. I remember walking through the gardens at age ten, slightly bored by the profusion of azaleas that bloomed in March and the clever twists and turns in the garden maze, the shrubbery on each side immaculately trimmed. The fact that I like wild, unruly landscapes—the Smoky Mountains with their dense underbrush and rushing, white-water streams or Soldier Creek with its weedy island and snapping turtles, Mama Dot's woods—I hide from this paper, praising instead sculpted pools with stone cupids and garden arrangements of wrought iron furniture in an antebellum setting beside an elegant mansion and manicured lawns. There are always oohs and aahs when people walk through the gardens and I want this appreciation of beauty to infuse my paper. Even writing the paper I feel special. I imagine the bones in my wrists as skinny as bird bones, my skin translucent, blue veins riding the surface of my flesh like thin, buried wires. I work hard on the paper, particularly the adjective phrases, using *restored glory* and *ancient beauty*, phrases which seem as precious as the ones I've read in magazines.

Briefly, I considered writing about Mud Hole, the first swimming creek where I went under, holding my breath, the water so dense with silt it was almost opaque. When I think about Mud Hole, I remember being thrilled at jumping in, swirling around in the darkness, a mystery even to myself. When I popped up above the surface, I laughed, and then went back under, my body stretched out like a pair of wide-open scissors. I learned to dog paddle in Mud Hole and watched the older kids swing out from a rope tied to an overhanging tree, then drop like bombs into the smooth brown water. Watching, I could feel the lust for danger rush through me, delicious, triumphal. Yet now I'm ashamed of Mud Hole, ashamed to have lived in a place so rural we didn't have a proper swimming pool. I know that if I think too much about Mud Hole, I might discover the secret of its pleasure, the chaos of unfettered delight, the body undisciplined, vulnerable, released from the day's armour, while walking through Bellingrath Gardens is meant to be instructive, educational: *This is how a rich person's garden should look. Notice the order, the sense of balance, the proportion. Notice how tidy everything is. All around you there are rose gardens and well-dressed ladies in stockings and gloves and three-inch high heels.*

When Father McCown comes in the next week with our stack of essays under his arm, the quiet, keen half-smile on his face, my body tenses with eagerness. He says with a burst of spirit that he's "very pleased" with our work and will read some of the samples out loud.

The first paper describes a back porch, bare except for a hammock where the narrator lies and listens to rain pelting the tin roof and sees lightning bugs swarm in spasms of blinking light. As he reads, I can see that young boy on a hot, steamy afternoon, the only sound the rhythmic creaking of the rope as the hammock drifts lazily back and forth. Stunned, I want to vanish, to dissolve into air. Suddenly I understand that good writing presents moments of being as if the writer has anchored one specific moment in consciousness, telling not just what she sees, but the feelings that the seeing evokes. I have done just the opposite: described a kaleidescope of impressions, never pinning down any emotion I've felt. Instead I used the thesaurus to look up fancy words for the ordinary ones that rolled out of my head. But I'm most surprised when Father McCown hands the paper he's just read to one of the fat businessmen. How can this ordinary looking man have written such incredible stuff?

In the second paper, a young woman describes her trip through Texas in the middle of August. She reports how she stopped at every drive-in restaurant on I-10 and ate a chocolate ice cream cone just to keep her going through that flat, desert land. She stops at the Lone Star Stop & Go in El Paso and Woody's Scoop-it-Yourself in Balmorhea, Texas. She even licks an ice cream cone while staring at the Davy Crockett Monument outside of Ozona, Texas. I can't help laughing at her obsession, so much like my own. I'm not as troubled when Father McCown hands the paper to a tall, angular girl with a ponytail and horn-rimmed glasses who talks frequently in class. I thought though that she'd write about something refined, a stone house facing the sea or an oak-panelled library full of leather-bound books, her father smoking a pipe as he reads the paper.

Father McCown puts the papers back on the desk and looks at us as if he wants to draw us closer. "Always remember that there is meaning in small things," he says softly as if it's a prayer. "The way a woman stands before her mirror to put on her Sunday hat, which is worn and droopy, can evoke great sadness or courage. The way a child talks about sucking his thumb can be the most important conversation in the world."

I feel my face glow with pleasure. I understand.

When I meet with Father McCown about my paper, he's tender but firm. "Too many words," he says in a business-like voice which surprises me. "See how much better it reads like this." And he reads aloud the pared down sentences, taking out the flashier adjectives I worked so hard to place, and the adverb *very*. The piece reads simply. Crisp phrases I can hear in my head. It seems so easy I can't wait to begin my next essay that night. Yet at home, sitting cross-legged on my bed, my mind is once again wrapped in fog. Each word seems necessary, unchangeable. I can't decide which ones to delete and I know the decision shouldn't be arbitrary.

The next night I re-write the essay, crossing out *very* and *something,* but leaving all the other words intact. I've written about the Smithsonian Museum in Washington, D.C., cluttering the paper with details about dinosaurs when I meant to talk about my confusion on seeing such monstrosities at age eight and my amazement at the number of stalls in the WOMEN's bathroom. How small I felt in that museum, an ant walking through a field of grasshoppers.

Although I don't expect my essay to be read this time, I'm again puzzled by Father McCown's choices. He reads about a woman's

trip through a shopping mall, how the vibrations inside the closely packed stores numb her brain but stimulate her feet and hands
and eyes so that she walks from store to store, touching and staring and buying. She says she feels "motorized" by the vibrations. I
consider this a rather superficial thought; what does shopping
have to do with literature? Then he reads another paper about a
shrimper casting his nets into Mobile Bay. In the early morning
light the shrimper says he watched dolphins following in the
boat's wake, "making those smooth, clean dives," and longed only
to throw himself overboard and swim alongside them. He also
describes the rhythmic motion of the waves slapping the sides of
the boat and the sudden loneliness he feels at the thought of his
new wife sleeping alone in their warm double bed.

To my surprise, Father McCown tells us we have to let go of
accomplishment. "You have to be willing to fail," he says, his face
rather severe, heat in his intense blue eyes. "You have to risk
exposing yourself, making mistakes and coming up empty. It happens to all of us." It sounds fatal, a rite of passage we all have to
undergo. I begin to worry about this. I've already failed twice, but
nothing much has happened. How long will it take? How much
more will I have to lose?

   At home, I take a deep breath and launch into the next assignment, which Father McCown has printed out on the assignment
sheet: *describe a turning point in your life, perhaps a time when you
experienced a major conflict of values which caused you to change
your views or an experience which changed the meaning of life for
you.* This paper is a lot of trouble for me. I can't think of anything
dramatic in my experience that I'm willing to reveal—I don't dare
tell about being a ghost—and yet I've fallen in love, a frightening
kind of love that burns through my system like fire. I have discovered the sound of words, the truth of them, though I can't seem to

find that truth in myself. And then late one night, staring at the pocked ceiling of my bedroom, I begin thinking about SHOE CITY, this discount warehouse in Pensacola, Florida where my mother and sister and I buy "irregulars" at reduced prices. Mother takes Jean and me there each August before school starts so we can buy a bunch of shoes for school. We hang our arms over the front seat of the car and discuss the new styles until we see the rectangular SHOE CITY sign flattened against the blue Florida sky. I think about the building: it always seems huge, a factory space, defined only by its free-standing shelves of shoes. Long rows of metal shelves divide the space, running in parallel lines from one end of the room to the other, with only a small area up front for a counter and check-out. Huge ceiling fans blow hot air in gusts so that as I try on shoes in the aisle, my hair blows in furious twists about my face while perspiration seeps quietly down my neckline towards my navel.

Mother always lets us buy as many pairs of shoes as we find, anywhere from four to ten pairs. Two years ago I came home with canary yellow flats, red tennis shoes with white laces, t-strapped navy blue sandals I could wear the first month of school and all kinds of party shoes: black suede pumps with flat, shiny bows, silver glitter shoes with a delicate squared toe and a sling-back heel, red patent leather with cut-out toes and a tooled design across the front. Yet this past August, something strange happened to me at SHOE CITY. As always Mother encourages us to find what we want and says she'll pay for the lot. As always, I stand in the aisle as I have in other years, six pairs of shoes surrounding me in a semi-circle, when suddenly my desire turns sideways. I know that Mother never wants us to do without as she did in childhood, but I understand at that moment how my needs are different. I need the opposite: to make choices, to discriminate. I have to begin *right now*. Here in SHOE CITY. In the past when Mother said I could take them all, I breathed a sigh of relief and yet after the first moments of pleasure I felt uncomfortably giddy as if I'd accepted something not quite my own. This year, I know I can't take them all. I feel the thrill of denial deep down to my toes. It's a perilous moment. Crazy, really. Here I am choosing restraint instead of opportunity. A lurch of independence shoots through me as if it's a BB ricocheting through my spine. I straighten my shoulders, push the corkscrews of hair behind my ears.

"I'm only taking one pair," I tell Mother. "The pair I like best. Nothing else."

"Don't be silly," Mother says. "Get what you need. They're inexpensive and I don't want to make several trips."

But I won't budge. I pick a pair of burgundy flats with heart-shaped cut-outs across the toes. They aren't really my favorites, but they seem significant, unusual, one-of-a-kind.

Immediately I turn on the light and write "SHOE CITY," describing it as one of the important moments in my life. I remember the thrill of it, how I was goose-bumpy with freedom, intoxicated by denial. What, I wondered, if limitation rather than excess was my salvation? Did that make me a saint or just a peculiar kind of sinner? Flushed with enthusiasm I scribble not only about SHOE CITY, but about bigger things: the whole indulgence of my life—from buying four kinds of hair conditioner to eating two desserts at supper to a closetful of new clothes. Of course, I don't mention the balancing act I perform inside my head, the tally of pleasures and desires versus the multitude of restrictions I practice to meet the perverse standards that govern my existence.

I arrive early for my conference with Father McCown and stand alone at the classroom window, watching new green shoots which have sprouted on bushes and trees. They look surprisingly fragile and small as if afraid to appear. I'm studying them so intently I don't hear Father McCown enter the room. When I turn he stands inside the door, his robes fluttering about his legs. His hair has been blown by the wind and he smoothes it down absent-mindedly, looking intently at me.

"I don't know why I wrote that—" I say, nervously picking at the waistband of my skirt. His look of quiet stillness makes me stop.

"This"—he holds up my essay—"sounds like you're telling the truth."

I nod, uncertain if this is a positive or a negative sign. The "truth" will place me, a girl from rural Alabama who doesn't know anything much.

"That's good. That's where you have to start," he says enthusiastically.

"It is?"

"Sure, writing's a kind of uncovering, you see, and if you start with false emotions or beliefs, there's nothing behind them but emptiness."

Again I nod. What he says makes sense. And yet I'm puzzled. How does a person know what stories she has to tell, what should be uncovered and what left behind? Isn't it dangerous to tell so much there's no turning back until you're completely naked and alone? How will I know when to stop? I ask him that, thinking that for me, someone whose self is divided in half, there must be some limits, some marker of restraint.

He sits down at his desk and looks out at the empty classroom. Neither of us speaks. His face seems vacant, frozen in its shell. He seems to have forgotten I'm there. He keeps staring at the chairs as if he's seeing something else. Maybe he's seeing the goats in Greece or that hot, dusty road. Or maybe my question has just been stupid, irrelevant, a high school question.

Then as if he's just woken up, he touches my paper with his thin, sensitive fingers, the fingernails rather long for a Jesuit. I feel again the thrill of his smile when he looks up at me, his face open and strong. "You listen," he whispers as if it's a secret between us. "You learn to listen to yourself. That's about all writing is." His eyes clutch mine. I can feel them pulling me in closer and closer to his vision.

But I won't let him. I shift subtly away from his desk. I look out the window at the night, the evening peeling back from daylight, dusk moving in slow like a fog. More than anything I want that release—to listen—but within it, I suspect, lie betrayal and defection. It would mean, I think, that I'd have to leave my home, my family, striding out into the world, waving a pink slip in my hand.

vanderbilt

Four months later Mother, Jean and I drive across the entire state
of Alabama and into the rolling hills of Tennessee. I can't wait to
get to college, to be *somewhere*—New York! Paris!—for being
somewhere, surely, I'll change. I'm convinced the place itself will
transform me, make me different, though I've packed all my old
beliefs and values along with my suitcase full of clothes.

I have my first inkling that things might not be *so* easy when
we pull into the Vanderbilt campus with its old brick buildings,
thick with ivy, poised like shrines on well-trimmed lawns. The
boughs of oaks and maple trees canopy the sidewalks and wisteria
blooms over trellises. Branscomb Quandrangle, the quartet of
dorms I've been assigned to, isn't only new and modern but as
luxurious and anonymous as a Hilton Hotel. Everyone who walks
through Branscomb Quad that first day looks young and rich and
white. The girls—already *ladies*—are thin and tan, tailored-look-
ing as if they've spent the summer playing tennis at the club and

shopping at Neiman Marcus and Papagallos. Parking our car in the driveway of the quad, where other parents are unloading their daughters from Cadillacs and Continentals, I don't see any other girl who looks as if she's dated only boys who drive their daddy's chicken trucks, who's spent her adolescence at the Hangout, the VFW Club and American Legion fish fries, who's never studied French.

But determined as always to succeed, I go out for sorority rush that first week because this, I think, is the social set-up for my college career. It's what all the girls from my hometown do and surely I can hide my nervousness for one piddly week. All my life I've heard only praise for sororities, these special clubs that stamp you like a good piece of meat. As I lie in my dorm bed that first night I remember the day the Egg Lady from our small town sat at our kitchen table, exclaiming over the good news that Betty Jane Rawlings had just been pledged by the best sorority at State.

"Isn't it marvelous," she said, drawing in her breath. She looked at us with nostalgic radiance, her small dark eyes glittering with satisfaction and envy. She had once been a social success, from a "good" Mobile family, but now that she was overweight, married to a farmer, reduced to delivering eggs, her experience was merely vicarious, watchful. And yet she still had the credentials to assess others; she knew when you were somebody and when you weren't. "It's so hard to get into a good sorority these days without a legacy," she went on, "but our Betty Jane made it. Of course, with that cute figure, we all knew she'd get the best. Even without somebody in her family to back her up."

We clung to the Egg Lady's words like honey. The idea of a self let loose in the social world held all the aura of salvation. A woman could be saved through social choice, could redeem her lack of family connections, her small-town origins by being exceptional, pretty, vivacious, having a good figure.

"How many pledges did they take this year?" my mother asked, turning her head towards the table. She was at the counter making lemonade, stirring the pitcher with a long-handled spoon. She asked the question as if it were of vital importance, though we all knew it was a mystery to her. She'd been trained as a scientist and had no knowledge of such things. She'd spent her time measuring chemicals into beakers, going to class with medical students; the idea of a sorority must have looked like the Presidency to her.

"Only twenty," the Egg Lady said. "They're very selective. Of course, you can't have a pledge class without the right number of girls." I saw twenty girls in white dresses seated at a table surrounded by an aura of candlelight. They floated in the air, unmoored, challenging gravity. Beside such an image, everything I did seemed cretinous. I chewed gum, turned the hems of my dresses up with scotch tape, could become engrossed in ridiculous things like a pile of ants eating up the remains of a beetle.

"Yes, Betty Jane has been a tribute to us all," the Egg Lady continued, sipping her lemonade, her sun-roughened hand picking up a chocolate chip cookie. She stared at it a moment, studying its shape, the curious protrusion of nuts, then sighed as if it were the only redemption left.

We took in sorority information as if we were Faulkner's Snopeses listening to a Compson talk about Jefferson. It was the same way my sister and I pored over *Mademoiselle* and tried every beauty secret—putting egg yolks and diluted beer in our hair to give it body and lustre as if some magic ingredient would assure us the final transformation. "And of course, they meet the very *best* sort of men. Ones whose daddies are doctors and lawyers and *captains of industry*." She closed her eyes at the fineness of this phrase. "You can't class yourself down in that sorority."

I wanted more than anything to unlock the mystery of Betty Jane Rawlings, to understand how a girl from nowhere could rise to the top, and yet at the same time, the whole conversation seemed contrived as if the Egg Lady had something to gain by delivering this news. I wondered what Betty Jane could accomplish out of a sorority except getting a successful husband. I imagined her married, giving dinner parties for one hundred people, serving liver pâté and oysters bienville in a room with chandeliers and oriental rugs, with black maids and butlers to serve and clean up. Already this picture fuzzed inside my brain. It wasn't what I saw myself doing.

But despite these considerations, we wanted to know what Betty Jane wore to the SAE luau party, what she said about the booster rally, what she ate in the dorms. "Did she get Zade to do her hair before she left?" I asked.

"Oh, honey, I don't think so. I imagine she went to some fancy-pants place up there."

My sister and I would raise our eyes to the ceiling, imagining ourselves finally *someplace,* a city where we could have our hair done right. In our imaginations there existed a place where we would be perfect, where we wouldn't have to sleep rigged for beauty, where everything would be just right.

My sister sent in a KD rec from Duke and I have a few other recs from women in my hometown, schoolteachers and bankers' wives and even the Egg Lady. Finally my day has arrived and I'm entering the privileged world of Betty Jane Rawlings. Along with thirty other girls I'm ushered into a lavishly designed sorority house decorated with upholstered furniture and swagged curtains, handed a cup of fruit punch and given the quick handshake by one of the "sisters." For the occasion, I wear my "Vandy" outfit, a green Villager dress, padded bra and pantyhose, small-heeled shoes and fourteen carat gold jewelry. Despite my nails bitten to the quick, I look as much like a conservative college girl as I know how to look, but inevitably I see there's a difference between how other girls are "rushed" and the occasional sister who ventures over to talk to me. No one has pimples, overgrown eyebrows or lipstick on her teeth. And yet there's something predatory beneath these pleasant smiles, the itch of aggression camouflaged by politeness, by the articulate gesture. "Where are you from?" a red-headed Nancy asks in a voice of pure honey while her eyes scan me with X-ray vision, tallying, I imagine, my assets and demerits. "Do you play tennis?" *Breathe in.* "Will you be riding at the stables?" *Breathe out.* I gaze at her, smiling, and have a sudden image of my sixteen year-old mother getting off the bus from Praco, dressed in her Junior League hand-me-downs, her hair curled, her face bright, her shoes polished as she waits anxiously for acceptance in the foreign world of college. Part of becoming something, I know, is a question of belief. If your imagination can shape the model, you have a chance of success. But in my imagination I don't quite fit the image, and from the coos and squeals of the "sisters" in the dorm at night I know in my secret self that I'm a fake, an impostor, still uncertain of my dreams. "I'll be taking riding at Belle Meade for P.E.," I say to Nancy, the red-head, but now her attention has wandered. When I look over at Marsha Taggart, her thick auburn hair hanging like a curtain around her radiant face, I see that she's surrounded on both sides by gushing "sisters."

Back in my room that night after this scene has been repeated at three other sorority houses, I wait listlessly for the cuts. I want to start feeling sorry for myself in earnest, but something restrains me. Maybe it's pride or a sense that "pessimism is self-defeating," that prominent illusion of the 50's. Or maybe it's something more private, a deeper horror of the class war being enacted under such innocuous circumstances. I felt the antagonism of the sisters, sensed my difference, and a wedge opens in my consciousness, barely a slit, but within that breech of light, I begin to breathe a different air, to see just a hint of relief. An immense excitement sweeps through my body. *What if none of it matters; what if this is the wrong game.* Oh, yes, I know this has been a test, but my mind senses that the real test lies tacitly behind this one, like a shadow gaining psychological density: what will I become by not fitting in, how will I change, reinvent myself? For a moment, possibilities dazzle me—the Theater Department, the Civil Rights Movement, New York—but then as suddenly as it opens, the slit closes—my parents will be so *disappointed!*—and I sit in darkness, pretending to read while listening to every sound in the air. It's not just me, but my parents' efforts that are at stake. When I hear a sudden screaming—a shriek of joy that bursts out into the hall, I know the bids have come in. The envelopes—both bids and rejections—are slipped under our doors. To me, it's like waiting for the atom bomb to drop. I anticipate the horror but can't quite claim it. Instead I tear a Kleenex to shreds, then begin picking up each ripped scrap. Finally, I hear the thud under my own door and scramble with my roommate to read my fate. But I don't want to know the result; the lull of limbo seems precious, a hiatus in the story before the inevitable crisis of rejection, where any miracle can happen. And yet here it is: my cream-colored envelope. I tear into it and see the five words I knew would be there: *I'm sorry to inform you . . .*

But I don't cry. Later I'll be bitter, but now I'm only ashamed. How can I tell my parents? Even as a child, I understand that both of my parents are deeply affected by the class system in the South, a patronizing conformity dependent on family background and inherited wealth. *Who was your grandmother's grandmother? Where did you say your people come from?* are questions I've heard all my life, questions asked to *place* you in the system. All my life I've read about *good* families and *old* families, both of which mean socially prominent families who have privileges I can't yet imagine. They keep silver in vaults and live in stately homes on private, restricted roads. They belong to country clubs and go on Mediterranean cruises. They send their children to private schools. I think of all the lessons I've taken so that I'll be prepared for this moment, this jump from invisibility into prominence. Now I'm oddly numb.

I decide to call my parents immediately, to get it over with. "Mom, I didn't make it," I say and wait through stunned silence. Only static bristles through the phone.

"Well, don't worry about it," she says, her voice low and controlled. "It's not the most important thing. It's just an extra."

"I know," I say, longing to hear at least a hint of indignation. Why can't I have the extras? What's wrong with me? But I *know* what's wrong with me. I'm not even real. And though Mother continues to reassure me that my college career is just beginning, I know this new world has slipped out of my hands by an error of my own clumsiness. Everyone will tell me it's not my fault, but secretly they'll believe it is, for I haven't learned how to be a successful middle class girl: to be light and charming, to keep my wits. I'm still a backwards small-town kid with scabby knees and a woeful glance, kicking my toes in the dirt.

And yet in retrospect, I can see that this failure with the social system is a great gift to me. It releases me from any allegiance to the Vandy coed style, the Southern lady standard. Eventually I learn to take pride in my outsider status, though this growth is a slow awareness. I wish I could say I immersed myself in a political movement, but in the late 60s Vanderbilt is a pocket of conservatism in the middle of our nation's chaotic change. While Berkeley's blowing up over the Vietnam War and Columbia's rioting, at Vanderbilt we're going to classes, worrying about dates and midterm exams. I remember Lynda Goodman, a girl from New York, walking down the hall late one afternoon in her mini skirt and black leather boots, muttering to herself as she kicked at her door. "This place is un-fucking believable," she said, and I thought I might be the only coed in the dorm to agree with her. But I'm not yet angry as Lynda Goodman is. I'm looking off to the side, trying to understand the many ways to walk in darkness; I've only learned to tiptoe.

I quit wearing the green dress. It's the day after the sorority cuts. I'm still embarrassed, ashamed of myself for being in a position which so publically exposes my unpopularity. I try to stay in my room as much as possible, avoiding the cafeteria—which is in the center of Branscomb Quadrangle. Instead I take the stairs down to the vending machines in the basement, staying away from the elevators full of gushing new pledges.

The basement's a maze of tunnels, some that lead simply to duct work and the repair/maintenance system. These spin out like spokes from the main tunnel where the vending machines stand, right under the lobby. Here you can select your food, then wander back to your room and eat in bed in a kind of blissful carnage, knowing that everything you're putting into your body is 100% junk.

I go down to the machines to buy my favorite treat that month—powdered donuts—but instead of bringing them back to my room I keep walking until I find a dark space in the tunnels, surely a section used only by repairmen. Beyond me, I can see heating and air-conditioning coils hanging in tangled loops; there's the damp odor of must, the occasional knocking sound of air whooshing through the pipes. I've been crying and my eyes are red, my face taut. I don't want to see anybody, not even my roommate, who's also been cut. As I sit on the concrete floor in the dark, I feel all the sadness drain away from me as if the girl I'm expected to become is dying right before my eyes. I'm witnessing her diminishment, her removal from my life, not with grief but with the quiet acceptance of her passing. She's dead and I'm alive. It's as simple as that. It occurs to me as if in a dream that I might let this person sitting on the concrete floor have her way. It's such a novel idea. I've been waiting to become someone else all my life. And here I'm coming face to face with my limitations and not rejecting them. I feel oddly peaceful as if the mirror of my thoughts is showing not just relief but a direction of hope. Perhaps I seem to be failing again and again because I've been choosing the wrong goals. Maybe the girl I keep hoping to become— that popular, self-assured young woman—is a mirage dreamed out of archaic books, ones that no longer fit the realities of my world.

But how can I be sure? What if there's no one to tell me, not now, not ever? It startles me to think that this might be my destiny, to discover new aspirations, perhaps to let some natural affinity guide me through life. Is this what it means to grow up?

And yet it doesn't end here. When I leave the catacombs of the basement, I walk, a somnambulist, up the back gritty stairs to the third floor where Michelle, my freshman counselor lives. I don't really remember going up stairs littered with candy wrappers, coke cans, and dropped pennies, but I remember standing alone outside Michelle's door. Red-haired and pretty, in one of the best sororities on campus, Michelle, a senior, is the essence of what I'll never become. I never think about being in *her* sorority. It's beyond my status, these girls uniformly beautiful and poised as if they've been hatched that way, emerging from their mothers' wombs with an elegant certainty. Though I've said little to Michelle, I have a sixth sense that she's accessible: I saw her in the cafeteria one day with her sisters, all chatting and laughing while

Michelle leaned casually away from them as she gazed towards the silvery leaves of the trees, her face lit with a quiet ecstacy. What did she see out there? When I looked, the trees were shaking—branches whipping furiously back and forth, leaves slapping, dancing riotously in the wind—as if they were being throttled. A storm was suddenly coming up. I smiled. Now, standing outside her door, I listen for the sound of conversation, and hearing none, knock quickly. Michelle looks surprised to see me, my red-rimmed eyes anchoring a pale, freckled face, a sloppy t-shirt over my jeans. It's not the usual way I present myself, but tonight I don't care.

"Hello," she says softly as if I've woken her up.

But I have no time for politeness, for apology; I simply ask if she'll come into the lounge and talk to me.

Michelle follows me downstairs into one of the many lounges, a room in the very back of the dorm, carpeted and curtained, antique desks tucked into corners and conversational groupings accenting the space. Dark green drapes cascade from the ceiling to the floor, blocking out the night sounds of traffic surging through the streets of Nashville, the hisses and squeal of brakes, the whining wail of a siren. The warmth of two lamps haloes the room, but I turn each one off until there's only the glow from the hall light sending its delicate probes onto the intricate patterns of the Oriental rug. I sit down, not on the couch, which is elegant and austere, but crosslegged on the floor as if I'm at home in Foley, ready to play a game of cards. Beside me, Michelle sits silent, waiting. There's an odd tension between us, and I have no idea what I'll say, why I've even gone to Michelle in the first place. But then she tilts her head slightly, and for a moment I feel as necessary and vulnerable as a tree in the storm.

"I've never been this sad before," I blurt, surprised at the urgency of my words. "I've just never been this sad." And then

I'm weeping harder than I've ever wept before, as if something solid inside me is disassembling, coming apart. In minutes I feel my eyes swelling, my nose filling, my cheeks streaked with tears, and I know I can't stop. I might never stop. But to my surprise, Michelle is holding me, rocking me, telling me it's okay to be sad, that I have a right to be sad, and then I'm holding onto her too, pushing my puffy face into the warmth of her skin because someone's finally told me the truth. I have a right to be sad. It's a revelation, like a puzzle piece that's been missing for years!

As I quiet down, Michelle sits with me while I mop my face with Kleenexes and blow my nose. She doesn't turn away from me as I do these things, but waits silently, intently.

"I didn't know you felt this way," she says. "All this week, I didn't know. You seemed, well, quite adjusted, getting along."

"I guess not," I say. And to my surprise, we both laugh.

We don't say anything more. After a few minutes we walk together to the stairs, a quiet intimacy between us as if we're old friends comfortable in our silence. The halls are brightly lit and at her floor, I become nervous again, afraid someone will see that my face is such a mess. Sensing this, Michelle turns quickly to me before she opens the door. "I want you to come see me any time you want to talk," she says. "*Any time,*" she repeats. I nod, agreeing, though I know that this one conversation is all I'll need; as I walk back to my room I stop to look out the window where clouds are breaking apart, feathering the sky. And I'm surprised at a sudden rush of happiness.

you southern girls

1968. Cambridge, Massachusetts

The summer after my sophomore year at Vanderbilt, when Jean announces she's going to Cambridge, I immediately declare I'm going too. Cambridge! It's like going to the moon. We both enroll in a special program at Radcliffe College designed to prepare women for the publishing industry, a non-credit program for university undergraduates who can pay the price. I'm sure there are serious students among us, women who intend to climb the rungs of the publishing ladder, knowing the entry levels will require certain editorial skills, but my sister and I dub it *Harvard Secretarial School,* and make long riffs through the air with our fingers, simulating a fast typing speed. Already we have lightning finger work from playing the piano for so many years. As a result of our secretarial finesse, we do homework thirty minutes before class each morning, stuffing blueberry muffins, freshly squeezed orange juice, raspberries and strawberries into our mouths while reading speed-writing exercises as if they're a simplified foreign language.

Afternoons and nights we roam around Cambridge, investigating all the head shops, the boutiques, the cafes and bookstores around Harvard Square. Everything is new to us: bands perform on the Square and in parks, couples lie on blankets, reading Sartre, Herman Hesse, Virginia Woolf, Samuel Beckett, while in another section of the Square, a theater troupe of half-dressed players practices an erotic dance. No one would dare mention a sorority here!

In the Square, we talk to everyone, our fast, thick-tongued voices attracting attention, but also bringing smug looks from the people we meet. *"Alabama,"* hippie-looking men smirk when they find out where we're from. "I wouldn't ever live *there.*" All this condemnation we know is due to George Wallace and his segregationist histrionics—his blocking the doorway at the University of Alabama to its first black students, Vivian Malone and James Hood, his racist diatribes, his lack of co-operation with Martin Luther King, Jr. and the Civil Rights Movement. In Cambridge, I meet such strident disgust with my home state that I begin to amend my answers to simply "the South," which brings rolled eyes and a general hardening of the jaws, but not outright contempt.

One day as we stop by a group of young men—longhairs, my mother would call them—talking freely, flirtatiously, Sergeant O'Brian, who moonlights as a security guard at our dorm, walks by. We wave to him, forever friendly. One of the boys is teasing me, pulling out the curls of my hair, saying, "Ya'll. Now what's the singular of ya'll?"

That night when we open the door to the dorm, waltzing in in a flood of talk, our hair curly, our arms loaded with packages, Sergeant O'Brian stands up behind his oak desk. He's big and square with a heavy Irish face, whiskers just beginning to sprout from his morning shave. When he blocks our path, we stop, ever respectful of authority. "Let me tell you something," he says, without introduction, his presence suddenly ominous, parental. The smiles leave our faces. Judgment and rules are exactly what we've left behind us. "You southern girls have got to quit being so friendly. You can't just smile and talk to everyone you meet."

This amuses us. Smiles again twitch our mouths. "Why not?" we ask. We've been taught always to be friendly and of course, friendliness includes flirtation. How else do women get what they want?

"Ever heard of the Boston Strangler?" He grimaces as he says the word, his voice peevish.

We nod our heads. "But that was years ago," I say.

"And it took years to catch him," he says. "After him, there's always another and another. Always some lunatic out on the streets just waiting for an innocent victim." He narrows his eyes, making the inference clear.

We aren't sure if what he says is true or not, but it was rumored that Richard Speck, who killed eight student nurses in Chicago in the early 60s, lived for weeks in Magnolia Springs. Although we no longer live there, it's only seven miles from our house and spooks us every time we think about it.

"Just do me a favor and quit saying hello to everybody you meet. I don't want you girls to get in any trouble."

We assure him we'll heed his warning, that we'll be fine, just fine, and in minutes we're laughing again, already forgetting his words as we wind our way up the stairs, discussing our conquests of the day.

The next day while walking through the Square during lunch hour, a black man I've seen around the park falls in step beside me. He's tall, thin, with just the beginning of an Afro, hardly enough to comb. I know I've seen him somewhere else, probably in a shop selling belts or tie-dyed t-shirts or perhaps in a bookstore checking out the new fiction. I'm wearing my new Boston clothes—a white satin blouse with an exquisitely pointed collar, low slung bell bottoms and a wide leather belt. For the first time I feel as if I fit in, belonging to the throng of people wandering the Square, looking lean and detached, East Coast hip. I'm used to flirting with many different men now, making veiled eye contact while listening to their silver-tongued spiels. They seem so different from the southern men, more certain of conquest, taking immediate verbal control.

"Bernard," he says, introducing himself but staring not at my face but at the satiny fabric of my chic blouse. He makes no bones about his stare as if I'm a new piece of goods. "Wanna catch a little time together tonight?" he asks after we've talked for a few minutes about the band playing several yards away and the Jean Luc Godard movie showing across the street. "Say around 8:30 or 9:00." I murmur yes, pleased, and he touches my belt buckle, says "see ya," and is gone as if all we need is this brief transaction.

Amazed, I walk back to Radcliffe, back to typing and speed-writing as if I've done something spectacular. I remember my mother talking to me in the kitchen right before I left Alabama. "I don't want you to date black men in Massachusetts," she said pointedly, tucking in the sleeves of a shirt to be ironed.

"But I can date them in Alabama?" I said, trying to trap her.

She said nothing, just picked up the pile of clothes she'd been folding and left the room, leaving me with a smart look on my face. I didn't brood on this. I'd suddenly lost interest in my mother and all southern lady demands. I've already discovered sex, something as primal as rage but much more accessible. Mother I'd assigned to the Dark Ages, someone I'd eventually have to confront. But not now. Now I wanted adventures.

And with Bernard, I have my chance.

I never think beyond this strategy, beyond the fact that I'm finally abandoning my southern roots. Not just abandoning, but defying them, doing exactly what I say I believe: erasing the color line. Although I've said for years that I think there's no difference between the races (it will take me years to understand the cultural context), I can't beat down the particular thrill of a black man's attention. I imagine us holding hands, perhaps dancing in some smoky all-night club, laughing as we lift glasses of gin and tonic to our lips, but the face I see in my mind isn't Bernard's, but my mother's, her eyes following every move I make as if even the most insignificant things, like wiping my hands on a napkin are suddenly important. This idea swirls in my head, my own ego swelling with appreciation. I tell no one, not even my sister about the date. During this last month, my sister has grumbled that I've followed her to Cambridge, that I'm a tag-along, a nuisance, but in her complaints I recognize a new jealousy emerging, a competition that excites me.

I'm to meet Bernard at 8:30 in the Square.

That night I wear a soft white dress with a lacy bodice and wide skirt, a feminine dress that makes me look fragile, almost delicate as if I'm tucked inside a fluffy white magnolia. I think that when Bernard comes we'll have dinner, maybe go for ice cream at Baskin Robbins or stroll around the many parks where bands play in the evening, enjoying the street life, dancing, flirting. A sweet southern dream. I imagine his compliments, my response, perhaps a quick kiss goodnight before I go back to the dorm. It's a hot night, the air still as if a cloak has been put over the trees, smothering their movement. Dusk chokes off the light, but in degrees so that darkness feels suspended just above the treetops. I wait for Bernard on a bench, spreading my dress out around me, uncertain about the tightness in my chest.

When Bernard shows up, he seems hurried, not quite as

smooth or as interested in me as he was at noon. He takes easy hold of my hand and begins walking me in a direction away from the park. He says nothing about my white dress, about the way it swirls when I walk. I wonder if he likes the tumble of curls in my hair or if he prefers the straight, severely parted hair of the hippie chicks. If he'd been immediately attentive, admiring my dress or my hair, I might have protested leaving the park so soon, but he seems distracted, less eager than I expected, and I follow him without question, matching my steps to his. We walk quickly through back alleys, past trash cans with garbage leaking out, past the line of shops I've become familiar with, only now I'm seeing them from the back where water trickles in gutters and dirt clots between the bricks. A stench of old garbage and mold hangs in the air. After fifteen minutes of walking fast with only minimal conversation, we arrive at a brick-fronted building like many others I've seen in Cambridge with a small shop underneath, something nondescript, a shoe repair place, a small used clothing store—I don't remember what. What I remember is the tension of Bernard's hand and my thoughts floating erratically inside my head. I see Mother leaning over the kitchen stool in Alabama, her face solemn, never severe, saying, "Please, honey, I don't want you to go out with black men . . . it scares me you girls going so far away." Then strangely, I see Ida as she was that day when I was seven, looking at me, stirring the cornbread mush in a big, white bowl: "Old Ida ain't never drowning in no Devil's Hole." Why do I think of Ida, a woman who hasn't entered my head in years?

By this time we're silently climbing stairs, then Bernard's opening a door with a fat gold key. The lock looks tricky and he has to jerk it, pulling it hard towards him before it springs open, revealing a small room with a bed, a desk, a table with books and records piled on top. The furniture is in such close proximity there's little room to move. One window frames the back wall, looking out onto another building of the same faded brick. I tell myself that Bernard is just bringing me here to change his shirt—he wears only a T-shirt already streaked with sweat—and to pick up some money for our ice cream. Without letting go of my hand, Bernard lifts the needle of his turntable and Jimi Hendrix's "Purple Haze" sweeps into the room. A sign above his bed says: *DROP OUT* in huge red letters. The only signs I've seen in my home town still say things like *STAND UP AND BE COUNTED IN THE FIGHT AGAINST COMMUNISM* and *JESUS SAVES US ALL FROM OURSELVES.* But in Cambridge, everyone wears signs.

I point to the poster. "I need to get one of those. Where did you buy it?" though I know you can get one at any of the shops along the Square. "You just can't find things like that in Alabama," I continue, nervousness filling my mouth with words. "In Alabama, they don't even know what it means. Drop out still means drop out of high school." I'm waiting for Bernard to laugh, to say something critical about Alabama, its racist policies, its backward education, its political orthodoxy, but all he says is, "Mmh," not even looking at me. Music suddenly swells into the room, filling out the corners, decorating it with sound.

"Have you lived here long?" I ask, wondering what else I can say, what leads this man into response.

"Let's dance," Bernard says, ignoring my question and before I have a chance to answer, his arms are around my waist, arms that hold me snug. I'm used to men starting out slowly, a drink, a hand held, slow kissing, seduction a subtle transgression of your boundaries. I know immediately that with Bernard I've entered another league. We can only move three paces each way without hitting the bed, the chair or the table, our feet erotically touching with each step. I tell myself to be calm, this is just a different style, an interlude before we begin our real date, and I'm determined to be patient. There's a smell of sweat between us, of dampness and heat. Before I can stop them, the words *Negro sweat* floats up in my brain as if uttered from my Mother's lips. I see Bernard's arms, the dark sooty blackness of them reaching around my waist. I want to tell him to slow down, but I'm afraid he'll think I'm rejecting him, holding myself above him, acting white. Still, I want to ask him questions, to find out who he is, where he's grown up, if he's grown up near water. I wonder if he knows that places like Magnolia Springs exist—I think of the smell of early morning at the river, of old leaves and damp pinestraw and the heavy must odor of decay—but there seems a great gulf between us, a space so wide ordinary speech can't reach.

As we continue to dance through that record and the next in a soft, undulating sway around the little room, I begin finally to worry about what we're doing and when we'll leave; as doubts throb stronger in my head I wonder what will happen to me, if he means to hurt me, if he knows I'm trembling inside, my skin beginning to prickle with chillbumps even though heat envelopes the room. I have a strong sense at that instant of my sister looking over my shoulder at me with surprise and jealous disapproval. In an uncomfortable moment, I see my tangled motives, my perverse, competitive needs: I've wanted to do something first, something my sister hasn't done. After Bernard's invitation, I felt a secret sense of superiority, of risk, of preference. *I have been chosen.* Bernard is my generic black man, my ticket to experience. I know at that instant that Bernard and I have nothing to say to one another, that the entire reason for our date has nothing to do with who we really are. But by this time he's kissing my ears, pushing back my hair, his tongue sliding in a slow, dazzling dance of its own over my skin as he leads me with a slow pressure of weight towards the bed. What Bernard wants to do is fuck. That word jumps out in my head as bold as his *DROP OUT* sign. I've only slept with Steve, my boyfriend back at Vanderbilt and I'm not planning on sleeping with Bernard.

And yet what I see in my head is another story: it's my mother and Ida fighting in the river, two grown women standing in water up to their waists, the current pushing against them, almost knocking them down. Mother has hold of the collar of Ida's white uniform and Ida has grabbed onto Mother's silk blouse. They're tearing at each other's clothes, swaying in the river, the water splashing up in their faces, plastering their hair. Then what I see is me, moving towards them, my flowing dress holding me back so that I move slowly like a woman in a dream. And yet all the time I'm pushing through the river, I know I can't make them stop. What they're fighting for is something beyond my control.

"I can't," I say suddenly, disentangling myself from Bernard's arms. I stand rod stiff, rigid, two inches from his body, my heels touching the steel rim of his bed, the lace on my bodice feeling crumpled, wet. I want to tell him why I'm here, what this is about—sibling competition, filial rebellion—but when I look at him, his eyes are hooded, and I can't make myself say the words. His eyes frighten me. They look through me as if I'm nothing, a fly trapped in a spider web.

It's a kind of dislike I've never encountered before. Cool on the surface but hot underneath. But then I think of Ida, her bland mask covering up the fury as she flung her apron on the chair and marched out of the kitchen. I look out the window at the brick building now darkening with night.

"I'm sorry, I can't stay here," I mumble, not able to meet his eyes. I think how silly I must look in my white frilly dress, the whiteness of my skin suddenly a tease, a rejection, everything I've meant to deny. Then even lower, "I can't do this." There's a thick silence between us. I feel his breath against my forehead, the tip of his shoe still butting up against mine. The moment seems to last forever, to take in my whole life. How protected I've been! My small town girlhood has given me a distorted picture of race as if it's a capricious thing, easily erased, rather than serious, historical, unavoidable. Tonight, race is everything.

Without another word, Bernard goes to the door and opens it wide. Then, not looking at me, he turns his back, sits down in his chair at the table and begins sorting through his records as if there's no one else in the room. He even hums to himself as night eases out the light of day.

I leave quietly, quickly, a humiliated beast, my head shadowing my feet on the stairs, then the concrete of the sidewalk. I don't really know where I am. I've walked into this place through back streets, following Bernard. Now I walk alone, taking turns which I have no memory of taking until I come to a major street with lights and cars. At one of the corners I get a taxi and speed back to the dorm. When it stops in front, I let out my breath. I hadn't realized I'd been holding it in.

At the doorway of my dorm, Sergeant O'Brian sits at the desk. When he sees me he doesn't smile as he's been doing the last few nights. He just shakes his head as if he can see the confusion turning inside my mind. "You southern girls," he says with a tired, irritable sigh. "You're a whole lot of trouble."

I nod, knowing he's right. I've been stupid. Perhaps worse than stupid. Insensitive, egotistical. At that instant, staring into his thick Irish face, I remember something my mother told me years ago about Ida. "Why did she leave us?" I asked, seeing her whirl into my room, snap sheets off the bed and roll them into a knot.

"Don't you remember," Mother said. "She was involved in some kind of crime at the quarry near where she used to cook. They said she killed somebody, but I don't know if that was true. All I know is that she quit coming to work. It took me weeks to find out what had happened to her. She was arrested in another county."

Killed somebody. I didn't believe it. I didn't yet know what might make a woman want to kill somebody. I didn't know how pain could build to a fever pitch, so hot it could crawl out of your skin as hungry as gasoline tasting the heat of a match. Walking up the stairs that night to my bed, it seems to me I don't know anything at all. The policeman's right. Knowing so little, you can end up "a whole lot of trouble." As my feet drag on the carpet, I wonder how you can decode all the messages that float around you, how you can ever know what you need to know.

As I pull the covers down and get into my bunk, beneath the cool, clean, regulation Radcliffe sheets, I feel as if I've been thrown head first back into my heritage, landing in the deep slippery quagmire of my own contradictions. "Alabama," I whisper repeatedly as if practicing for the next day's review. "I'm from Alabama."

draft notice

1968. Cambridge, Massachusetts

In the end it's not Bernard or Cambridge that changes my life irrevocably, but a single day in July, the weekend my Vanderbilt boyfriend, Steve, comes up to Boston for a visit.

While I'm at Radcliffe, Steve's been stuck in Tennessee, working in his father's construction company, loading trucks and driving the forklift while waiting impatiently for graduate school acceptances and his July 7th draft physical to put everything in its place. Vietnam hangs in the balance. All the boys in West Tennessee are expected to go, to refuse would be considered downright unpatriotic, indecent, immoral. Although we've had heated all-night discussions favoring draft resistance in Nashville, in his hometown Steve becomes moody, cynical, vacillating from week to week about what exactly he can do. He applied late to graduate school and now with absolutely everybody applying, his acceptance is uncertain at best.

At night when memories of Vanderbilt flood my thoughts, I

see him as he was that first month we dated, rushing towards me in a mossy gray sweater and tight-fitting jeans, an old leather jacket, cracked and scarred, flapping against his chest. Sometimes he'd pick me up and swing me off the ground, my feet flying in the air. Then I'd feel a buzzing inside, a tingle in the nerves.

Today Steve's flying to Boston for the Fourth of July weekend. On my way to meet him, I slouch in the back seat of a taxi, ignoring the expense. "Get us a room," he insisted, having made money this summer. "Everything. The works!"

Waiting for his plane to arrive I check out my appearance not only in the wavy bathroom mirrors but in the stares and quivering gazes of other travelers. I'm thin and blonde, flat-chested and sleek-hipped just like the Twiggy models appearing in every women's magazine. Who would ever have thought that the waif would be so admired, so coveted, so overtly sexual? Women give me as much confirmation as men, but in a totally different way. While men gaze appreciatively at me in my satin shirt and herringbone bell bottoms, women look at me with an X-ray stare as if memorizing my style, rating it on a secret score card tucked inside their heads.

I don't see Steve at first in the stream of passengers pouring out of Gate 10. In my head, I've fixed him as I last saw him at Vanderbilt—in jeans and a workshirt, his thick, brown hair drifting over the limp edge of his collar, an introspective look on his face. When I finally see him, I stop short: this isn't Steve, this short-haired, 1950's frat-boy in a button-down collar and khaki pants. I feel deceived, outraged at this disguise as he rushes towards me, a flat smile plastered on my face. But immediately, sensing his anxiety, I feel guilty for such petty discriminations. After all, July 7 hangs in the balance.

As we embrace, his body so near yet so foreign in his Mama's boy clothes, I say, "Jesus, let's get you undressed," though I don't mean it as sexual innuendo.

"Won't take a prayer meeting for that," he says, hugging me close. I see that there are brown gobs stuck between his teeth as if he's been eating mud. Then I notice his pockets bulging with Babe Ruths, Snickers, Butterfingers, Hersheys, M & M's.

"What kind of diet are you on?"

And now he pulls me closer, his mouth to my ear. "Gotta kick up my allergies. Everybody's got letters from their doctors, but they're saying it won't do. You've got to have an attack or something. Stop breathing, have a seizure. Fall down dead." And then I understand. Our weekend will be devoted to wrecking Steve's health.

By the time we hit the room, 8th floor in our medium-priced hotel, Steve has transformed from a backwoods country boy, improperly dressed and out of style, to my old lover with gentle brown eyes and thick brows which grow straight up just above the bridge of his nose. In the taxi he smoked one cigarette after another and ate two candy bars methodically as if they were tasteless, but it's his suitcase which holds the biggest surprise. A bulky dark leather affair, it bulges on either side. When he opens it, I expect clothes—Steve's a clothes horse—but instead more khaki pants are wedged between three bloated brown paper bags. "What's that?"

"This," he says, staring intensely at one lumpy sack, "is my last hope." And he pulls out an Electrolux vacuum cleaner bag packed full of dust and dirt. "My inhalation system." He smiles. "Every thirty minutes I breathe into this thing for five minutes with the supreme hope that every little scrap of dust filters down to my lungs. Crafty, huh?"

"Diabolical. Machiavelli would have approved."

"And Thoreau."

"No, he'd have said, 'go to jail. Sit this one out.'"

"Well, I'm not going to do that." Steve looks out the window at the pale clouds drifting towards the bay, lapsing into a privacy so deep, I feel excluded. "My father would disown me," he says finally. It's a simple statement packed with grief, and I will realize later, fear. "He thinks it's a *just* war, that all this resisting is plain cowardice, a bunch of lint-heads and longhairs." As if contemplating the stark consequences of his father's faith, he reaches quickly for one of the vacuum cleaner bags and begins to breathe deeply, closing his eyes like a baby nursing at its mother's breast. Dust flies out in puffs, spreading into thin, wavy clouds.

At this time I know very little about his father, only that he inherited a lumber and construction company from *his* father and built it into a multi-million dollar business. The one time I visited, he'd seemed like an aging Marlboro man, full of purpose and cranky authority, believing in a 19th century work ethic as the only viable political creed. Around him, Steve was stiff and polite and to my surprise, almost pandering. "No sir, I'm not smoking much" (Steve smokes like a chimney!). Steve's grade point average suffered because his father insisted he major in business for his first two years, an area in which Steve has almost no aptitude. His first battle with his father was over switching to political science, a decision that barely rescued him from defeat. As I look at Steve breathing in the bag, I know he won't bolt to Canada, won't burn his draft card, won't protest except in the most private, irrational way. Like me, he believes in the rule of negative justification: only after you've suffered a significant setback of bad luck and ill will can you expect any sort of blessing. It's this unspoken premise which binds us together, an alliance with the patriarchal gods of the Old Testament who bellow out punishment and retribution. In my heart, I know that neither of us believes in reason and rationality, but in the darker whirlpool of superstition: not black cats or ladders, but the more archaic fear that there are lions inside us straining to be let loose. It's our own aggressive baseness we're certain of and its trickster sister, lethargy, which holds it in check.

In that instant I see him face down in a rice paddy, blood streaming from his throat, body fragments hurtling through the air from the force of a land mine. I don't know much about the specific battles in Vietnam, though I've read in *Time* how the North Vietnamese have kept the marines isolated at Khe Sanh, how the mists float in from the hills, spreading out like a veil, cloaking the marines in fog. I try to imagine what it would be like to sleep in the cold damp air of an underground bunker, the earth falling in my eyes, in my mouth, turning to grit between my teeth when the shelling began. But I can't. I've never even been in a storm shelter. Foley is too close to sea level for basements. We don't have bomb shelters or anything underground. Only Charlie Hudson, the guy I dated freshman year at Vanderbilt, made me think of Vietnam. "Mr. Texas," I called him because he was tall and handsome with thick dark hair and a pronounced slouch that came, I told him, from leaning against fence posts out on his father's 10,000 acre ranch. Actually, he was just a rich cowboy whose family seemed etched in bitterness. We only dated for a few months, but when we saw each other I couldn't help but notice that there was always an edginess to Charlie, a sense of abandonment and failure. He cut classes, ditched his fraternity, would stay awake all night to work at the campus radio station and then sleep all day. Sometimes he didn't show up for our dates. Sometimes he showed up an hour early, "starving," he'd say, "we've gotta get out of here and eat." When I heard through the gossip mill that he'd quit school and gone to Vietnam, I wasn't really surprised. All the other men I knew were spending most of their time avoiding Vietnam, but Charlie wanted to show his old man he could hack it. Live Free or Die. And then right before I left Nashville for Cambridge, I heard that Charlie had been killed. I imagined him doing something daring—taking the lead on a patrol of those hills outside Khe Sanh or leaning out of a chopper to get a better aim (he really did want to prove something to his father). But I knew it could just as easily have been a stray bullet that hit him while he slept in his bunker or something awful, something unbelievable, like a booby trap which sent him exploding into the trees. I've seen scenes of torture, amputation, napalm fires on TV. And now my concern is more focused: How can I prevent this from happening to Steve? Is it possible that I can save him? I look at his button-down Oxford cloth shirt, his shiny Bass weejuns, the sharp line between his hair and neck, white as a chalkline. Outside the windows a tall, angular man in a white t-shirt and beard stares up at the hotel. I'm sure he can see me, is staring only at me, radiant in my white satin shirt. And in that moment I understand the conditions: I must be true in thought, word, and deed. I will save Steve by my sacrifice, by purity and loyalty, and then oh, yes, then he will be obliged to save me too.

Steve coughs, his eyes now bloodshot, his face pale with worry and fatigue. "Come here," he says, not with passion but with the restless energy of raw nerves. We're both a little awkward with each other, trying to find the old rhythm of our talk. We make love, a fast, fumbling, rocketing madness, me holding together his limbs with my fingers as they try to jerk loose from my grasp and scatter to the corners of the room. I pull on his hair, grabbing the short thick mass as if to secure it with pressure. "Ouch," he whispers, but I refuse to surrender and whether in retaliation or from his own nightmares, Steve crushes himself into me, bruising my lips, rubbing bare the skin between my legs. It's despair fused with sweetness as if in minutes we've lost the innocence of our child-hood and now face the insolence of adulthood.

Sweating, hoarse, we lie beside each other, tense and bruised. My mouth feels swollen, thick. There are scratches across my breasts, a hairline mark on my stomach. Steve's skin blooms in patches of red where I've pinched him. Around the edges of red, the skin is ghastly white as if it's been bleached. Steve is quivering as he reaches beside the bed for the vacuum cleaner bag, letting it rest a moment against his chest. A trickle of sweat rushes towards it, staining the outside. Seeing this, Steve lifts it quickly to his nose and breathes, dust whirling in eddies towards the ceiling, drifting back down like plaster against our skin. Time bends itself into fragments: I see myself a month earlier with Bernard, a black hand crushed against the white lace of my dress, then the police-man from the dorm looking in the door, shaking his head as I walk up the stairs. I'm wondering at my own indiscretions when Steve breathes out a stream of words.

"What?" I raise up on an elbow and hover above him. The bag lies almost limp against his chest. I look into its eye as if some intelligence lies there, a consciousness that could direct me. But Steve grabs the bag again and inhales, closing his eyes, rushing I guess, towards his own private void.

He lets out a long, slow breath. "I said," he looks up at me, the red pinch marks on his skin beginning to fade, "will you marry me if I flunk the draft?"

I stare at the eye of the bag. I want to be inside it, to hide in the dust and debris. No one will ask me to make a decision then. I feel Steve's hand on my thigh, then stroking my belly, the soft soreness of my breasts. "Willya?" he says, and I hear the sadness in his voice, a choking explosion of fear as he grabs me to him, a cor-ner of the bag crushed between us, scratchy and coarse, held tight to our skins.

"Yes," I say, stroking his back, but what I feel inside is the beginning of a storm.

At the airport on Monday afternoon, Steve looks as if he's just walked out of a deep freezer; he's pale and blue, cowed by an exhausted numbness. His shoulders slump, his mouth automatically chews the thick chocolate of a Mars Bar. Other candy bars bulge from his pockets. As we wait for his flight, we're silent. I have begun to eat the chocolate bars too and automatically my tongue flicks between my back teeth. Steve's flight is late. Each moment we wait glues us to more misery. When his flight is finally called, Steve hugs me tight. "Last boarding," the intercom announces, then he touches my cheek, his hand cold, clammy; he turns quickly and walks through the dark corridor without looking back.

It isn't until Friday that I hear from Steve. I know the minute his exuberant voice pounds the air waves that he's failed.

"1-Y, babe, a deferment," he says, "and you know what that means!"

I think of marriage, but I know he means escape from the horrors of Vietnam. I wonder if he's forgotten his proposal, if I can be wiped away as quickly as a chocolate streak. In a perverse way I now want him to acknowledge his proposal whereas a week before acceptance seemed like a sacrifice.

"Should I buy a white dress?"

"Buy everything," he says, evasively.

In my dorm room in Cambridge, the air is rich with the smell of new-mown grass. Grasshoppers jump in the shrubbery. Someone plays flute, trilling, beneath my window. I lie on my bunk and think about Steve. Now that his desire seems ambivalent, mine has returned. Once again I see him as he was at Vanderbilt, a beautiful, underground maverick, holding the frat world at bay. I can feel the weight of his hand across my thigh. That weight will draw me into a new life, away from irrelevancy, from the flat farm land of Alabama. A remote voice whispers to me that this is absurd, that I'm about as ready for marriage as I am for climbing Mt. Everest. *You have to prove yourself through dilligence and struggle.* But since I've identified no special passion, the dilemma and struggle remain abstract, and in the end, this dissenting voice is shouted down by the hope that this is my ticket away from the South. I hold fast to the belief that there's life outside Alabama and Steve will take me there.

When we talk the next night, Steve is rhapsodic about the future: he'll become a professor of political science and I'll finish my B.A., get a Master's, the two of us living in a manner that transcends our parents' lives. "Beautiful," he whispers over the phone. "We'll be beautiful together." And I see Steve sitting in the old faded, blue chair in his treehouse apartment in Nashville, a board full of books laid across its arms like a bridge. A coffee mug sits on one side and Steve, in granny glasses and old jeans, looks up at me when I arrive as if he doesn't know who I am. He's been doing research on Kefauver, the senator from Tennessee, one of the "civilized minority" who bucked the Southern tradition of the 50s and supported anti-poll tax and anti-lynching legislation as well as school desegregation. Steve was researching his years as chairman of the Senate Subcommittee on Anti-trust and Monopoly where Kefauver investigated pricing in the drug, steel and electrical industries; he was obsessed with Kefauver and over pancakes and coffee detailed how Kefauver's investigation led to legislation regulating drugs and the conviction of business executives in the electrical industries for price fixing.

I love this part of Steve, the rebel, the serious scholar, outraged by political corruption. The truth is, I hope we'll be outraged together, and this is the thought I carry uppermost in my mind, this desire to show them all.

❧

"I don't want to move," Steve says the second day of our honeymoon. He refuses, in fact, to leave the bed except for necessary trips to the bathroom. "It's peaceful and dark in here. That's all I want." He orders everything from room service—shrimp remoulade, oysters bienville, champagne, even the washing of his pajamas. Yet he's neither passionate nor attentive. Instead, he walls himself off from the world, from me, withdrawn inside a protective shell. I know he's recovering from the claustrophobia of the wedding week where we've been presented and entertained, with no time alone and nothing settled about our future. We don't even know about graduate school yet though every day I call Steve's parents for news. While he broods and sleeps, I think about his old bedroom in Nashville, the tiny room with the bed shoved up against the windows, the tree limbs brushing against the glass. The first time I stayed there I woke to blasts of sound like a huge gust of water bursting through a pipe.

"It's the kid downstairs playing the tuba," Steve smiled. "He's getting better. It used to sound like a snowblower stuck in the snow."

And we giggled, pulling the covers up over our heads, the lovely feel of Steve's breath in my hair.

While Steve sleeps, I try on my nightgowns in the bathroom, posing beneath the fluorescent lights, then secretly, leaning seductively on the ledge of the tub, in the dim glow of the night light. The oyster-white satin gown looks appealing with one strap casually sliding off the shoulder, but I'm less certain about the cool blue silk with ecru lace. It still seems to sag in the bust, so I twist the straps with bobby pins, pulling the bodice tighter, then stand back to see the effect. I imagine Jean nodding her approval. I almost laugh except a storm of worry has already gathered in my head. Oddly, it's not Steve's lack of passion that overwhelms me, but his lack of control. How are we going to show everybody that we don't need them if he won't get out of bed? While he broods, I walk the streets of New Orleans, primping in store windows, wondering how I'll get us to Colorado.

But we aren't going to Colorado. On the next to last day we learn that Steve has been accepted only at Utah on conditional status, given the lateness of his application. No financial aid. No money. We're all on our own. Now worry is replaced by sadness. I can see it in the paleness of his skin, in the way he keeps staring out the window, then quietly smiling as if he's just understood some hilarous irony. He slumps onto the unmade bed. "I'm going to build houses in Reelfoot," he says finally, and then he laughs, gushes of laughter spewing out of him like vomit.

"But you *hate* those kind of tacky houses your father builds, those cookie cutter traps," I say, ignoring his fit of mirth. His father has railed against graduate school, shaking his head at a son who'd turn down the gift of a prosperous business.

"I know," he says, suddenly sober. "I hate them but I'll hate myself more if I don't give it a try."

"What does that mean?" I say. I am shocked into stillness. I can hear the water dripping in the bathroom, the squeal of the maids' carts out in the hall.

"A year," he says. "That's all it will be. Schools won't give me aid until next year."

"No, we can't do that. I *want* to go West," I say, feeling the first flutter of fear. How dare he deny me my chance to be different from who I am. If Steve refuses graduate school I'll be stuck. It doesn't seem possible to leave a marriage after only one week.

Now Steve sits on the edge of the bed and lays the trap before me: he looks at me with a pain so deep I know it's genuine; it's a pain I recognize, a pain I feel beneath the layers of my skin. It's the pain of disappointing your parents, of pushing out to sea on your own, defining yourself, ignoring them. It's the old trap of loyalty, slow suffocation through family demands. It's the fear of belief in yourself. I see his father's tight-lipped smile. Only now am I beginning to understand his father's hold, the threat of expulsion. As we sit together on the hotel bed, I know suddenly that I'm inside another marriage, one different than the marriage I pledged just a few days before to honor.

That night I lie down beside Steve in my blue jeans and t-shirt (I've abandoned the idea of pretty nightgowns). Now I too stare at the ceiling, full of insomnia and anxiety, knowing we aren't pledged together as rebels but are simply two children still afraid of our parents.

PART THREE

1997. Foley, Alabama

"I'll never break down," Mother tells me as I'm getting ready for bed. It's years later, after my divorce, my breakdown, my beginning attempts to write. The lights are low, the room a blue fog of stillness. I lie in bed, soft as fruit, unable to move.

I nod, not sure what else I can do. I'm visiting for a week at the end of summer, sleeping in my old room with its fussy pillows, its dust ruffles, its low-slung Victorian couch.

"I won't allow that," Mother continues, and I feel her stiffen as if a hairline crack is traveling through her body, causing fissures, the shattering of nerve.

When I look at her full, white nightgown floating like a cloud around trim ankles, above velvet slippers, I imagine the two of us standing before the many rivers and bays of Baldwin County: Magnolia River, Fish River, Bon Secour, Pirate's Cove, Wolf Bay, Cotton Bayou, Soldier Creek. I run my fingers down an invisible map until I feel a familiar lightness, a happiness that knows no bounds. "You'll be all right, Mother," I say, opening my eyes. "And so will I."

a spy in the house

And yet I did break down.

It's like a hammer that comes out of nowhere, a sledge hammer smashing me to pieces, breaking me apart. Each whack says I can't copy the life of my mother, my father, my brother or my sister. But more than that, it says I'll have to take cover, have to find ammunition, protection, spies. There's a war going on and if I don't fight I'll die. I don't understand the war, don't know which side I belong to, and yet secretly, I'm relieved it's finally come to this. For so long I've let everything wash over me as if I were already dead. Now I'll have to wake up and pay attention.

It begins not long after my divorce, after four years of marriage to Steve in a small southern town in western Tennessee. When I first saw that town, after driving through miles of cotton fields, their white fluff bobbing beneath a fierce August sun, my mind lurched hopefully forward then swung into reverse. The town had neither a river, a lake nor the hills and valleys and winding curves that create beauty but was a flat little burg that might have flourished before the Civil War. When Steve and I drove to the house his father was giving us—a small ranch-style house which sat on a bare patch of earth like a Bandaid on the back of a suntanned thigh—I banged out the back door and wept. How had I ended up like this? In this pedestrian life? This shoe-box house? I looked at the treeless yard, the bleakness of a single crow blazing the sky.

At age twenty, I'd arrived here with so many questions; now at twenty-four, I was leaving, the answers blowing like dust in the air. My marriage to Steve had turned a corner, become sticky, greedy, but arid of desire. A few months before we separated, I quit my job as a caseworker at the Department of Public Welfare—the place I'd worked for the past two years—and for several weeks I had nothing to do but stare into the emptiness of each hour.

But there is a particular day I remember, the day Steve leaves for good. That morning I sit on a kitchen stool, one of those tacky plastic kind with a thin, padded seat and aluminum legs notched in the middle like knees. From this perch, I watch Steve move loads of stuff—clothes, records, books, sheets, towels—out the door and into his car. I feel insanely calm, as people often do who've just been in an accident and can't yet assess the damage. Distracted, I look up at the stain on the ceiling as if there might be a secret message printed there while Steve makes his monotonous trips back and forth to the car. I know that once he stops, another mood will descend. I'll have to admit that I've failed, that I'm neither loved nor desired, but a woman alone, sitting on a stool, staring into nothing. I can't quite imagine myself alone. It will be like seeing myself squashed inside a dryer, tumbling over and over in a dark, tight space.

A bubble in the sink pops. Then I hear the car motor catch, a sound of such quiet finality, I stiffen. Now I can set the house on fire. I can immolate myself. I look at the stove. The curtains. It won't take much. But I can't move. Pain's an old friend, a frequent companion. And suddenly I think of Mrs. Chauncey, my fifth grade teacher who thumped my chest with her index finger and said, "*You* have no common sense," raising one high-arched brow. In my mind I begin to make a list:

I've never had any common sense.
I've never had breasts.
I've never had a good conversation with a man.
I've never had a decent tan.
I've never pleased my family.
I've never had an orgasm.
Masochism, I realize, can have a certain style.

When Steve comes back the next day I'm again sitting on the plastic stool, holding a burnt piece of toast in my hand. I'm not eating it, just holding it as if trying to decide on a reason to throw it away.

Steve looks even more decisive by morning light. He seems surprised to see me sitting in the same place as if I too should have left in the night. "Forgot the dimmer switches," he says, nodding towards the lights. He begins to unscrew the little knobs that fit over the light switches. I think about the night he put them on, how excited he was, obsessively lowering the brightness until the room had the glow of candlelight, the softness of moonlight. He was really nuts about those dimmers. To him soft, modulated light cast the world in a more romantic perspective, and in fact, our ugly house seemed more charming in muted light.

"Don't forget the ones in the hall," I say now, lifting my head. I'm glad he's taking the dimmers. I want to see myself in cold, sterile light. Or else hide in darkness. Perhaps, I think, this is the beginning of my real education, and I feel a tingling in my feet, just beneath my socks.

Steve drops the screwdriver on the floor. Its clatter shatters my thoughts, and when I look up again, he's staring at me as if trying to figure me out. Two dimmer switches bulge from his pockets. His hair is still thick and dark and shiny. I want to tell him that something's changing in me, something small, cellular, inevitable. But I'm still hurting, sad. I say nothing. Instead I tap my foot against the rim of the stool and turn my body away, hearing only faintly the inevitable wheeze of the door. Alone, I watch the afternoon light brighten into patterns on the kitchen floor, then fade into inevitable darkness.

The next day I sit on the doorstep and think. It may be the first time I've thought in a long time. I see myself at the very beginning of our relationship, believing there's something noble and anguished about our love, a love born of the Vietnam War, of drugs, and childhood sadness as if each of us felt cheated inside the family nest and hoped the other would provide that craved sense of belonging. Now I look out at the lawn, the grass overgrown, a savannah of greenness and think how happy we were as students. After my classes at Vanderbilt, I'd walk to Steve's apartment, climb the stairs to the upper story of a two-story white frame house, anxious to get inside, to be warm, to see him studying with a cup of coffee besides his books. Maybe we'd listen to the Doors, talk about Martin Luther King Jr. or about the frat rats and their predictable, pedestrian lives. We planned to leave the South, to find our way to San Francisco or Seattle, but instead we'd landed right back here, in a life that was predictable and pedestrian and confusing as hell.

After my divorce I move across the state of Tennessee, deep into the mountains where icy streams cut through glaciated rocks and wildflowers bloom alongside the blacktopped highways. I live in an apartment in the woods surrounded by maples and oaks and pines. I love coming into this place where there are so many birds and trees, and for the first few months I surprise myself by being happy in a monkish sort of way, alone and ambitious, studying art at the university, drawing still-lifes, stitching and dyeing fabric, cutting designs into soft blocks of wood. I've fallen in love with fabric design and spend hours in the studio, painting wax onto silk screens, mixing dyes, printing tiny swatches of cloth along with other women who seem oblivious to everything but this work. We are acolytes to something bigger than ourselves, something better. On Saturdays I walk into the hills and watch clouds of birds swim across an October sky. I pick up a ruby red leaf and put it in my apartment window. I collect stones and feathers and tiny pieces of flint. It's the first time I've ever done such things, and I'm immensely pleased with myself, not only for surviving the divorce but for actually enjoying myself.

I'm in this first flush of pleasure when, quite suddenly, I wake to twisted strands of hair lying loose on my pillow, limp wads clogging the drain when I take a shower, clotting my comb as I rake it through my curls. Jesus! Losing my hair isn't something I can fathom, so I try to ignore it, fluffing my hair to cover its new thinness, assuring myself it's some kind of yearly shedding, a spring cleaning of the scalp. I've read about such things in beauty magazines, the way hair sheds every few years, a natural thinning, making way for new, healthier growth. But a week later when I reach down to the drain after my daily shower and feel a thick wad of hair lying there, I scream. I can't afford to be ugly; I'm only 24 years old.

Immediately I go to a dermatologist, embarrassed yet frantic to explain that my hair's falling out. It's the first time I've marked "divorced" on an official form and it looks like disastrous freight, a weight I can't bear to carry. But the doctor doesn't seem to notice. He comes in all starch and bustle, staring at me as if I'm a specimen, reading my chart, then explaining that my curly blonde hair "might" be shedding because of the strong estrogen birth control pill I took during the four years of marriage (and subsequently stopped taking only a month ago). He recommends I comb my hair only once a week, wash it every two weeks. "Wear a bandanna or hat if you feel uncomfortable with how it looks."

And this is exactly what I do. I rush to a department store and splurge on three bandannas, then avoid the mirror when I wash my hair. Though the process upsets me, I cling to my residual hope, an irrational faith that this is temporary, some catastrophe of modern medicine. After all, it's probably caused by the pill and now I've stopped taking it. Soon, my hair will grow back (though the doctor doesn't actually *say* this), and I'll throw away the bandannas, render the whole thing irrelevant, buried in memory. To my relief, the mirror reassures me: I'm a girl dressed in tank top and jeans, a bandanna on my head, large gold hoop earrings dangling from my ears. I'm thin, *svelte,* older men would say and I take pleasure in their comments, in the fact that they still turn their heads when I walk by. But I don't allow myself to date, to make friends, to do anything so risky. When under siege, I do what I've been trained to do: I work, everything spread out on my dining room floor—art books, fabric, silk screen designs, notebooks, ruler, popcorn, coke.

Most often I kneel on the floor, refining the scale drawings for my interior design class, drawings that require infinite precision, the use of a special ruler and Rapidograph pencil. Every night I pore over these drawings, erasing and re-drawing until I'm positive they're exactly right. And yet when I arrive at class on Tuesday night, I'm surprised that my drawings look messier than my classmates', my lines lacking a hard-edged crispness, an Oriental certainty. I must be doing something wrong, and I resolve to correct whatever it is. Always I believe I can improve, can force myself to be at the top of the heap. It's all a matter of determination, a test of will. Our professor, Mrs. DeVinnis, takes up all of our drawings each Tuesday, and tonight, at the end of class, after looking at mine, she asks me to stop by her office the next day. It's the middle of the semester and I'm gratified, certain she'll give me pointers for improvement.

When I arrive at her office, Mrs. DeVinnis looks up from her desk, smiles, and puts away a book she's been reading, placing it carefully in the second drawer of her desk. "I've been looking at your drawings," she says, picking up a stack that I recognize as mine. When she turns to me, moving slightly in her seat, a look of discomfort crosses her face, her eyes shadowed with dread. Her lip twitches in the corner, and I'm surprised at this because she's usually so calm, so careful, a controlled presence standing at the front of the class, delivering a lecture on drafting techniques. She's the kind of woman I know I'll never be, and I both admire and resent her, though I haven't acknowledged it until this very moment. I admire that she's so poised, never rattled, never untidy, but attractive and graceful and correct. And yet I resent her for these very same traits, for the potential boredom of them, the way poise becomes static, tidiness mechanical, and control so lacking in immediate drama.

"Occasionally," she begins, "I meet a student in my class who simply can't draw straight lines, can't "see" the drawing in the way an interior designer and draftsman must see it. This is not due to lack of persistence or intellectual awareness, but perhaps something of eye-hand coordination . . . I'm not sure what the reason is, but when I notice it, I have to point it out." She pauses and inevitably both of our eyes go to my drawings where I see, not smudged lines, but an innate tentativeness, a faint swerving where lines intersect. Just above my drawings a crisp clean illustration of an interior room is tacked on the wall. The difference is palpable.

"I would not be a credible teacher," Mrs. DeVinnis continues, pulling her eyes back to mine, "if I didn't tell you that I think this isn't your field. I can see that you work hard. I see the time you've spent on your drawings, but I don't think they will ever come up to the required standard." She pauses again. "I tell you this because it's not something you can correct, or at least, I haven't seen other students correct it. And so I want to encourage you to consider other areas of design, ones that don't require the kind of precision and tension of drafting."

I nod, but there's no feeling behind the nod. I'm too stunned to reply. Instead, I look at my notebook, blank and ready, and quickly close it on my lap.

But of course, I plan to prove her wrong. I plan to defy the truth of that last statement: no one can correct it. Walking back to my car, I feel the delicious pull of stubbornness fed by disappointment. And suddenly I recognize this as a familiar moment in my life as if disappointment is my mentor, the one thing that instills desire. In sixth grade, I used to hear my sister praised for her performance at the piano, Mama Dot saying, "this is excellent, you're *feeling* the music with your fingers," and for a week, I'd practice and practice, waiting to "feel" it too, until eventually I'd lose interest. But this time. . . .

I clean the dining room floor of all other projects, and put the drawing board and drawing paper dead center. I begin my first night of practice. I am going to will myself to be good. Every night I work for several hours. Every night I erase, start over. I've barely begun the extra work on my drafting when the very next week my face erupts in craters, oozing boils and tight little pimples disguising my nose. It happens so suddenly it's as if I go to class one day a fairly normal person and come back a monster. That afternoon, I stand on the soft oatmeal carpet, staring at myself in the mirror in silent disbelief—*what kind of joke is this* —

then in a moment of hysteria I know it's all my fault, my problem: I'm a failure, a loser, a woman who can't draw straight lines. I sit on the side of the tub, hands covering my face, imagining people staring at me, eyes widening, mouths open, and suddenly I'm crying convulsively, gasping and hyperventilating, unable to stop. But deep beneath the crying is a rage so frightening, so huge, I don't dare let it out. It's the kind of rage that demands destruction, smashing my hand through glass, breaking furniture, cutting myself with scissors. And yet I hold this rage back, keep it like an ugly dress in my closet—I won't use it until I have to—and call my mother instead.

"What am I going to do?" I ask, sniffling into the phone. "I'm so ugly I don't know what to do." I imagine Mother's face, cautious at first, her eyebrows drawn together in suspicious concern as I attempt to make the horror real, to pull her down with me into the damp basement of my despair, until quite suddenly, a look of absorption defines her. Her voice softens; attention lingers. No matter about the roast beef in the oven, the laundry that needs to be sorted. Then, only then, is she mine. And yet even as I'm crying, I know this is slightly artificial as if I'm an actor in a play, fulfilling a familiar role while hovering just above me is a black cloud of disgust, the red fever of fury.

"You'll just have to go back to the dermatologist," Mother says in a soothing voice. Even hearing her, I feel some of the tension spill from my shoulders, dropping like a weight to the floor. I relax a little into the couch. "I'm sure he'll put you on several weeks of antibiotics." She sounds calm and sensible. "And then you must be patient because the antibiotics will take a few days to start working." Mother reassures me that my skin will get better, that the doctor will know what to do, that I can call her anytime. "I'm sorry this is happening to you, honey, but please try not to worry."

Relief floods through me. It's not my fault. I'm not to blame. "Sorry this is happening to you," Mother actually said, and I replay this sentence again and again in my head, sighing and repeating, *I'm not the subject. I didn't cause this. It's not my fault. It will take only a few days to heal.* And like a pricked balloon, all the rage leaks out as I crawl into bed, pulling the covers over my head, lying in the dark, waiting for the doctor's appointment tomorrow, waiting dumbly for rescue.

"It's probably hormonal," the doctor says, staring blandly at my face, pressing his hand against my cheek. He pushes my nose to one side, squinting at the ring of blackheads there. "It's probably the result of going off the strong birth control pill."

Even I see the irony of this: my hair fell out because I was *on* the pill; now my face breaks out because I went *off* the pill. But who cares about irony? All I want to do is slap someone, but who is there to slap?

"But we can't be sure," he says, looking now with curiosity at my thin body as if there's something I'm hiding he wants to see. "It could be stress." He strokes his chin absentmindedly, pressing again at my cheek. "Regardless, it'll take six months to a year to clear up," he says as if predicting the weather. "You've got that sensitive kind of skin."

Numb, I go to the pharmacy and fill my prescriptions, then drive home and cook a big pot of spinach. Not even fresh spinach, but the frozen kind, stiff and unpoetic in its hard white packages. I don't know why I choose spinach. Perhaps because it helped Popeye. Perhaps because there's no reason to be rational and pragmatic any longer. Now there's something dark and dense shadowing my life, a primitive curse, and for weeks, I don't allow myself to think about the shadow, but live like an automaton: showering in the early morning darkness, going to class (who cares now about straight lines!), coming home, eating spinach, then calling my mother. After Mother and I sign off, I drink a gulp of tequila, flinching as I feel the heat of the liquor going down my throat, settling in my stomach like a splash of tenderness; then I lie on my bed, tipsy and strangely content, letting myself drift off to a dreamless sleep.

But one night I don't drink the tequila. Instead, I take off all my clothes and face the mirror, seeing what I already know to be true: my breasts are never big enough to attract attention. With my bandanna off, my hair's so thin you can see my scalp; but worse to me is the acne that spreads in flowery clusters across each cheek. I stare and stare into the mirror, moving in for a close-up, then pulling back, trying to wish all the ugliness away, believing I can will myself into relief. I close my eyes and wait. I touch my toes so that when I look in the mirror, my face is flushed with color. But it makes no difference. There's only the fire of welts and bumps and swollen blackheads, the fine fuzz of thinning hair. Embarrassed, I quickly put my clothes back on and sit in the dark, knowing these are symptoms, deficits, but the THING is deeper still, this ugliness a sign of my internal confusion, my self-disgust. Though I've never admitted it before, I know there's nothing underneath me, nothing holding me up. The only thing inside me is a voracious hunger for praise, a furious rage at failure. Later it will occur to me this ridiculous need for approval is a kind of addiction, chock full of obsession and self-destruction, exhilaration and greedy shame. Like any addict, I never let myself see the whole picture, never admit I'm using my mother's sympathy the way an alcoholic uses drink: to whisk away the bad feelings and substitute artificial hope. I never tell myself that approval is ephemeral and the only way to have it is to give it to myself.

And of course, it never occurs to me to see a psychologist, to admit there's anything wrong other than physical distress. Part of my training is to tough it out, to whine and carry-on, but to keep moving forward, improving myself. Most days I rush from my apartment to class then back to my apartment, wearing a bandanna, looking with awe at the Venus of Willendorf projected onto the screen then dully at the candy wrappers and squashed gum on the floor. I don't dare look at anyone else. At home I try to finish my final project in interior design, sketch new patterns for Sister Mary's silk screen class, and read art history, but in the middle of the Mycenaean culture, I jump up to check the mirror, to see if anything's changed. When I glance at my reflection, I'm so ashamed, I take out three of the four light bulbs surrounding the bathroom mirror so that I'll see myself only as a dim, shadowy figure emerging from the bath. I decide my *real* self has left my body, has paused just beyond me, waiting for a reason to return while this imposter self is merely standing in, drawing in my notebook, doing projects, taking up slack. I live this deceit for several weeks until one morning I step into shimmery sunlight, the sky motionless, cold, the shadow of my life coming starkly into focus. *Maybe this is your real life. Maybe this is all there is.*

I can't move. I think at first that I'll have to yell for someone to insert the key into the door, then help me lie down on my bed, moving each leg quickly, quietly onto the mattress. I won't notice the dirty clothes on the floor, the dust on the lamp shade. I won't notice the dull silence, the absence of sound. I will only ask whoever it is to call my mother. "Tell her to come get me," I'll say, and then I'll fade into unconsciousness. Right in the middle of these thoughts, I jerk awake and walk to my car. I'm suddenly determined to leave school, but to do this—at least *this*—on my own. Still, I'm afraid to ask Sister Mary, the taciturn nun who teaches our silk screen class (she's on sabbatical from her Catholic university in Minnesota), for permission to leave the semester early. I'm sure she'll see ugliness as a superficial excuse for escape, a sign of my spiritual weakness rather than my emotional collapse. Yet when I approach her with the possibility, she takes one look at my face and says, "Fine."

I'm shocked, and as suddenly, angry. I turn quickly so she won't see my surprise. Secretly I despise her terse suggestions, her sharp-edged designs. Regardless of her permission, I'm determined to complete the semester, and I live that weekend in the art building, finishing my final silk-screen print—a primitive ogee pattern printed on coarse burlap; I eat yogurt in the hallways while breathing in the heavy fumes of inks and dyes, and turn in my final drawings to Mrs. DeVinnis, no longer determined to defy her.

On Monday, packed and exhausted, I leave Knoxville forever, rushing towards the flat, pine-studded vistas of Alabama, entering my parents home and my girlhood bed with relief and dread, stunned that everything inside me has stopped.

Oddly enough, relief comes from my dermatologist. He's a quirky little man, stubby-faced and blunt about everything, recently becoming an artist in his own right. He talks obsessively about this new discovery as if medicine is only a sideline, a day job while art is transcendent, a reward. He's what I call a "hands-on" derma-tologist, his fingers mashing zits like my mother used to do to my brother, leaving me lumpy and bruised, blood crusting my face as I stumble out of his office, hiding in the elevator, then out to my car. Yet while he works, we talk about the "pots he's throwing" or the design commissions I'll soon be getting, a conspiracy I allow myself because it's easier to talk about work than about myself. In fact, he never says a word about my face or hair, acting as if the way I look is irrelevant. Every day he sees teenagers with perma-nent acne, "real craters" that will doom them to scars and wrin-kles, while I'm a mere "pizza face," one of the temporaries, my acne hormonal, a physiological adjustment I'll have to suffer for a year or so until my system comes back into balance. Every other Thursday I sit in his waiting room, feeling both relief and panic as I stare at the young kids whose faces bloom even in the dim, interior light as they sit glumly on the couches, thumbing through old magazines.

When I come home from his office, I closet myself in my room, drawing the drapes, shying away from mirrors as well as from any contact with my parents. My face is puffy, disfigured, red welts forming where the pimples have been lanced. Sometimes I put ice inside a washcloth and hold it to my face, the cold a sudden searing pain turning quickly to numbness.

One Thursday, Mother invades this private landscape, standing backlit in my doorway, rubbing a Kleenex in her hands. "Why don't you wear a little make-up to cover up your bumps," she says cheerfully as if this might be *just the answer.* "Everybody wears it now. The women in your father's family wouldn't dream of coming to the breakfast table without first putting on their face."

"And that's *all* they bring to the breakfast table," I sneer, hunching deeper into my pillows. Of course, I know next to nothing about the women in my father's family, but to me, Mother's suggestion is a contradiction in terms: make-up is meant to emphasize your beauty, not hide your flaws; any suggestion to the contrary seems heretical.

"You never try to help yourself," Mother says, twisting her Kleenex into a knot. "There's no reason you should make things harder than they are."

"You're ruining that Kleenex." I point to the wad in her hands. "And besides, things couldn't get any worse." Like most idealists, I believe in the purity of terms. I am ugly and deserve no disguise. I will not wear make-up. I will not please my mother. This is the closest we've come to talking about what's happening to me and though I never initiate discussion, I resent that such silence prevails. In my secret fantasies, Mother takes me back to the place of childhood intimacy where I lived a marsupial life. Now I say shamelessly, "I don't want any advice. I just want to sleep."

Relenting, Mother dims the overhead lights. "Well, try to get some sleep, honey. This will all be over with soon."

Though I long to have faith in Mother's prediction, to see myself soar beyond adversity's reach, I know in my heart that the antecedent of "this" includes not only the ugliness of my body, but that unacknowledged fear of identity that's buried inside me like a seed.

As I lie in my girlhood bed—the drapes drawn, the room dark though it's the middle of the day—I know I'll have to kill a part of myself so that another part can live. But which part? Which part needs to die? It's this question that obsesses me, confounds me, this act of surgery I must perform on myself. Frightened, I lie absolutely still in my bed, waiting for the house to settle.

Later that night while Mother and Daddy are sleeping at the other end of the hall, I tiptoe into the living room and sit cross-legged on the couch, trying to remember the girl I once was. I stare at the grand piano which floats in the shadows, its luster hidden by the quiet darkness of the room. I've always loved that piano even though I've no particular talent for music. I can't hear rhythms, have no ear for pitch or tone or the inflection of mood; I seem to have inherited a tin ear, a sliced mushroom fitted against the side of my head. But even more than loving the piano, I remember being frightened of performing, staring at my hands as if they were foreign bodies—jellyfish stingers, lobster claws, frog legs—incapable of manipulating those smooth ivory keys. In the early afternoon on his day off, Daddy often asked my sister and me to play for one of his doctor friends, either Dr. Coleman, an OB/GYN, who was learning French and spoke foreign phrases with a boozy Southern accent, or Dr. Fogel, the radiologist, stout and dark, who went on hunting trips with my father each fall and smelled of Cuban cigars.

One spring day when the sky opened up and bled a steady torrent of water like a celestial leak, Dr. Coleman's car was parked in our drive. As we drove in behind him, rain dripped from the eaves of the house, gushed down the water pipes, flooding Mother's caladiums and irises and all the low spots in the yard. I rushed in the house, wanting only to pull off my wet socks and shoes then go splashing through the puddles in the park or to curl up in bed with a book, stuffing oatmeal cookies in my mouth. But coming in the door, closing up my umbrella, I heard the voices of men in the den, Daddy and his doctor friend. Almost immediately, Daddy asked my sister and me to play something for them, a look that said *Please, girls. Right now.*

I stared out the window, peering into the blinding rain, praying for a thunderstorm with lights blinking and limbs breaking. There would be frogs croaking beneath the branches, the grass glistening with moisture, the fold of the land deepened by shallow lakes of steaming water. "I've been paying for piano lessons for four years," Daddy's voice brought me back to the present, and immediately I sat down while Dr. Coleman stood at my side, drink in hand, *observing* (I imagined) my technique. He stood close, his eyes keen, smokeblue behind thick glasses. His body was short and husky, but he carried it lightly, almost like a dancer. I could feel his breath across my face as I played Debussy's "To a Wild Rose," a simple but haunting piece which surely would have pleased English ladies after tea. When I finished, my sister chose something complex and tuneless by Bach.

After our performance, Daddy, oddly silent, got up to fix another drink, while Dr. Coleman, after swallowing the last sip of his bourbon, asked if we knew anything by Mozart or Grieg. He sat down on the bench with us and fingered the keys, starting a melody and asked my sister if she knew a particular contemporary composer, someone who had recently given a concert in Mobile. I knew I should listen; I might learn something valuable, a clue to sophistication. And yet while he talked, I looked out at the rain-flooded yard, watching the steady drill of rain bend the branches of the pine trees, their arms hanging down in defeat. More than anything I wanted to be outside, sloshing around in the puddles, splashing water at the squirrels. I saw myself twirling in the yard, the rain cleansing me, baptizing me, washing the outside away. If only I could rush out into the rain, I'd be happy, whole, and yet something restrained me as if I were imprisoned, detained, my heart a frozen stone in my chest.

What held me inside that house?

Now in the darkened living room, I want to tear these restrictions apart, to know precisely what held me back. Are these old inhibitions part of the war? Was I just too timid to rush out into the rain, and if so was that my nature, or had something slyly inserted itself between desire and enactment? I try to think about this rationally, to remember myself as a child staring out the window, and yet what comes to me isn't my life at all, but a vivid image of my mother at fifteen sitting in small white church in Praco in a red crocheted dress, a hymn book in her lap. It's a story she told me once and as she spoke, I saw something furious and sad behind her eyes; remembering it, I snuggle deeper into the couch, having no idea what this memory has to do with me.

"I made myself a special dress," Mother said years ago, "because I wanted something beautiful, something all my own, not hand-me-downs or dresses bought at the commissary." She became friends with a woman in the community who taught her how to crochet. Who knows what this woman might have been like? And yet I imagine her with the dry smell of talcum powder in her bosom, a widow with clean floors and rickety chairs, whose hands fly with the needle. Ecstatic, my mother bought red thread and began to crochet a dress. I can see her working at the dining room table, her head bent, her eyes intent on the pattern while fireflies flicker outside in the dark. She leaves the room of bothersome children, of too much noise and too little hope, and steps back into another world where she's both dainty and bold, wearing a dress that announces her worth to the world. Many Saturday nights she works, creating her dress inch by inch until it has length and shape, with little caps of sleeve that float like petals across her upper arms.

When she first tries it on, her mother glances briefly at her and nods, not exactly approval but tacit acceptance. Of course, the only place she has to show off this dress is at church, the little white framed building that sits on a clearing just beyond the red dirt hills, the steep, graveled road.

In my mind the day is warm, the wildflowers in bloom up on the hill. Maybe Mother wishes she could pick the blue violets or the marigolds to take with her, a vivid contrast to her red dress. She walks carefully, trying to avoid the clouds of dust that blow across the road when the wind springs up. The day is fair, with slanted lines of sunshine, clouds drifting idly across the sky. Mother enters the church with a sassy step, pride awakened in her body, her dress new and bold. As she walks up the aisle, she imagines entering a larger world, having the confidence to stand straight and tall. She's never known what it's like not to be ashamed, not to feel confused by the sensations of her body, but today the very air seems to caress her. Her shoulders are small, her breasts rounded, her legs shapely and strong. She sits in the pew beside her brothers and sisters, feeling the first hint of vanity and pride. In the quiet of the church everything is amplified, sounds and smells and even the swelling of her own dreamy heart. When she stands to sing, she's aware of women behind her, two old women with rough skin and heavy legs, stalwarts of the community who sit in judgment of everyone else. She imagines their awe; *they* will never be young again; *they* will never be beautiful girls in red dresses with stars in their eyes. And with the sound of the organ, she lifts her voice to the ceiling and sings:

Sweet riv-ers of re-deem-ing love. Lie just before mine eye,
Had I the pin-ions of a dove, I'd to those riv-ers fly;

After the song, the women stir behind her, rustling their programs, smoothing their skirts. One sighs as if making amends to Jesus then leans over to her friend to mumble in a too-loud whisper, "That poor child. . . wearing that ugly red dress." The air heats up, becomes magnetic. My mother, frozen, presses her back against the thick wood of the pew.

"It's a shame," the other says. "She looks so pathetic, all homemade and not. Her mother don't know no better."

And then the clincher. "All those children!"

Now Mother is no longer breathing. But her eyes do the work: she looks down at the carefully created stitches, the red threads interwoven, worked with such loving care. Through the stitches she can see bare skin. Her flesh! For the first time, she notices that the dress sags on one side, drifting to the left, the stitches uneven, some clumsy and thick, others tight and thin. Now as she looks at the dress, its loveliness is dragged right out of her. All she sees are her brothers and sisters, that great long line of them, straggling and poor and shamed, lolling behind her ever-pregnant mother.

As I imagine my mother's embarrassment, a dark fury surges inside me. I want to protect her from ever feeling such shame again. I want to save my mother so that she can continue to save me. It's not a new thought but suddenly I'm on an elevator slamming to the ground, shaking up everything inside. Tremors rush through my body. *I want to save my mother.* My body is loose, light, as if I might drift into the air. *Is that it?* Have I been living a life based on my mother's humiliation, trying to overcome and redeem us both? *You must be appropriate at all costs, mindful of the codes of respectability and achievement. That alone is the road to entitlement!* And I've interpreted this sanction literally: You must stay inside and perform. You must work longer and harder than anyone else for sacrifice alone can save your mother! Outside there's nothing but rain and puddles, nothing but the pleasure of twirling in the storm, the relinquishment of pressure, release to the physical world. I stand up and stare into the empty darkness. For a moment the air coagulates and then dissolves back into just air. And I say these words out loud: *My ambition is not even my own.* I'm still merged with the ugliness of Praco, the skimpy red dress, the old coats, the bad teeth, all the monsters of the past. But if I don't have these things to hold close, what will I believe in?

This thought so frightens me I barely hear the little voice that says, "Yourself." But that's impossible. Everything in me has broken down. Been erased. Besides, I need something bigger than myself: I need the rage and fury of the past to give me grit; I need the dirt and dust, the heat and bugs. I need to believe in hell!

Exhausted, I slump back on the couch, too tired to listen to the voice that comes up through a fog of memory. "You have to let go."

"What?" I ask as if my unconscious is another person, someone I might not trust.

"You have to let go and get on with it."

But I'm not quite ready. I slump deeper into the couch as if burying myself inside a cocoon. I'm not ready to breathe my own oxygen, to tear the slats of my crib. No, I'm still a bald-headed baby waiting for the next transfusion. My mother once saved me and now I must save her, at least the part of me that *is* her. Or do I?

I see the girl afraid to splash through puddles, the girl who longs to keep her mother safe so that mother will eventually save her. This past is a second skin. Now I have to step out of it, cut it away as if freeing myself from the lining of a dress. But how can I do that when I'm ugly and penniless, when everything that's held me up has been lost?

I begin to grope in the darkness, feeling my way through the house. I find the circuitous path to the door. I am close, so close. "Open it," a voice says. "You have to walk out the door."

I don't know how long I stand there. I may have slept for awhile, curled up on the white sofa. When I wake I look outside the window where morning light pierces the sky. Dew spreads across the ground and fog circles the bank of trees. I see the limbs of an old oak tree swagged beneath a heap of Spanish moss, swaying gently in the breeze. I remember reading somewhere that the moss is a rootless parasite that will eventually kill the tree, yet as the fog lifts and the pale sky brightens, I stand silently staring at it. In the sudden light, I think it's beautiful.

city of angels

1977. LOS ANGELES

I don't think anyone fully resolves a troubled past. Certain pieces of the self come unraveled, never to be reclaimed. Other pieces are amputated, useful only with a prosthesis. New pieces come to fruition as if they've been grafted on and you wear them warily, hesitant of ownership. But some unflinching part of the self survives, wounded but hungry to define itself again and again and again.

That's the part that got me out the door.

After a year in Atlanta, then Birmingham, I move to Los Angeles to study art. It's the first act of independence I've taken in years, and though the war isn't over, the advantage has shifted, making me alert, determined to survive. I'm not saved, but like Lazarus, I've risen from my bed. I've chosen a direction.

West.

Driving into that madhouse of L.A. traffic, I'm first stunned and then thrilled by the throbbing motion of the freeways, a mesmerizing movement which seems to go on and on into infinity as if people here have so much energy they have to wear themselves out. Colors are saturated—neon pink, Valentine red, fluorescent blue—rather than faded and worn as they are in Alabama. There's nothing chaste, nothing hidden. It's all out in the open under an impersonal sky. By now my hair's grown back in; I wear it long and curly, no need for a bandanna or wig. My skin's cleared up and I turn this new face to the morning sun. No make-up. Not even a smudge of mascara. I'm as pure as an Easter lily blooming in secret soil. I roll down the window, letting the hot, dry air lift my hair from my shoulders and toss it around.

I've come here by a series of moves—flitting from apartment to apartment in Birmingham, teaching classes at museums, working in fussy boutiques, sewing curtains and dust ruffles, mounting flat, thick-painted pieces of art—until finally I applied to UCLA and Florida State University. Florida State was my safety net, a school that offered a master's degree in gifted education, but the MFA program in Art and Design was where I wanted to be.

"I don't want you to go so far away," Mother said one day when I'd come home for a weekend visit. "It's just too far. You know how you always like to come home."

What she said was true. After my breakdown, my parents' home seemed the only place that was safe, a neutral retreat, the familiar net of my past surrounding me, enclosing me. And yet I wanted to study art. I'd sit in my old girlhood room plugged into the catalogue of courses and feel as if someone had given me an extra pull of oxygen.

"Go to Los Angeles," my brother—now a lawyer in Mobile— said the next day at lunch. He took a swig of iced tea, looking intently at me. "That's what I'd do." I was shocked at his statement, but pleased, taking it as an act of faith. Though I hadn't been close to him for most of my life it surprised me how relieved I was to have his support.

"You think so?" I asked.

"Absolutely."

A lightness surrounded me. If he thought I could go, then what was holding me back except my own fear of the dark?

With this small encouragement and my father's agreement to help with expenses, I left.

The early days in Los Angeles are blurred by the unrelenting sun, but the nights are burned into my memory: pink with smog, a luxurious spread of dust and heat. Looking out over the palm trees, you can see the particles drifting, floating, lingering in the air. Jacaranda trees sway in the breeze, the fronds twitching as if an animal's scurrying up their trunks. Beyond the trees, the lights of the city blink on in a carnival of brightness. I stand at my apartment window and see the night come awake, a rosy smog alive only at the rim of the world. As I watch, I feel hopeful, trusting; in exile I believe I can create myself.

When I walk into the art building at UCLA I'm met by a stack of canvases, bulky sculptures, padded design tables, and a double row of looms. No one's ever recommended art or the creative life to me. At best, art is suspect, subversive; at worst, it's a marketable decoration, something to sell in boutiques. I'll never forget that the mother of one of my friends had a Picasso print retouched to match her sofa or that neighbors make driftwood lamps and decoupaged trash cans. No, it's better to be a doctor, a lawyer, a teacher, something practical, marketable, while art—well, that lies in the wild zone, the archaic, the untamed, the irresponsible. Worse, this is the period when conceptual art is at its craziest: one of my professors, Chris Burden, shot himself in the arm to explore the nature of pain. Several years earlier he'd locked himself in a school locker for two days, scrunched up in that small, singular space with only food and water, a hole cut in the bottom, a bucket in the locker beneath. It became a sort of midnight confessional with people wandering in late at night to tell their fears, their worries, the dark edges of their stories to a man hidden inside a metal cage. Another professor shaved her head in protest of the beauty myth, then flew from airport to airport to record people's responses (this long before the baldness of chemotherapy was publicly discussed). The artwork at UCLA is autobiographical, political, self-conscious, irreverent, and students and faculty remind me of the kids from Organic School, only now they're older, freakier, driven by a confessional lust for exposure.

To my surprise I adjust quickly to UCLA, working steadily at the studio, going to galleries on Melrose and Robertson, and to Market Street in Venice where everyone's barefoot, dressed in the briefest of clothes. As I watch, a skater swivels in and out of the pedestrians, wearing a bikini with fringe splashed across her breasts. The fringe sways with her movements, back and forth, back and forth, in a mesmerizing frenzy. I can't imagine being dressed like this, but in several months, I barely notice. On weekends there are always performances: Alvin Ailey, Meredith Monk, Philip Glass, Tom Waits, a Mamet play, a Beckett play, lectures on Modernism, Gertrude Stein, Hemingway. I feel as if I've been famished and am presented with a feast.

But mostly what I do is work, silk-screening felt and linen, manipulating pieces into sculptural forms, some with hard-edged preciseness, others collapsed with a kind of rip-and-tear punctuation complete with burned edges and frayed corners. Often I stay late in the studio so I can talk to Beth, who appears about 9:00 with her dog, Kipper, a half-breed German shepherd that follows her everywhere.

"C'mon, boy," Beth says and Kipper plops down by her loom. "Thata boy," she whispers, scratching deep inside his coat until he groans. "Good boy." Kipper sighs and settles contentedly into sleep.

I sit across from Beth in the weaving lab, straddling a bench, my own loom threaded with coarse string and jute. Beth's loom is still covered in a sheet and together we fold it so she can get to work. Every night Beth works from nine until midnight when she and Kipper both climb inside her van and settle in for the night. They have special places to park, in driveways and parking lots, permission given from friends and institutions.

"Wanna cup?" Beth asks, holding out an empty mug.

I nod as Beth measures out coffee, plugs in her pot. With her, I'm completely relaxed as she talks about her work, her life, even her mother's suicide, a fact that always jars me to attention. "You know, my mother was depressed all of my life," she says tonight, not looking at me, waiting for the coffee to perk. She seems solemn, sad, her face sallow in the overhead lights, old acne scars making her look older, wiser. I turn towards the windows, breathing deeply, the smell of eucalyptus flooding the room. I love it when Beth tells me about her life. It makes me feel normal, though I never say a word about my own family or what I'm frightened of. "In some ways Mother just wasn't there at all," Beth continues, wiping out her favorite blue cup. "My sister was the one who tried to take care of Mother, but she also had to take care of me because my mother just couldn't. Of course, when my sister left for college, Mother and I were pretty hopeless." Beth laughs. "We couldn't get meals together or coordinate the laundry. It was just like living in my van. You can see I was brought up to live this life, to fit myself into whatever cubbyhole I could find." She talks about her family as if they've left years ago, and she's an orphan with Kipper, though on weekends she often drives north into the mountains to visit her sister. She seems happy, content with her choices, and I watch her constantly, trying to detect signs of despair. But Beth remains unflappable, steady in her desires. "Art's my home now," she says, looking at the pictures of moss-covered bark she's tacked over her loom. "Art and Kipper."

That first year in L.A. I too make a home in the art department, staying late in the studio, helping other students when they get in a bind, talking to Beth. I surprise myself by being happy in this place where students walk around at all hours, paint and sawdust clinging to their clothes, where the talk always comes back to art.

When Beth isn't there I run up to fifth floor to see Annie, the lanky blonde painter from New York who paints surfers, beach boys, "my brave little hunks," she calls them, laughing, sliding her hands seductively down her suntanned thighs. Pictures of surfers collide with snapshots of street life in Manhattan, the only place besides L.A. that Annie's ever lived. "Ground Control to Major Tooooooomm" oozes out of her tape deck and seems to vibrate the air; when I knock, Annie puts down her brush and stands for a minute looking at the perspective, a surfer careening off the frame of her painting, the wave just beneath him so real it makes you feel he's riding it to the edge of the world. "Does *not* love me," she says, sticking out her tongue.

Sometimes when I leave Annie's studio, I take the elevator down to first floor to work in the photography studio. Being there is like being inside a cool, dark cave, the smell of chemicals making my nostrils pinch as I move into one of the darkrooms. After exposing an image, I stare intently at the transformation, the print emerging gradually as if it's acquiring a soul. Mostly I shoot self-portraits, close-ups of my face, trying to find something I've sensed the edge of, but have been unable to capture before. Sometimes it comes across as dreamy rapture, other times what emerges is the cynical smirk of a skeptic. I become obsessed with these pictures, printing them larger and larger until I can see, floating in the fix, the curious question in my eye staring back at me.

I work steadily, as steeped in solitude as I used to be when roaming Mama Dot's woods. There I watched birds and trees, the shape of a leaf, a trembling drop of moisture sliding down my arm. Here I'm studying the intensity of expression on my face. One night I develop a print that I call my Caddy Compson photo: my face turned to the side, gaze downcast. Waves of hair veil my cheeks; a white collar is crushed against my throat. This girl seems reckless and damned, ready to flame, one eye in shadow, the other just waiting for a dare.

That night as I walk out of the studio I feel as if I'm re-entering the world. I stop in the darkness beside my car, looking up at the faint glimmer of stars. Maybe this is all I need: a darkroom, my face, and solitude.

Something is happening to me in Los Angeles, something I can't quite make sense of, something I've never felt before, or at least, haven't felt with such intensity. It's a sense of goodness, an inner radiance soaring through my body, moving from my toes up through my legs, my stomach, my chest, my throat, and spilling out of my pores. In certain moments I'm lighter than air. I can move in any direction, see any sight, think any thought and it will be the right one. When it happens, I'm often alone, walking towards the ocean, sending the sand spraying out from my feet, or just getting out of the shower, water still dripping from my body. I believe the goodness has come to me as a gift, and in these moments it wipes out all the badness I've believed to be there, all that wretched self-abasement, that insistent loneliness that makes me rush out of my apartment just so I won't have to be by myself. I want to find a way to release the goodness more often, but of course, I never do. It happens only spontaneously, maybe because I forget to think about what's wrong with me, what's hurting, biting me in the ass.

When I first got to L.A., I took the bus from my apartment into Westwood, got off to run some errands, then caught the bus back to my apartment. On the ride back, in the middle of a group of anonymous people, people not paying the slightest attention to me, I felt the whole world open up. I looked out the window at the rather predictable California landscape and saw not square box bungalows and apartment buildings but eucalyptus trees and bougainvillea and hibiscus, not endless highways but little neighborhoods tucked into side streets with ivy crawling up the porch railings and kids' bicycles lying sprawled in the grass. It was a moment of bliss. Perhaps that's all these moments are: the sudden insistence of hope, not artificial hope, but something new that's burning through me. I'm living in a new place—a world as far from southern tradition as I can get—and art seems, at least at the beginning, clean.

At the end of the first semester, all the graduate students hang their art in studios so that faculty and other graduate students can wander in and look at the work. The faculty, of course, comes by to conference with you, to critique the work and discuss its possibilities, considering what courses you might take, which artists you should look at, what techniques might be worth fooling around with. I remember being very nervous that day as I look at the two pieces I've hung in an empty classroom, the California sun blazing through the slats in the blinds, forming thin rectangles of light on the floor. The first is a textile that looks like some cross between a topographical map and the skin of an animal. It's rough, irregular (the edges frayed, burned), visceral, and it practi-

cally covers one entire wall. Beside it is a hanging so totally different it seems inconceivable that the same person could have made
them both. The second piece is a four by five foot rectangle, a
low-relief sculptural piece that looks as if it's been apprenticed by
Agam. Its dominant colors are various shades of red bleeding into
yellows and turquoises, each tiny piece silk-screened, cut up, and
reassembled so that the assemblage forms both a sculptural relief
and a movement of color. I've worked with such fever on these
pieces I have no idea of their worth or success, but now when I
look at the "skin" piece, I see it needs more textural movement,
more of the delicate overlays I've become fascinated with. The
sculptural piece is more successful, but I like it less. A weaving
project remains unfinished on my loom, though I've stayed up
many nights, alongside Betty, trying to complete it, getting a rash
from the raffia all up and down my arms.

Standing there looking at these pieces, I wonder if there's any
chance of success, or if I'm just fooling myself. All I'm certain of is
that making them consumed me, got me high in the way drugs
are supposed to do, but now that the pieces are practically finished
I'm blind to them. Clueless.

When the faculty comes in—four professors in the Design
Department—my body feels light enough to toss out the window.
I try to listen as one of my professors, an exceptionally beautiful
woman artist who graduated from Cranbrook several years before,
begins to talk. She critiques the textures, the lines, the way the
movement is working, "a sensuous, serpentine rhythm, the background fading into the foreground . . . almost Oriental," she says.
I barely hear her words; instead I watch her face which seems to
be saying she's pleased. The men talk too, getting up close, then
moving back to stand as far away from the pieces as they can get.
As they talk, slowly I bring my body back into the room. I'm alert
and curious now, all the panic gone, and I'm surprised when I

hear my mentor saying, "We'll want this piece for the show . . . it should be prominently displayed."

Excitement ripples down my spine.

That night I come home late from the studio to find my roommate entertaining a friend of hers, a playwright and director, who is directing a play at one of the many theaters in Los Angeles. They are standing in the kitchen when I come in, hungry, tired, longing only to fix myself some supper and read in bed. But when I see the man's face—olive skinned with dark, expressive brown eyes—something softens inside me and I want to rush up and kiss him. If only I could kiss him the day would be complete. I talk with the two of them briefly, then take a shower, putting on my nightgown, getting into bed. But I have one of those moments . . . a luminous, prescient moment when I'm lighter than air, floating around the room, seeing and feeling everything even as I'm contained within this body. Art seems to me a world of promise where what has been lost can be reclaimed, the past no longer a noose, but a treasure chest of images and ideas. Or perhaps I've finally learned—as Father McCown suggested—to be still and listen. As I turn on my bedside lamp and pull out a book to read, I'm conscious of the cool air rushing through the open window, the halo of light beside my bed, and the veiled quality of goodness that surrounds me, protects me.

When I hear a knock on my door, I know it's the playwright. At that moment it seems only right that he should knock on my door. I sit up. "Come in."

He apologizes for bothering me, but asks if he can speak to me for just a minute. As he comes nearer, I feel golden, as if everything inside me is shining through. "I just have to look at you," he says softly. "I just had to see if you are real. I thought you were an angel."

And in that moment, I am.

Weeks later I step out of the art building into the brisk hustle of Los Angeles, where eucalyptus leaves rustle in the ocean breeze and the skeletons of buildings rise beneath the steady glare of a white, blistering sky. But what I see are Mother and Daddy in the kitchen in the early morning hours, Mother in her silk robe, a cup of coffee in one hand, her face bent to the morning paper, Daddy striding—dressed in a suit and tie—towards the coffee pot, pouring his first cup into a pristine white mug. "Cream?" Mother says, and without looking at him, passes the carton of Half-and-Half across the table. For minutes, they barely speak, merely shift the pages of the morning paper back and forth until Daddy says laconically, "One egg, fried," and Mother uncrosses her leg, clutches her robe as she gets up, tightening the silk sash which has loosened in sitting. It's only when I imagine Mother breaking the egg, her hands strong and certain, that a wave of homesickness washes over me, and I see not the palms and bougainvillea of southern California, but the sun-scorched fields of Alabama, the NEHI signs rising like scarecrows beneath a hazy sky, then the blue dawns of Magnolia Springs, the fleshy scent of magnolias drifting through the windows.

"Do Alabama," my friends keep saying when I tell them about the drive-in, the VFW club, about Mr. Smits and his black-caped women. "Tell your own story."

I'm horrified at such a thought. I believe that by choosing art I've chosen myself, set the course, cleaned out the closets and dusted the shelves. I don't want to see what remains in the dark. Instead of going home for Christmas, I go to New York, to galleries and shows, seeing Andy Warhol's Divine, a Joseph Beuys' retrospective, having coffee and pastries in Soho, walking deep into the dirty streets of the Bowery. As I wander around New York I realize that if Joseph Beuys can make art out of felt and fat because he was shot down in the Crimea and these substances helped save him, then I can make art out of the drive-ins and VFW club dances, the woods and rivers of Alabama. In a symbolic way these things helped save me too. It's the first time I admit that the context of place defines you both in history and art. It's the first time I recognize that exile can mean obsession. Now that I'm no longer in Alabama, no longer going to Sunday dinners of fried chicken and homemade biscuits, no longer hearing the "ya'll" of my culture, it stands out in stark relief. Until I left Alabama I hadn't thought much about being southern. I hadn't needed to because everyone around me inevitably was. But in Los Angeles and New York, I recognize that the South has its own "funny ways" that define how men and women act towards each other, how they perceive themselves.

By California standards, southern women look "put together," too formal, overdressed. Even prissy. By now I've discarded my nice southern clothes, my pants suits and linen trousers for jumpsuits, shorts, leotards, sandals and jeans. By summer, I'm convinced I've claimed myself and in a fit of nostalgia, plan a three-week trip back to Foley, to a town that hasn't changed much in fifteen years, except that the potato sheds have been torn down and a new redlight added on Highway 98. Candy, the one-armed taxi-driver still parks his cab in front of Wright's Drugs and Mr. Smits still teaches the telephone operators how to shoot a gun.

The first week I'm home, Mother and I accompany Daddy to a medical conference in New Orleans; I'm thrilled at the thought of finding new items for collages, voodoo dolls and Cajun menus, Creole lace and gambling dice. On the drive, I can close my eyes and smell the thick odors of chickory coffee mixed with the musty stink of garbage. Of course, it's also the place I can look the worst in the world, my hair frizzed into a crown of tight knots by the sultry air, the humidity so high the air feels as wet as rain. I used to get depressed by the sheer ugliness of my hair, the way my bangs frizzed, the sides kinked, but I tell myself I'll be different this time, no longer using my hair as a barometer for my moods.

In New Orleans, the heat is searing but the humid air sweet to my skin after a year's worth of desert dryness. When my hair begins to fuzz, instead of worrying so much, I get out my camera and take pictures in Jackson Square of the wisteria and honeysuckle vines, the con artists working the tourists, the women in large hats, shading themselves from the sun, men holding up a newspaper to their eyes. At the hotel, Mother and I unpack, have lunch with Daddy, then decide to wait until the sun's gone down before venturing out again. While I swim in the hotel pool, Mother washes her hair and Daddy studies his course material for the conference on geriatric health care.

I remember sitting before the dressing table at our hotel, staring at a golden sun melting into the white haze of the horizon. While watching the sun sink below the city, I wind my wet hair into a bun. I've changed into a tight, stretchy leotard, running shorts and tennis shoes and now stand before the mirror, assessing myself. I'm particularly proud that I can jump out of the hotel pool and dress quickly, not bothering with the usual fifty minute ritual of female beauty. I'm excited that the acne is gone, that I'm whole and clean. I lean closer and swab my bare face with Refresher, removing any trace of chlorine. Indeed I'm different. I look like a Southern California girl, taut, bare, athletic; I could have been rushing out to the art department or to the corner store to buy a magazine. I know that my parents and I will meet again to dress for dinner, Mother and I in expensive dresses, Daddy in a good suit and tie, but for now I'm ready to scavenge. Excited, I don't see Daddy standing in the doorway, his tie loosened, a bunch of papers in his grip. I cock my head in the mirror, aware only of the slight curve of my breasts beneath the stretchy fabric, my long legs tightly muscled, already freckled. "Daddy," I say, glancing up, smiling at him.

But he doesn't return my smile. He simply stares at me, his brows knit together in a peculiar frown. I should have seen this as a warning, a thunderstorm brewing, but since I've decided on this visit not to depend on approval, I'm much less wary. "Ready for your—"

"Christ," he interrupts, "you look like a whore!"

I don't move. When I look in the mirror I see a girl in a too-skimpy outfit—too much leg, too much skin—but simultaneously my mind spins out like a net capturing his words, translating them into words of my own: *I'll never please him.* I listen to the silence of the room, see my face ghost-white in the mirror. "What?" I ask, caught off-guard, a finger to my lips.

"You heard me."

I inhale a deep breath, then say quietly, "You don't know what you're talking about. You don't know what a whore is, what—"

Mother walks into the room, her hair in curlers, a strange irridescent blue cream smeared over her face. "Sure he does," she says, her voice like a small surgical drill boring into plaster.

For a brief moment I stare at both of them, ignored, irrelevant, the current of tension lifted above me, caught in the narrow grasp of their gaze. Then I run into the bathroom and slam the door, the old sense of shame rising like a tidal wave, washing over me, hiding the undertow of rage that lives just beneath the surface of my skin.

Daddy leaves immediately for his meeting and Mother, trying to calm me, takes me down to the restaurant, where, under her particular etiquette, we order iced tea and shrimp cocktails, the shrimp like little pink dancers hooked over the rim of the bowl. But I can't eat. "He should never have said that," I whisper. "I don't want to be punished for my looks." After moving to California I've tried to pay less attention to physical appearance, ignoring my usual scrutiny before the mirror, but in fact, I haven't detached at all, but simply moved in the opposite direction. This has been a test, a trial of my new persona, one I'm trying to nurture into existence. I look into the sympathy of Mother's face, pained and fixed with resignation, and it seems to me we both are victims of something we can't name. In the end, my mother's emotions are fueled by mine, and we leave New Orleans that afternoon, taking the car back to Alabama, letting my father find his own way home.

Three days later I know Daddy's gotten a ride home with other doctors but I haven't seen him since that afternoon in New Orleans. I'm staying with my sister, and as I sit in her bedroom, I remember the day we moved from the red clay hills of northern Alabama to the flat swampy fields of the south. Mother was still unpacking and had sent us to town for lunch. I sat with my father, brother and sister on the slick red seats of the Foley Cafe, seats which weren't quite high enough for me to reach the table. The waitress scurried by, putting down plastic glasses of water, handing out menus, calling my sister "honey" and "sugar," and smiling at me, her mouth red and full, beads of moisture spreading across her upper lip. When she left I moved forward to lift my glass, but my hand slipped on the plastic and water spilled down the table, splashing everywhere, even onto my father's pants' leg. "Jesus Christ!" Daddy said, and I felt myself grow huge, my head exploding towards the ceiling, my hands like baseball mitts. I stood above everyone, without language, without thought, a thousand wings beating against my chest.

Once again I'm huge, awkward, wrong. But this time I call Daddy's office and ask his nurse to put me on his calendar. This time, I'm determined to speak. The next day when I open the door to his office, I see him standing in the hall talking to a patient. Behind him, through the half-open door, the white flash of nurses' uniforms distracts me, the sounds of pain—"Aaah-aaagh"—and disease punctuate the air. "You've gotta fix this, Doc," I hear a patient say, holding out his arthritic hand which twists inward like a claw. I want to say the same thing. Am I not still the doctor's daughter, his flesh and blood? I've prepared my analysis: what we have is a conflict of style and generation—West Coast to Southern, 1970s to 1950s, Modern to Victorian. I intend to explain this eloquently, to say how we've both gotten it all mixed up like a Marx Brothers' skit, yet when I see his white-coated figure, so full of authority and ease, I feel like a swimmer, holding my breath, realizing I'll never make it to the end of the pool. He stands before me, arms crossed at his waist. He looks impatient as if he's been interrupted from the real demands of his day. "Please, Daddy," I say, trying to hurry, "I think you were being rude about my looks, but I wasn't thinking about how it's different here than in California. Women look so different. They wear lots of make-up and stuff. And they dress up so much. I always forget about that." Of course, I haven't forgotten at all, but I don't want to admit that this has been a test.

Nothing changes in his body. Not his mouth, his eyes, his hand. I watch for a signal, a comma to slip between my words, but I see nothing to stop me.

"You see, I was trying to hurry," I continue, "trying to get out on the street to see—" I'm about to say *art,* but when I glance up, his eyes remain opaque, and I sense something's hardened between us. I know he has patients waiting, that he'll be fretful until everyone has been seen. "—to see the street life," I say lamely.

Suddenly he leans forward, his knuckles cracking on the desk like the sound of pecans breaking open. I have no idea what he'll say, but his face is flushed; his stethoscope swings in the open air.

He looks intently at me and I can see the anger glinting from his eyes. "You were trying to embarrass me," he says.

"Oh, no," I begin. "Really, that's just what I—"

But he stops me with the palm of his hand, his lips tight against his teeth. Then something changes in him. He becomes cooler, more distant as if he's looking at me with a critical lens. He taps a finger against the desk, then says with a gravity of a judge delivering a verdict, "Don't come home until you can get your picture in the paper."

There are moments when the self breaks loose from reality, when it's spirited into another realm and looks back dispassionately at the scene. You watch yourself flinch and shudder, see your eyes deepen, intensifying, shooting forth little arrows of scorn. Your left shoelace is coming undone. There is a letter lying under the desk, highlighted by a seam of sunlight coming from the windows. You wonder at the slowness of everything, the sound of a nurse's footsteps moving closer and closer, the exhalation of your father's breath, the intercom calling "Dooooc-tor Fossss-terrrrr." You are watching as he turns, pivoting like a ballerina at the end of a dance, aware that you are rooted to the floor as if caught in a fresh layer of cement.

And then the moment snaps, and you're inside yourself, running, running out into the sun, throwing up with screams and black, useless words.

Getting off the airplane into the hot, dry winds of Los Angeles, I feel relief, glad to see the smog hanging thick and low on the horizon, drifting towards the Hollywood hills. With impatience I pick up my bags and get a taxi to a UCLA dorm; I've sublet my apartment for the month I planned to be in Alabama, and now must call this place home.

When I step into the dorm room and stare at the faded green

bedspread and scarred chest of drawers, the empty closet and pale yellow window shade, I'm frightened again. Looking down at my pale knees, at my feet against the green bedspread, I know I can't stay here. I jump up, grabbing my purse, and run out of the dorm before I can feel the terror swimming beneath the sadness. I know where I'll go. I want to dance.

At the dance studio in Venice, California, I lie on the mat while the instructor Ariel encourages us to feel our muscles lengthening as we stretch. "Let yourself leeen-gthen," she says softly, pulling the word out long and slow. I'm tight as a rope strung between two trees. I push myself to new limits, tightening my toes and widening my legs in a split.

"Lighten up," Ariel calls from across the room. "Don't forget to bbbbbreathe."

But I can't lighten up. My breath exhales in short spurts, shallow and dry. And in an hallucinatory dream I see a snake slither across the floor, moving with terrific speed. I'm so startled, I draw back, terrified. But in that moment I turn to stone. Only my eyes blink and I watch as the snake slides forward, curling around my ankle, circling the shaft of my leg, making a bracelet around my calf. Some invisible part of me tightens. Deeper still, I sense a shudder, a volcano of emotion stirring in the darkness. I want to pull myself into a knot, to fling the snake into the air. But my body will not move.

"Don't forget to bbbbbreathe," Ariel says again, looking straight at me.

By the end of the week my ankles swell like tree trunks as if I'm a victim of elephantiasis. By the second week I've moved back into my apartment, sleeping on the living room couch and crawling to the kitchen for supper, then back to my bed to prop up my swollen feet. They lie motionless before me, thick and formless as slugs. Although the doctors are afraid of kidney damage, I know that anger went in like a spike, then exploded in the soft tissues of my legs, destroying my means of locomotion. *Stand up and be counted,* I've just been told. Now I can't even stand. As always, my body's astute in its metaphors, but I recognize it this time. The war is moving deeper into the woods.

turning

So this is rage. I look at it, sniff around its edges. This time I don't feel sorry for myself, don't fall down that trap door, hoping someone will hold my hand. Instead, I sit in the den staring at my puffy piano legs. I can't yet separate my thoughts into clear emotions, but replay that scene in my father's office again and again until the battle seems perfectly clear: it's him and me. But somewhere in my psyche, I know it's not my father I'm fighting; he's merely a prop for what infuriates me, makes me think I'll never be whole. Puzzled, I watch the light leak from the sky and darkness descend, the sounds of people outside my window, laughing and talking as they get into their cars, until finally I admit I'm fighting something in me, the way I seek approval, the way I want to be loved. In some complicated way, I know I initiated the conflict with my father, not consciously, of course, but slyly, my mind pulling at a thread, unraveling it right to its source. "Do Alabama," my friends kept saying, and Alabama for me wasn't just scrub pines and bayous, dirt roads and potato fields, but the seat of a power struggle, a monstrous battle for my own self rule.

Susan sits across from me on a fouton chair, her back straight, her legs tucked neatly underneath her. She doesn't look the way I thought a female therapist would look: someone subdued, tranquil, dressed in gray or brown like a female bird. Instead she wears a peach silk blouse and linen skirt, her thick blond hair cascading down her back. She looks poised and professional, the way I've always wanted to look. But I'm tired from crawling around my apartment, eating cheese and crackers and tomato soup, things I can fix quickly while sitting on a stool. The swelling in my ankles is gone, the pain eased, and I sit across from Susan, sprawled, staring at my knees.

"Could your father be afraid you're straying too far from the family role, defining yourself differently?"

"What do you mean?" I eye her suspiciously.

"Well, you've told me that you're not terribly concerned with settling down to a middle class life, having a full-time job, getting credit cards, buying furniture . . . that you're trying to live the life of an artist."

"Maybe," I murmur.

"And your mother," Susan asks, "how did she react?"

"Oh, she tried to console me," I begin, "but—" Then I stop, silent, startled. I have the sudden image of Mother trying to soften Daddy's words, to lighten their meaning. Always, this has been her role, the one who intercedes, who re-interprets behavior, making peace in the family, contriving forgiveness. And this is what I've been addicted to—a sense of rescue—but this time I need to believe what I've seen and heard. My father has given me the bottom line, no window-dressing, no sugar-coating, and though I don't want to admit it, my mother stands symbolically behind him, silent, waiting. What surprises me is that it's the ultimatum I've feared all along, and in an odd way it's a relief to have it out in the open: Success is all that matters. In a family like mine—a mere generation away from poverty—there's too much at stake for a daughter's clumsy improvisation.

As I think about this, I look out the window of Susan's office, listening to the noises of traffic, the buzz of life. I feel silly, absurd to have forgotten that I'm not yet financially secure. Though I have a teaching assistantship it's never enough to live on in L.A. where rents are so much higher than in Alabama, and my father frequently sends money to help me out. It's here that the first flush of panic rises in my throat. I haven't made myself independent at all, I've merely shifted the terrain.

As I leave Susan's office, walking back to UCLA, I feel limp, exhausted. I stop to watch a street musician play his harmonica, but its sweet sadness disturbs me, and I stare blankly into the crowds thronging the streets, men and women in designer suits, students in blue jeans and tank tops, bums holed up in doorways with empty bottles, children admiring a spastic clown. I feel completely lost, as if I have no connection to the world.

Waking, I can barely breathe. The air is thick and wet. It slides like honey over my face. I can't think, can't see through this veil of moistness. I walk blindly out into the yard, down to the river, my shoes soaked, beggar's lice stuck to my socks, coating them like gloves. There's no sound but the chatter of sparrows and the sputtering of a motor somewhere further down river. The grass is velvet. Even the ant hills—like tumors clamped to the sides of trees—look collapsed, the dirt grainy, damp, the little holes like the pores of skin. It takes a long time to walk across the back yard, but when I arrive, the river smells

like sweat, mist traveling on its flesh like steam swirling above a pot.
And when I see it I'm happy.

Can it be true that I've lost not only a family but a place that's frightened and absorbed me for over twenty years? Sometimes when I can't sleep, I get out the map of Alabama, running my fingers down the rivers, the Tombigbee, the Alabama, the Tennessee. I find Lake Martin, then press my thumb into Mobile and see the little foot of Baldwin County nudging its toes into the Gulf of Mexico. I follow the causeway through Spanish Fort, Fairhope, then pull it along the Greeno Road into Magnolia Springs. In my mind I recreate Moore's Store and two brothers behind the counter eating sardines, their fingers oily, hair bristling from their ears. I wander down to the river to watch the afternoon clouds move in, the water turning gray and choppy, the sky chilled. Finally, when I'm ready, I plunge into Foley, the potato sheds gone, the park full of blooming lilies, the houses bigger, prettier, the red lights blinking. And here I come to a stop, full of longing, as alienated as those Rothko canvases I saw one Saturday in the Los Angeles County Museum. Only now do I understand why they're saturated with a sadness too huge to name.

"All I've done is circle the kitchen, waiting to be noticed," I tell Susan on the next visit, "and all my parents have done is wait for me to get out of the kitchen and do something remarkable." I put my head in my lap, unable to bear the revelation of my thoughts. My head feels like dynamite, a hole cracking open at its center.

"Perhaps," Susan says, "You need to pay attention to yourself."

But I'm tired and lonely and looking for easy answers. "No, I have to fight back," I say, lifting my scowling face. "I have to do battle."

Susan looks quietly at me, her face thrown into the shadows. "I know you do, but if you want to do battle, you'll have to take off your armor," she says. "You'll have to fight naked and alone." She pauses. "You'll have to do what you think your parents couldn't do."

My eyes must show my horror because Susan says more gently, "I'm speaking metaphorically, of course. This is what all children have to do,"—and she looks out the window at the bruise-blue sky where clouds drift by like tangled threads—"that is, if they want to grow up."

I limp out of her office, confused. I've always thought of doing battle as clarifying my defenses, being honest about my weaknesses and strengths, then going forth righteously, weapons revealed. But Susan means something quite different. When I leave her Westwood office, I wander through the neighborhood towards my apartment, both oblivious and conscious of my route. All around me there are windows wide open, the sounds of talk and laughter, snatches of songs, a shrill shouting. A boy rushes by on his bike, whistling, then shrieking like a hungry bird. I pay no attention. Susan says I'll have to go naked, and I see myself as a little girl running under the hose, delighted in the sun's warmth on bare skin, the ruffle of grass beneath my feet. And then it hits me. She means . . . she means I'll have to give up their protection. All of it! I'll have to say no in every possible way not because I want to, because it's the most ordinary thing in the world to let go. I stop suddenly, unable to move, one foot touching a soft patch of grass. I'm as silent as a snake. All my life I've seen myself as lost and broken, and though none of us ever spoke of this directly, it's always been there, a secret truth hiding in the dark. But now I feel a deepening in my self, something understood: I've evaded responsibility because I didn't believe my life could exist, and because I didn't believe it could exist, it didn't exist. Instead, I piggybacked my mother's past, my soul wrapped up in that hard, flinty place with its seething rage, its shaming fear. And I did this for the oldest of reasons: the fear of being invisible, ignored. Not the child who marches in her underpants the three blocks downtown to have a coke float, but the child who pleads, "Mother, will you help me?"

That night I'm standing in the dark skirt of a river, the waves gathering around me in rippling folds. It's the kind of river I used to swim in during the hot summer days in Alabama, diving deep into the darkness of blind creatures until my lungs scream for air. In my dream I'm partially submerged, only my head and shoulders revealed. Just beneath the surface of the water, I'm writing, recording a journey, some glimpse of my passage to this river. To my surprise, my family is nearby, sitting together on the dock as if they're at the kitchen table. "Hurry," they call. "C'mon, you've got to hurry up!" and they're laughing and talking, gesturing to my empty seat. But my hand will not behave. It's the current, swift-moving and constant that jiggles my grip, makes my wrist an acrobat, requiring all my concentration. I glance back at the dock where my family waves to me, urging me to finish and come take my place. I smile at them but continue writing, working my hand through the tumble of waves. But even as I hurry, I hear in the distance the splash and slap of water. When I look in the opposite direction, away from the dock, from the wild, stalky weeds growing near the shore, I see a rising shimmer, something emerging— is it beckoning?—and slowly I begin to turn.

It's during the time when I first see Susan that I begin dating a man I'll call Brent Morris. We met at a Westwood bookstore one Friday night when I was browsing the new fiction section for a book. That evening I moved through the store as if I were gliding through water, slowly floating, my mind twenty million miles away. I stopped at the sales table, idly picking up books, but it was when I dropped one that a man standing nearby turned his blond head towards my fragile hips. When he looked at me, our eyes met, locked, and then I picked up the book, opened it, but couldn't read its cover, the print blurring to squiggles, a ripple of pleasure racing up my spine as I felt him moving closer. I believed I knew who he was from his stare, as if we'd spoken volumes of words, felt each other's bodies in the dark. He stood silently beside me for ten minutes—his breath smelling of Chiclets and beer—then asked if I wanted to get a cup of coffee in the coffee shop nearby. It's such an immediate attraction that we see each other every night for a week, either in Westwood or at my apartment. We talk every day. The second week we both have work to catch up on and go out only twice, with plans to meet at a restaurant in Venice on Friday night.

Sitting across from him at the Rose Cafe, I notice he's nervous, uncomfortable, avoiding my eyes. His cheeks have that ruddy look of a fresh shave, the blush spreading into his hairline. "I've got something to tell you," he says, and suddenly I imagine a wife, a small child, some impossible complication.

I take a small breath and fold my hands beneath the napkin on my lap.

"I'm . . . well, I'm not who you think I am," he says haltingly, looking directly at me for the first time that night. His eyes are clear blue, the color of a lake at noon. I've looked at those eyes as mirrors of my own. But now he's nervous, clumsy, knocking the knife off his plate.

Expectation hardens in me. I sit stiffly, waiting to hear about the wife in the Valley, the guilt, the necessary parting. I think about how easily we've come together, our nights of passion, floating together on my narrow single bed, then talking, staying up late, whispering in the dark. But the story he tells isn't the one I've expected at all.

"When I was a little boy, I always wanted to go to law school," he says, a half-smile playing across his lips. Idly, he pushes the food around on his plate, shoving it to one side. "I once found an old briefcase someone had thrown in the trash in our neighborhood and I toted it home to my room and kept it under my bed. I cut out articles from the paper when there was any kind of famous trial going on. I even had stuff from the McCarthy trials, old stuff with a young Nixon trying to horn his way in. I never told anyone about the briefcase, but just kept stashing things inside it. I also had all kinds of stuff about Lee Harvey Oswald and Jack Ruby, Sirhan Sirhan, James Earl Ray, the Manson trials. I thought I would grow up and be the person who put those kind of people behind bars, the slime, you know. The real killers. I never told anyone about the briefcase. It was my dream, you see, my secret."

I nod, glad that his dreams have begun to come true. Our very first night together at the coffeeshop, he tells me he's saving money for his second year of law school at UCLA. This summer he's working at a Radio Shack to keep the wolf from the door. We've talked some about the political scene, about civil rights, about environmental issues he worried about, having grown up in Colorado.

He looks away from me now, around the restaurant, some David Bowie song on the stereo, the clink of silverware and jewelry, the sudden spills of laughter from people in other booths. "That briefcase," he says suddenly, turning back to me. "It was all I had." Now he looks moody, withdrawn. I think he might just get up and leave.

"What?" I say. "I don't know what you mean."

"It Was All I Had," he says again, emphasizing each word. "Jesus, I'm not in law school. I've never been in law school. I work as a manager in a Radio Shack in the Valley. I finished high school, went to junior college, then dropped out. I grew up in

Lancaster, for god's sake, in a desert town and I couldn't stand to be there anymore."

We look at each other without speaking, my mouth a soft, round O. I'm stunned, and for the first time in my life enraged, absolutely furious that he's lied to me, betrayed what seemed essential in a relationship: that we trust each other's stories.

"But why did you do that?" I ask. "Why did you pretend to be something you weren't?" I remember his telling me about studying late in the library, how he liked the intimacy of the room when only a few students were there, how he could slouch down in his chair, close his eyes and just think. How peaceful that was. Like being alone in the woods. His own family, he said, were hikers, outdoors people, environmentalists in Colorado who cared deeply about the land.

Now he looks down at his plate, his body slumped. "I didn't think you'd like me. I didn't think my real self would be enough for you."

I feel horrible. But still furious. Like me, Brent's admitting his hunger for acceptance. And part of my fury is that he's right: I like the fictional story better than the real one. I don't want to fall in love with a manager of a Radio Shack. I prefer the more romantic and ambitious figure of the political law student. I've known him as one person and now he's become another. Honesty severs me from desire.

"He wasn't so much trying to deceive me as trying to deceive himself," I tell Susan one Friday afternoon not long after I've stopped seeing Brent. Susan nods and with her nod a jolt of recognition slams through my body. All my life I've shown the world the fictional life of a pleasant middle class girl, anxious to please, ambitious and competitive while beneath this version I've lived another life entirely. Down deep, I'm furious, desperate, as hungry as the rest of my family, but my hunger's turned inward, clawing, making scars. My only releases are sudden moments of independence when I act on impulse, moments when I slip through the net of cultural training. And yet when this self emerges, as she did in New Orleans—dressing as I felt like dressing—all hell breaks loose. My father is furious at me *for removing the masquerade I've worn all the years I've lived in his house.* Like Brent, I must have seemed the betrayer when I took off the mask and said, "Surprise!"

Years later this knowledge will be the impetus for our reconciliation, the beginning of a deep friendship between my father and me, a love stronger than either of us could have imagined.

It's my thirtieth birthday and I'm in the kitchen baking a cake. It's the first cake I've ever made for myself and as I lick the beaters and put the cake in the oven, I feel a secret thrill at making my way in a big city, finishing a Masters in Fine Arts in art. "Stayin' Alive" is playing on the radio, and I'm doing a little shakin' as I throw the beaters into soapy water. And yet as I walk from the kitchen down the hallway to the bathroom, ready to take a shower and prepare for a night with friends, an avalanche of sadness strikes me with the force of a blow. I can't move. I've entered a zone of resistance so familiar I sit down on the carpet, my body trembling, my back against one wall, my eyes fixed on the blankness of the opposite wall. What I see is my family sitting at the kitchen table while I stand hesitantly in the open doorway, trying to decide whether to enter or not.

In a flash I watch my mother, her face drawn into a frieze of agony, her fists knotted in her lap. Someone has just hailed my father as wonderful!—"You can see where those kids got their smarts!"—choosing him over her, holding him up like a hero, a man who waves triumphantly to the crowd. How he soars! How it galls her to a fury of ashes! Isn't she smarter, isn't she the fulcrum around which we're all balanced? But there's no way to prove it, nothing to do but get busier and busier, taking on more and more community work until the lesson of Praco is revived; you must work longer, harder than anyone else! And yet when she was a young girl, surely there was a prize attached to her work, a prize that glittered and glowed when she thought of it at night, lying beside her sisters in their lumpy double bed. That prize would bestow blessings of independence, the glory of her shining achievement. And then . . . aaaaaaah, yes, then they'd stand up and take notice, then they'd stop all their rattling fury and see she was the Golden One after all. How she'd show them! Such a feat of revenge!

The breath goes out of me. I'm suddenly cold, shivering, sweat like icicles on my brow. My god, this is exactly what I've tried to do. I've always assumed that success was my ticket of entrance, that it alone could promise me self-respect, but now, as if I'm holding a crystal ball, I understand something quite different. Respect, if it comes, will result from the very act of turning away, moving into the unknown.

And for the first time I don't want to save my mother. I want to save me. I recognize this as a fundamental, necessary change, something that's been a long time taking root. For most of my life it seemed a terrible betrayal to reject the world my mother worked so hard to affirm, a rejection too huge to assume. As I sit in that dark hallway I see how I've been at war since childhood, one part of me trying very hard to be the daughter my parents desired— ambitious, carving out my place in the middle class, protecting myself against poverty and failure by acquiring credentials to ensure my upward mobility. But another part of me cast a critical eye on just that progression. This part of me stood in the woods looking at a butterfly, entranced by its flight, unable to say why such a moment was crucial, but knowing it was.

And yet I couldn't release myself from that other world. Always I believed you had to be eccentrically talented, outrageously gifted in order to leave the fold and strike out on your own, and I spent all my time trying to develop some talent, trying to live up to my own outrageous expectations, but with the strictest adherence to form: you make yourself into something marvelous while sitting placidly on the lawn and *then* you leap over the fence into the woods. Now a cool wind blows through my body. What if you can reject expectations first and discover talent later? What if the very assessment of expectations is the whole point of growing up?

I draw my knees up tighter to my chest, breathing slowly, deliberately. This means I'll have to trust my own feelings, have faith in my own experience.

And in this moment, I know which part of me has to die.

As I walk into my room, glancing out at the darkening sky, I notice the street lights are just coming on, a milky haze, the moon so light it looks etched in chalk. Bougainvillea float near the window, red blooms trembling in the ocean breeze. Night is beginning. My birthday. A celebration. From the kitchen comes the delicious smell of Devil's Food cake. I close my eyes, breathing in its heady fragrance, and when I open them again it's as if I'm waking from a long, confusing dream.

epilogue

"I Love You Mama, So Please Don't Cry"

We drive through the wild greenness of southern Alabama, the frazzled weeds and lush pampas grass crowding the concrete slabs of the highway. Mother and I are on our way to New Orleans, and we sit in our air-conditioned car, staring out at land so wet it shimmers in the white-hot glare of the sun. Mosquitoes rise in clouds from the fields. Doves fly overhead. When we turn the air-conditioner up high, frosty streams blow toward our faces, and we feel cool and happy. Foley is one hundred miles away.

Now that we're far from home, we talk freely, discussing whether my niece will go to medical school, then how Mother left Praco almost sixty years ago. "I would never have gotten away if Mrs. Elgin hadn't helped me," Mother says, her voice charged with emotion as though she's uttering a confession.

"How exactly did she help?" I ask, curious as always about Mother's escape.

"Oh, she told me I was smart, and that I could do something with my life." Mother's face is serious, sincere, and then suddenly she laughs. "I wish you could have seen her. She had short hair, I mean, *really* short, cut like a boy's. She didn't care what it looked like at all . . . and she always sat with her legs wide open, even when she was playing the organ. The boys used to sit in church and look up her dress." Mother smiles and I think of Mrs. Elgin as her Mama Dot, this woman who flouted southern femininity, who demanded independence. "And I wanted to believe her," Mother says with surprising fierceness, but she looks away from me, out the window so I can't see her face.

Somewhere in the distance a truck horn blasts and a covey of birds flies overhead, scattering like scraps of cloth. I watch until we cross the state border a few seconds later. As we drive through Mississippi, the sun glares cruelly at the water-soaked land, and I think about Praco, trying to imagine the everydayness of Mother's young life. I see her walking through the summer weeds to the outhouse, looking down at a dirt-scraped path, searching for snakes and frogs. Maybe this is why she hates wildlife, the outdoors, all types of spiders and ants crawling nearby. I see her squat in the outhouse, watch her eyes close against the smell of lime, the smell of excrement, the thought of darkness at the bottom of the hole. And then I imagine her sitting primly on Mrs. Elgin's sofa, her hands touching the fabric, stroking it delicately when Mrs. Elgin isn't looking. She's never seen good upholstery before, not the linen and polished cotton of the Elgin's house. *When I'm grown up, my own house will be just like this,* she thinks, *with a living room and dining room all clean and neat, with china figurines and a piano near the window.*

I smile. At least she got that.

Water lies stagnant in the grassy swamps of Louisiana, the roots of cypress trees tangling above the surface. Everything looks soft and spongy, ready for decay. As we get closer to New Orleans, I think about the video on Toni Morrison's novel *Sula* that we watched just before we left. A professor from Brown University was discussing the day Nel and her mother Helene go to New Orleans to Helene's grandmother's funeral. In this scene, Helene, the paragon of propriety in Medallion, Ohio, has gotten onto the wrong car of the train, the "white" car instead of the "colored" car, and in trying to correct her mistake, she's stopped by the conductor. "What you think you doin, gal?" he asks, implying that her mistake is intentional. Nel watches as her mother blushes, but what astonishes her is that Helene, the most prominent black woman in Medallion, turns a coy face to her tormenter, smiling a dazzling smile. At that moment, Nel realizes her mother is custard, that beneath all that propriety and elegant bearing, she's as soft as jelly.

I look at my own mother. She's wearing a blue-linen pants suit with silver disc earrings and a filigreed watch; she too looks elegant, the ideal of propriety. I think of the times I've seen her go soft, turn away from a neighbors' snide comment, hide her emotions in mopping the floor, but more and more I see that beneath this deference is a tough, resilient core. She's never been rebellious, has prided herself on being a lady and a good doctor's wife, but all along she's spent most of her life like Nel, observant, watching, trying to find a new story, one different from her mother's.

"Did you ever see your mother act like Helene?" I ask. "I mean, see her humiliated and afraid?" I think of the stories her sisters have told me of her mother crying late at night over her philandering husband, the man who was both the curse and love of her life.

Mother frowns at the thought. "I *never* saw my mother as anything but harsh." She turns away from me towards the window as if searching for a thought in the landscape of swampy grass. "Of course, I understand now that she had little choice in her life. With so many children she had to be strict, but she whipped us every day. At least she did me."

"Why?" Though I should know better, I'm always surprised to hear about her mother's hardness.

Mother frowns again, her face in shadow. Then she looks at me shyly. "Talking back," she says. And we both laugh.

"That's not a bad thing," I say. "I wish I'd done more of it myself."

As we drive through Slidell, across Lake Pontchartrain into the city, I smell the musty mold of the swamps, the scent of chicory coffee mixed with garbage and the salty sea-smell of the docks. We walk to Jackson Square, to the French Market for iced coffee and beignets, but the heat's so intense it covers us like a drape. I find myself breathing shallowly, slowly, and we walk, wilted, back to our hotel, hurrying only when we're almost to the lobby. After we've settled in for the night, Mother curls up on the bed in her red pajamas, pajamas she tells me have to be dry-cleaned. I roll my eyes at the extravagance, but she doesn't see me. She turns instead onto her back, one hand over her forehead, a position I recognize from my childhood when she had migraines.

"I'll be in bed in just a minute. I've got to brush my teeth," I say and leave the room. In the clean white bathroom, I brush my teeth and wash my face, but when I come out I'm surprised to see Mother crying.

"Mother, what is it?"

She shakes her head. "I cry all the time now," she says. "I try not to, but I just feel like such a failure. So many things I don't know what to do about."

Though she's been the scaffolding of our lives, she believes she's left no visible mark. I think of her standing in my girlhood bedroom, her shoulders slumped, her voice tense. "I can't stand it," she's saying about her life. "I just can't stand it anymore." And something changes in me. I feel like a little girl again, a girl who wants to comfort her mother. But instead of saying, "Don't cry," I whisper, "Cry. Keep crying," because of all the emotions withheld, all the secrets kept close. Sometimes now I think of her as the keeper of a lighthouse, always on lookout for a shipwreck, knowing a powerful storm will eventually come. She's expected to be on guard, to anticipate trouble, to stifle her own feelings and get the job done.

When I look at her now, I see the lines around her eyes, the lipstick still smudged across her lips and think that with all her vigilance, the shipwreck did indeed occur. Not with roaring seas and a shattered ship, but more quietly, pieces fragmenting, floating apart. A difficult marriage. Not knowing what to do or be. And that sack full of secrets. We've never talked about the sexual molestation in her childhood, how silence was the only thing she could claim. We've never talked about why she hates to be touched, why friendship is denied, why she never left my father. Sometimes I think we've never talked about anything at all, that inside us there's a lifetime of conversation, years of stories to be told.

"I wish you'd write a story," she says, surprising me, interrupting my thoughts. She's never asked me to write a story before. "I want you to write a story and call it, "I Love You, Mama, So Please Don't Cry." She gives me a weak smile as she says this, and for a moment I think she wants me to write a story to give her hope, the kind of hope she's never had. But another part of me knows that the story my mother wants isn't the story of salvation, but a story of courage, of saving herself. And suddenly I see her again as that young dark-haired girl from Praco, the one who learned so early not to unburden her heart.

It's raining. A light blowing rain streaks the windows of the house. The children are playing in the front room, making puzzles, and late in the afternoon my mother sneaks out, running down the path into the storm. The wind rushes through the hills, swooping into the hollows, scattering rocks and pebbles in ditches by the side of the road. Thunder booms in the distance, but she moves quickly up another path until she reaches the slag heap. It's a pyre of rubble, rock and coal, slippery and sharp. She climbs it steadily, the wind blowing her hair, catching in her skirts so that they flap around her legs. Rain occasionally wets her face but she keeps climbing, not looking down until she's at the top. Only here can she survey her kingdom: mining trucks dirty with coal, air that rains filth and dust, then the roofs of camp houses, tin and shingles and tar rising through the trees. The storm blows cinders across the road and gusts through the straggly bushes and bramble. There are no tulips, no pansies, no roses ready to bloom. No robins, hummingbirds or cardinals singing in the trees. There's nothing but ugliness, the yawning mouths of the mines and soot that dissolves into rivers of black sludge. But today she doesn't hate it. A new and amazing thought has caught inside her mind, a thought so simple it comes straight from the heart. *I am myself, nobody else.* She looks out over the hills, knowing this place has pressed against the deepest part of her soul, knowing it has crushed and mangled her, nourished and protected her. But it's not all that I am, she thinks. Inside there is a quiet place. A center. And no one can take that away. Not even if they break into my body; not even if they try to crush my spirit or crumple my heart.

I stop here and stare out the window at the wind blowing the branches on my oak tree. The leaves flutter against a clear blue sky, a bird pokes its beak into ragged bark, but that's not really what I see. In my mind, I watch as my mother turns her face to the rain, letting the wetness seep into her skin, letting it leak into the clean place inside.

But perhaps this isn't my mother's story at all.

PATRICIA FOSTER is an associate professor of English at the University of Iowa. She is the editor of *Minding the Body: Women Writers on Body and Soul* and *Sister to Sister: Women Write About the Unbreakable Bond* and co-editor of *The Healing Circle*.

Deep South Books

The University of Alabama Press